The Consuming Flame

F. W. KENYON

The Consuming Flame

THE STORY OF GEORGE ELIOT

HUTCHINSON OF LONDON

HUTCHINSON & CO *(Publishers)* LTD
178–202 Great Portland Street, London W1

London Melbourne Sydney
Auckland Bombay Toronto
Johannesburg New York

First published 1970

*This book has been set in Pilgrim, printed in Great Britain
on Antique Wove paper by Anchor Press, and
bound by Wm. Brendon, both of Tiptree, Essex*
09 101440 9

Part One

1

JUST before dawn she woke up laughing. Lying very still in bed she wondered, almost fearfully, what had caused the laughter, for never before had laughter torn her from sleep. Terror, yes, but never laughter. Then quickly she recalled the dream and laughter got the better of her again. It was, she realised, a true dream with no fantasy in it, an exact repetition of an event of the night before. Remembering the event as well as the dream, she saw herself sitting in front of her mirror addressing her reflection thoughtfully but with amusement in her eyes.

'At sixty-one I, Marian Evans, better known to the world as George Eliot, have decided to marry for the first time and become, as they say, an honest woman. Honest indeed! Why, most of my friends are just as shocked by my decision as they were when, at thirty-four, I made up my mind to live openly in what is called sin. Not surprisingly my brother Isaac who ostracised me all those years ago is grimly pleased, and making a rare joke in his letter remarked that Father was no longer turning over in his grave.'

Happily Marian fell asleep again, but within an hour she was wide awake, panting in the grip of one of the night terrors which had plagued her all her life. Marriage, legalised marriage! Was she doing the right thing? John Cross, the man she had agreed to marry, was all of twenty years her junior. The early morning sunshine, giving promise of a beautiful April day, was streaming through the window, and that, as sunshine always did, made Marian feel better, more in control of herself. Struggling between contempt and compassion, she remembered that one kind friend, referring obliquely to John Cross's age, had uttered the single word 'Scandalous!' another 'Indecent!' while yet a third, with a sad shake of her head, had said, 'A genius, yes, but headstrong, always headstrong, *that* is Marian Evans.'

Marian pondered over the word 'headstrong'. Just or unjust, it brought back memories of her mother; memories, too, of the first night terror which she had ever experienced.

'I was only five at that time,' she whispered.

2

'YOU may sit down, Mary Ann,' Robert Evans said, smiling on his young daughter.

'No, let her stand,' his wife Christiana said imperiously. 'You pamper her too much, Robert.'

The child remained standing, her lips quivering uncontrollably. She hated the name Mary Ann and thought: I shall change it as soon as I can think of something better.

'Your father's softness,' Christiana Evans continued, addressing her daughter sternly, 'is one reason why I have decided to send you to boarding-school.'

Mary Ann looked aghast; her heart began to palpitate painfully. It was frightening to think that at boarding-school she would be separated from her beloved brother Isaac.

'I won't go,' she said, glancing appealingly at her father. 'I won't.'

'You are much too headstrong,' Christiana Evans reproved. 'That is another of my reasons.'

Robert Evans sighed lightly. His wife was an invalid and must be placated whenever possible. If Mary Ann was really headstrong, which he doubted, it arose out of fear, uncertainty and her mother's often ill-disguised dislike of her.

'We are sending you to Chrissey's school,' he said gently. 'You will at least have your sister to look after you. And besides, you are a clever child, far advanced for your years. The sooner you go to a real school and get some real education the better.'

'Now you are flattering her,' his wife said in disgust.

Robert Evans sighed lightly again. He loved Christiana dearly, but he was, and always had been, a little in awe of her. She was his second wife and socially his superior. She came of good yeoman stock, whereas he was the son of a peasant carpenter. The fact that the humble carpenter, by dint of hard work, had become a master builder, and that he himself had prospered, made not the slightest difference. Held in high esteem as he was in the district, his feeling of insecurity and inferiority at home had persisted from the beginning of his second marriage. At fifty-one Robert Evans had the face and figure of a much younger man. He was well-built and physically strong. His eyes were alert, his complexion ruddy; he spoke, as did his wife and children, with a Midlands accent, though not very pronounced. He was born in 1773 at Roston Common, a Staffordshire village. There his father, a Welshman, had set up business, and there Robert, in the course of time, had taken over the business. Branching out, he became Francis Newdigate's agent and helped to run the New-digate estate at Kirk Hallam. Industrious and diligent, he eventually became the agent of other landed gentry. In 1801 he married Harriet Poynton who was in service at Kirk Hallam. Two children were born of this marriage, a boy and a girl. Later, when Francis Newdigate inherited Arbury Hall, an estate in Warwick-shire, that gentleman took the Evans family with him and established them at South Farm which was part of the estate.

Robert Evans's first wife died in 1809. Four years later he married his second wife, Christiana Pearson. Three children were born of Robert's second marriage: Christiana (known as Chrissey), Isaac and Mary Ann, the latter on November 22nd, 1819. A few months after Mary Ann's birth at South Farm, Robert Evans took his family (with the exception of the two children of his first marriage, Robert and Frances) to live at Griff House, a large red-brick house in another part of the Arbury estate on the road between Nuneaton and Coventry. Robert junior was eighteen; he had never got on very well with his step-mother and was glad to escape to Kirk Hallam to look after his father's business interests there. His sister, equally glad to escape, went with him to keep house for him. As a result, Mary Ann saw very little of her step-brother and step-sister and had never felt close to them. They were almost strangers, if kindly ones.

Christiana Evans moved impatiently in her habitual chair by the fire and drew her shawl more closely round her thin shoulders. Often she felt frustrated because ill health prevented her from taking a really active part in the running of the house. She spent a great deal of her time knitting; she was knitting now, angrily.

'Chrissey went willingly to boarding-school,' she said, addressing Mary Ann above the clicking of her knitting needles. 'Why not you?'

'*Because* . . .' said Mary Ann.

'Because—*what?*'

'Isaac.'

Christiana Evans thoroughly understood. The eight-year-old Isaac, her favourite child, was Mary Ann's hero, she his willing slave. She followed him everywhere, insisting upon joining him in all the madcap games he invented. And in some strange, indefinable way Christiana resented it.

'Isaac is too old now to play with a little girl,' she pronounced.

Appalled and disbelieving, Mary Ann flung herself at the piano, seeking some means of self-expression, of violent if unspoken protest. She climbed on the stool, threw back the lid and crashed her arched fingers down on the keys with all the force at her command.

'Temper!' her mother reproved.

Mary Ann took not the slightest notice. She knew not a single note of music but she continued to attack the keyboard violently, almost ecstatically. The result was a cacophony of jangled sound.

'A horrible noise,' Christiana said. 'Stop her, Robert.'

'Music, beautiful music!' Mary Ann roared, and in that moment, to her, it was.

Robert Evans lifted the child from the piano stool and held her close for a moment before setting her on her feet. She glanced up at him admiringly, thinking how handsome he looked in his dark cutaway coat with its velvet collar and high narrow waist.

'You shall have piano lessons at school,' he said. 'Will that please you, my little wench?'

'No!' Mary Ann said promptly, then she felt a sharp stab of guilt, for she loved her father dearly, almost as dearly as she loved Isaac. 'Yes, Father,' she amended contritely.

'Yes or no, it scarcely matters,' her mother said. 'Go to bed at once, Mary Ann.'

'It—it's too early for bed, Mother.'

'Do as I say and be thankful I haven't asked your father to give you a thrashing.'

Mary Ann smiled secretly; she knew that if that had happened her father would only have pretended to thrash her. Nevertheless she went slowly to the door, dragging her feet, and lingered in the hall, listening unseen to her mother and father.

'What a plain, even ugly, child she is,' Christiana said, 'and how much worse she looks when in a temper.'

'Her first show of temper, Christiana. She was frightened, that was the cause of it.'

Christiana ignored this. 'Clever, you say? Well, she will need to be. But cleverness and ugliness, what a disturbing combination

—disturbing to a man, I mean. I doubt if you will find her a really good husband when she grows up.'

'She has fine eyes and lovely auburn-brown hair,' Robert Evans said placatingly.

'To say nothing of your great beak of a nose.'

'Merely a miniature of it,' he laughed.

'It's bound to grow,' Christiana said unhelpfully. 'It will be a relief to have her at school,' she went on querulously. 'Perhaps I shall begin to feel better then, but I doubt it. I have never been really well since she was born. Her birth destroyed my health.'

On the verge of tears Mary Ann fled up the stairs to her room, and presently one of the maids was sent up to put her to bed. The girl, a pert fifteen-year-old, looked at Mary Ann teasingly.

'Dear me, have we been misbehaving?'

Mary Ann shook her head. 'I was only making music.'

'If *that* was music,' the maid chuckled, '*I'm* a born lady.'

'I felt it *here*,' Mary Ann said, pressing her hand against her heart.

'As for me,' the maid said, tapping her forehead, '*I* felt it *here*. Just about gave me a splitting headache, it did.'

Mary Ann very nearly laughed, but she was remembering all that her mother had said.

'Am I really ugly?' she asked tremulously.

'Well now, Miss Mary Ann, to be honest you ain't no raving beauty, but there's something special about you.'

'*Special*?' Mary Ann asked in amazement.

'I can't rightly describe it, that I can't. It's just something I feel, so to speak.'

'In your heart?'

'That's right, now you mention it. In my heart.'

But Mary Ann was still troubled. 'Is it true—I mean, is it *my* fault Mother is an invalid?'

'Well now, it was a real difficult birth. You didn't seem to want to come into the world.'

'I wish I hadn't!'

'Now, now, that's a silly thing to say, Miss Mary Ann. It's a fine world for a little girl in your position. And I'll tell you this, your poor mother was ailing before you was born, so you can't be blamed altogether.'

Vaguely comforted, Mary Ann said: 'Ask Isaac to come and tuck me in.'

The maid shook her head regretfully. 'It isn't allowed. Go to sleep now. You'll feel a sight better in the morning.'

Mary Ann flung herself on her stomach and buried her face in the pillow, but she waited until she heard the maid close the door before she gave way to tears. Trying to comfort herself she thought about all the nice things that had happened to her at Griff House. They were centred, of course, on Isaac. Yesterday, a repetition of all the weekdays she could remember, she and Isaac had gone together to the dame's school across the road from the gates of Griff House. The school was a small cottage; Mrs Moore, the only teacher, had rosy cheeks and smelled like ripe apples. Before going to school they had watched the mail-coach pass by from Birmingham to Stamford. The four, high-stepping greys drew the coach at the unbelievable speed of ten miles an hour, or so Isaac claimed; the coachman and the guard were dressed in exciting scarlet, and there was a post-horn at the back of the coach. It was always a thrilling sight, suggesting as it did the vast and fearful world beyond the confines of Griff House. Isaac wanted to be a scarlet-clad guard when he grew up, if only for the sake of being able to blow that great post-horn, but Mary Ann hated the very thought of it. It would take Isaac away from her and she herself wanted to remain at Griff House forever. After school, at three in the afternoon, they had watched the mail-coach pass by again and had waved to the guard. Then they had played in the farmyard and fished in the round pool at the back of the house where Mary Ann, much to her brother's admiration, had caught a great, fat perch. Later they had watched the sturdy cart-horses dragging the coal barges along the nearby Coventry canal, and finally, before the evening meal, they had built a fort of old furniture in their special playroom, the large mysterious attic of Griff House.

Dwelling on all this, entranced by it, Mary Ann fell asleep, but she woke in the middle of the night in a panic of apprehension. Tomorrow, or the next day, or some day soon, she would be dragged from her private heaven and thrown into a strange, unwanted world. Terror-stricken, she trembled violently, far beyond the escape, the tenuous comfort, of tears. She longed to go to Isaac, to slip into bed with him, but she had suddenly become afraid of the dark. She was pale and silent at breakfast the next morning and scarcely able to eat. Later, when Isaac took her to the gates to wait for the mail-coach, she clung to his hand pathetically.

'Isaac, I'm going to drown myself in the round pond.'

'Well, I suppose it's deep enough. But why, Mary Ann?'

'Because I'm being sent to Chrissey's school.'

'It's only three miles away.'

'No, it's three *thousand* miles.'

Isaac laughed cheerfully. 'If you drown yourself in the round pond you'll turn into a perch. Then I'll hook you, Cook will fry you for breakfast and we'll all eat you hungrily.'

Mary Ann smiled wanly. 'I wouldn't mind if I turned into a *pretty* perch.' And she added, hopeful of an encouraging reply: 'Do *you* think I'm ugly, Isaac?'

'You're my sister,' he said candidly. 'It doesn't matter.'

'You *do* think I'm ugly!'

Isaac looked faintly uneasy. 'You're my best friend as well as my sister. *It doesn't matter.*'

'You're *my* best friend too,' Mary Ann said passionately.

'Besides,' the boy added generously, 'you're not ugly when you smile.'

Partly consoled she said: 'Promise not to forget me when I go to boarding-school.'

'That's easy. Promise not to forget me either. I'm going to boarding-school too, in Coventry.'

Tears welled up in Mary Ann's eyes. Boarding-school for Isaac as well. So there it was, even if she remained at Griff House there would be no Isaac to play with. She fought back her tears. In a way that made being sent to Chrissey's school seem not quite so cruel.

'There's always Saturday,' Isaac said.

'Saturday?'

'Chrissey comes home every Saturday. So will you.'

'And you too, Isaac?'

'Of course. Father said so. Look! Here comes the mail-coach. I wish it would stop. I wish the guard would let me blow the post-horn.'

But Mary Ann was no longer listening and she scarcely glanced at the mail-coach as it sped by. Saturday! That would be the one important day of the week, the day to wait for, long for, with all else forgotten.

'Isaac,' she said stoically, 'I won't drown myself, after all.'

3

CHRISSEY EVANS, very much the young lady at ten, looked at her sister without sympathy. 'You were crying in the middle of the night,' she said pityingly. 'There in the dormitory. You kept the girls awake. I don't know what you had to cry about, Mary Ann. Were you homesick?'

Mary Ann shook her head in proud denial. 'They laughed at me again yesterday. They're always laughing at me.'

'That's because of your accent. They laughed at me at first because of mine. You must do what I do, child, try and speak like a lady.'

'What,' Mary Ann asked earnestly, 'is a lady?'

'A lady is not a servant,' Chrissey pronounced. 'I mean, a lady is not just a woman.'

Mary Ann digested this. Chrissey certainly spoke differently these days, as if something peculiar had happened to her tongue or her throat. Refined, that was how Chrissey described it herself.

'The girls might laugh at you but they love you,' Chrissey pointed out.

Mary Ann scowled, then tried to smile: Chrissey had said only yesterday that when she scowled she looked very unattractive. It was true that the girls loved her and pampered her and sometimes, because of her gravity, called her Little Mamma. But they were all so old, Chrissey's age, most of them, and alarmingly large, so large that it was almost always difficult for Mary Ann to get close enough to the fire to keep warm on a cold night.

'Cheer up,' Chrissey said airily, 'tomorrow's Saturday.'

Mary Ann tried to smile again. Saturday, but would Isaac be at Griff House? During the three months that she had spent at Chrissey's school Saturdays had become more and more disappointing. Isaac had made friends at his boarding-school in Coventry and often spent the weekends with one or other of them. Last Saturday had been particularly disappointing. Isaac had come home but he had brought a boy with him, a fat, freckled-face grinning boy, and had scarcely noticed his adoring sister. 'I'm too old to play with a little girl,' Isaac had said. 'Mother says so, Mother is right.' She was very much a baby, Mary Ann supposed, but she had cried herself to sleep that night.

'I'll give you lessons, teach you how to speak correctly,'

Chrissey offered, and using one of her big words added: 'It will save you embarrassment.'

On the point of refusing, Mary Ann remembered that Isaac had begun to speak differently too.

'Thank you,' she said politely.

To her great joy she found, on reaching Griff House the next day with Chrissey, that Isaac had come home and not brought a friend with him. Quivering in anticipation of a joyous romp in the attic, she looked forward to a day spent entirely in her brother's company, but when she asked him to take her fishing he shook his head decisively.

'Father gave me a pony. I'm going riding instead.'

Mary Ann tried again. 'Let me ride the pony too.'

'You're not old enough.'

'How silly, Isaac, of course I am.'

'Not big enough, then.'

'You think more of your pony than you do of me!' she burst out.

Instead of denying this Isaac said: 'It's because I'm growing up. Mother said so.'

'You don't love me any more,' Mary Ann said brokenly.

Isaac looked momentarily puzzled. ''Course I do, but in a different way. I'll always protect you, Father said I must, but, well, I'd rather ride a pony or play with boys than have a little girl running after me.'

'I don't want you to protect me,' Mary Ann said defiantly. 'I can protect myself.' But she doubted it and felt a great quaking fear in her heart. All she wanted was to love Isaac and be loved by him in the old familiar way. The change in him was bewildering. The world she had known and rejoiced in had vanished. She felt lost and cruelly treated. She would, she knew, be afraid to go to bed that night and lie alone in the dark.

'Take me to watch the mail-coach this afternoon,' she begged.

'No,' Isaac said promptly. 'I don't want to blow a post-horn any more. I don't want to be a guard. I'm going to be an estate agent, like Father.' He looked at his sister incuriously. 'What do you want to be when you grow up?'

Much at a loss, Mary Ann said: *Somebody.*

'Important, you mean?'

'Yes, Isaac, *important.*'

'That's silly, Mary Ann. You can be a wife, and a mother, or not get married at all, like Cook. A girl can't ever be somebody important.'

'I don't want to be a cook.'

'Then you can keep house for me, like Frances does for Robert.'

That, she thought, would bring her close to Isaac again, but perversely she said: 'I don't want to be a housekeeper.'

'Then I'll find you a husband, so there!'

Alone that afternoon Mary Ann watched the mail-coach pass by. The entrancing sight still excited her and for the first time in her life she had no wish to remain at Griff House forever. The thought frightened her but persisted. The coach, if it stopped for her, would take her to Coventry and another coach would take her to the vastness of London, a very wicked city, her mother had once said. Frightened still, and apprehensive, she was moved also by a strange, searching anticipation. She was having piano lessons now, showing great promise, the music teacher had said. Could she possibly become a great pianist and play before hundreds of people in London? It was wrong of her, she knew, not to believe Isaac, but she felt rebelliously sure that if she worked hard at school she would become something more exciting and important than a wife and mother, which would be like playing with dolls, or a cook or a housekeeper.

She watched the mail-coach until the dust from the hooves and wheels blew away, taking with it, in part, her dream of future greatness.

Later, still alone but trying not to feel lonely, she searched for the gardener and asked him to give her a fishing line. The round pond was very still and desolate. There was no joy in fishing without Isaac at her side. Aimlessly she dangled the line in the water and presently hooked a perch, but after watching the struggling fish in consternation for several moments she landed it, unhooked it and threw it back. What if she *had* drowned herself and turned into a perch? It was a terrifying thought. All she wanted, herself, was to be free.

4

'I AM very proud of you,' Robert Evans said after studying Mary Ann's latest report from the head mistress of the boarding-school. 'Very proud of you indeed.'

Mary Ann, now eight, very nearly nine, glowed with pleasure. Praise from her father had come to mean more to her than praise from Isaac. Isaac was inclined to be condescending these days, whereas her father was always kind and gentle.

'You can't call it a *good* report,' Christiana Evans said from her chair by the fire. 'Mary Ann is slow to learn, *that* is clearly indicated.'

'Ah, yes,' her husband said quietly. 'But she is younger than the other girls. She can't be blamed for finding it hard to keep up with them. And it does say here that she can read quite well and play the piano better than ever. An ear for music and especially an ear for words. That's what it says. What does it matter if she's poor at arithmetic and can't remember all the dates they try to cram into her little head?'

Christiana ignored this. 'As far as *I* can make out she hasn't learned much more than to speak with an affected accent.'

Mary Ann bit her lip. Her accent was the same now as Isaac's and Chrissey's, but her mother never sneered at them. It was unfair and cruel.

'It isn't affected,' Robert Evans said, asserting himself for once. 'It's just plain good English, without a trace of county accent in it, except when she's agitated.'

And that, Mary Ann thought, was often enough.

'Have it your own way, but there's one thing I hope and pray.'

'Yes, Christiana?'

'That Mary Ann won't become a snob.'

'Snobbery is for the servants,' Robert Evans said sagely, 'not for Mary Ann. Not for me or you. Not even for the gentry. It starts at the bottom, it always has.'

'Yes, I think you're right,' Christiana said surprisingly, 'but there's one thing I can't understand. Mary Ann hasn't made any friends at school. It's *unnatural*.'

Mary Ann frowned over this. She longed for one special friend to whom she could be all in all and who would be all in all to her, just as Isaac used to be, but the search, a constant one, had yet to give her such a friend.

'Unless you make friends,' her mother said, addressing her directly, 'you'll be lonely all your life.'

Mary Ann frowned again. Now that she had learned to read easily and rapidly she was never lonely or unhappy, except at night when the nightmares attacked her. Reading had made it possible for her to lose herself in a world of her own creation, a world full of strange people, places and events. Aesop's fables had so impressed and excited her that she had read the stories again and again and had even memorised them. She was no longer sure that she wanted to be a great pianist; to be a great writer, like Walter Scott—she was reading *Waverley* avidly—might be much more satisfying.

'You're such an *untidy* girl,' her mother went on. 'Your hair is always out of place, and your room is always in a dreadful mess five minutes after you come home from school. You're more like a boy than a girl. Why can't you be like Chrissey? *She* is always neat and tidy and feminine. Of course she's pretty, I grant you that, and prettiness helps. But you could *try*. You're the despair of my life, Mary Ann.'

'It isn't "Mary Ann" any more,' the girl said suddenly and daringly, 'it's "Marian".'

'Fanciful,' her mother commented. 'You were christened Mary Ann and Mary Ann you'll remain.'

Intimidated as she was, the girl repeated the new name under her breath, then repeated it aloud: 'Marian.' Still savouring it she knew that she would always be grateful to the girl at school who had suggested that she should put 'Mary' and 'Ann' together and make 'Marian' out of them. It made her feel like a new person. It had a heart-warming ring, like a chord of music, and she felt sure that Marian Evans would amount to a great deal more than Mary Ann Evans ever could.

'*Marian* it is, then,' her father said indulgently, with an appealing side-glance at his wife. 'I'm so proud of you, Marian, that I have decided to send you to a new school. You deserve it, my little wench, and I'm sure you'll find the change beneficial.'

Mary Ann looked at him anxiously. Often enough she longed for change but almost always she feared it.

'A new school, Father?' she faltered.

'Miss Wallington's Academy at Nuneaton. There'll be girls of your own age at Miss Wallington's, and you, I vow, will soon outstrip them.'

Mary Ann inclined her head gravely. Girls of her own age and the chance of competing with them on equal terms, that would at least be exciting.

'You shall have a short holiday at home first,' Robert Evans promised, 'and go with me on my rounds. That is,' he teased, 'when you can spare the time to take your head out of a book.'

'Mary Ann!' Christiana Evans said peremptorily.

'Yes, Mother?' Mary Ann asked, with downcast eyes.

Christiana's expression softened. 'That you have become such a great reader at an early age is admirable and exceptional. I, too, in that respect, am proud of you.'

Mary Ann blushed but was quite incapable of expressing the pleasure which her mother's words had given her.

5

It was midnight. Miss Maria Lewis, head mistress of the Wallington Academy, closed the classroom door loudly, but her action, a deliberate one, did nothing to draw the new pupil's attention to her entry. She studied the girl in silence for a few moments. Marian Evans was seated at a desk reading a book with the utmost concentration. Pen, ink and writing paper were close at hand. There was evidence that at least a second candle had been lit. Maria Lewis approached the desk with a heavy tread but still the girl remained oblivious of her presence. As a final resort the head mistress coughed loudly; Marian looked up in sudden consternation.

'Miss Lewis!'

'You should have been in bed hours ago,' Maria Lewis said, but not severely.

'Yes, Miss Lewis.'

'How can you possibly work well tomorrow if you remain awake half the night?'

'I shall manage somehow, Miss Lewis,' Marian said confidently.

Maria Lewis smiled and thought it more than likely. Marian Evans had made amazing progress during the few weeks that she had been at the Wallington Academy. She was quietly industrious and evinced a deep interest in almost all subjects. There was every reason to believe that she would eventually become one of the cleverest of the thirty pupils.

'It is breaking the rules,' Miss Lewis said, 'to remain up after bedtime. Are you aware of that?'

'Yes, Miss Lewis.'

'Then what shall your punishment be?'

'Am I to pronounce my own punishment?' Marian asked daringly.

Miss Lewis tried not to smile. 'Perhaps I should forbid you to indulge in any private reading during the next three days.'

Marian looked aghast. 'Not *that*, Miss Lewis, please!'

Maria Lewis nodded slowly. 'You share my own pleasure in

reading, the only real pleasure I permit myself. I permit it to such an extent that it *could* be called a sin.'

'A *sin*, Miss Lewis?'

'It depends, of course, on the nature of one's reading. Tell me the title of your book.'

'*The Pilgrim's Progress*, Miss Lewis.'

'I thoroughly approve.'

Marian found herself warming to Maria Lewis. 'I can't live without reading,' she said pleadingly. 'Please punish me in some other way.'

Maria Lewis noted the eagerness of the girl's voice and at the same time the look of uncertainty, even insecurity, in her eyes. She studied her more closely. She was indeed very plain, with a rather large head, a long, almost hooked, nose and a thick lower lip inclined to stubbornness. On the other hand her hair was beautiful enough to make any other girl envious; her voice rang pleasantly, even when she was deeply disturbed, her smile was engaging when she was in the mood and her grey-blue eyes, not too widely set, invited confidence and love. Plain, yes, but an inner beauty shone through the plainness.

'Very well,' Maria Lewis decided, 'you shall write out ten times my favourite psalm, the fifty-ninth. I hope it will become your favourite too.'

'It will, I promise,' Marian said, without being able to recall the fifty-ninth psalm.

'We must do something about your accent,' Maria Lewis went on thoughtfully.

'My accent, Miss Lewis?' Marian asked in surprise.

'It is not as good as you might think. There are times when there is no doubt at all about where you were born.'

Marian remembered something that her father had said. 'That's only when I'm agitated, Miss Lewis.'

'Then we must first try to iron out the agitation. I see that you have been writing as well as reading. Many pages by the look of it.'

Marian nodded eagerly. 'As much as I could remember of Walter Scott's *Waverley*.'

'Why that, Marian?'

'My sister Chrissey lent me *Waverley*. She got it from a friend. It had to be returned before I could finish it.'

'And did you aim,' Maria Lewis asked mildly, 'to invent the rest of the story from the point where you were deprived of it?'

'Yes,' Marian admitted.

'Successfully?'

Marian shook her head in despair. 'No, Miss Lewis.'

'Then you are not as conceited, not as vain, as one might have thought,' Maria Lewis said, resisting the impulse to embrace the girl but touching her lightly on the shoulder. 'I have a copy of *Waverley* in my private collection. I shall lend it to you if only in order to prevent you from feeling thwarted. Now, my dear Marian, go to bed and make good your promise by working really well tomorrow.'

Marian went happily to bed. There would, she knew, be no night terrors that night, no waking in panic and apprehension. She loved Miss Lewis and was ready to worship her. She felt that she had made a real friend at last, a friend who would be all in all to her and to whom she herself, she hoped fervently, would be all in all.

'I shall model myself upon Miss Lewis,' she whispered to herself in the darkness.

6

'MARY ANN has become a prig,' Isaac pronounced. 'That's all the four years at Miss Wallington's have done for her.'

'Come, now!' Robert Evans protested warmly.

'A *religious* prig, that's what I mean, Father.'

'Scarcely that, Isaac.'

'A religious *fanatic*, that's what I really mean.'

Marian stood near the piano, just as if not present at all, listening to herself being talked about. She was glad that her mother, who was taking to her bed more and more these days, was upstairs with the doctor in attendance and unable to support Isaac in his criticism.

Robert Evans turned and smiled at his daughter, drawing her into the conversation. 'I don't think there's anything fanatical about you, Marian. Religious fervour can hardly be called religious fanaticism. But whatever it is, I have no complaints.' He paused and laughed teasingly. 'It makes you go willingly and eagerly to church every Sunday instead of under duress.'

'It isn't a laughing matter, Father,' the thirteen-year-old Marian said soberly.

'Who would have thought,' Isaac asked in disgust, 'that Mary Ann would turn into an Evangelist? That isn't a laughing matter either.' At sixteen, very nearly seventeen, Isaac had High Church leanings and as a result, for a reason which he had never been able to explain, considered himself very much a man of the world. 'She thinks all the pleasures of the world are sinful,' he went on accusingly. 'All she wants to do is to go about with a solemn face, never laugh and do her best to convert everybody to her own way of thinking. We have Miss Lewis to blame for it all.'

Marian blushed angrily. Isaac had said that before and it was hateful. Besides, she did laugh on occasion, but if not very often it was because there was very little to laugh about in a world full of wickedness. Miss Lewis herself, the kindest and wisest person in the world, had said so many times.

'An Evangelist is not a fanatic,' she argued stolidly. 'An Evangelist is a person who brings the good news of the gospel to the world.'

'The sinful world, dear sister.'

'Yes, Isaac, the *sinful* world. Deliver me from the workers of iniquity, and save me from bloody men.'

'Marian, Marian!' Robert Evans protested.

'So they've taught you to swear at Miss Wallington's,' Isaac laughed.

'I wasn't swearing,' Marian said indignantly, 'I was quoting from the fifty-ninth psalm.'

'Well, in that case...' Robert Evans shrugged.

'I'm not a sinner, even if you think I am,' Isaac continued.

'I think,' Marian said hotly, 'that you are a very misguided young man.'

'Now, now, no quarrelling, children,' Robert Evans said equably. 'And, Isaac, setting aside the religious question, let us give praise where praise is due. Your sister is the cleverest girl at Miss Wallington's, just as I expected her to be.'

Isaac smiled and chucked Marian under the chin. 'Oh, I agree, but why haven't you made any friends at Miss Wallington's? Is it because you're too clever for all the other girls? Too religious as well?'

'There's Miss Lewis,' Marian said defensively. 'Miss Lewis is a very good friend.'

'I can't understand you!' Isaac exclaimed. 'Thirty girls at Miss Wallington's and your only friend a woman years and years older than you. It isn't natural.'

24

Uneasily Robert Evans felt obliged to agree with his son, though not entirely with his wife who had stigmatised the friendship, apart from the religious aspect of it, as unhealthy. He had wondered of late what to do about it and now, influenced by a recent report from Miss Wallington, he made up his mind and hoped that his decision would fail to hurt Marian too severely.

'Marian,' he said gently, 'I have decided to send you to another school, a better school.'

Marian was appalled. 'And—and separate me from Miss Lewis?'

'A good thing, too,' Isaac said enthusiastically.

Tactfully and truthfully, Robert Evans said: 'You need and deserve greater opportunities, Marian. Miss Wallington herself said so. You can learn very little more at her school. She said that too.'

Marian bowed her head and fought back her tears. To be deprived of Miss Lewis's love and sympathy and understanding— it would be worse than losing an arm or a leg. She looked up and held her father's eyes in dumb appeal. Sensing something of what she felt he said:

'There'll be nothing to prevent you from visiting Miss Lewis occasionally, and you may write to her whenever you wish.'

'Thank you, Father,' Marian said brokenly.

Feeling sorry for her, remembering that it was his duty to protect her, Isaac took her by the arm and led her out to the garden.

'Let's go fishing like we used to,' he suggested.

'No! No, no, no!'

'Fishing isn't a sinful pleasure, Mary Ann.'

'Yes it is!'

'You eat fish, don't you?' Isaac reasoned. 'That means you allow somebody else the pleasure of doing the catching. You and your Evangelists! St Peter was a fisherman, wasn't he? And don't forget how Jesus fed the multitude at the Sermon on the Mount.'

'Oh, Isaac,' Marian sobbed, feeling lost and terribly unsure of herself, 'you don't understand.'

'About Miss Lewis, you mean?'

'About *anything*. And I can't *make* you understand.'

'It's my opinion you don't really understand yourself,' Isaac said shrewdly.

Marian wondered uneasily if her brother could be right, and that made her feel still more unsure of herself. Life, she thought, was hard and cruel and scarcely worth living, unless you were as holy as Miss Lewis or as self-satisfied as Isaac.

'I shall go for a walk *alone*,' she said forlornly.

'And I,' Isaac chuckled, 'shall read the fifty-ninth psalm, just to make sure you weren't really swearing.'

'No!' Marian said vehemently.

'*No?*'

'I mean, Isaac, I won't allow you to make me laugh.'

7

CHRISTIANA EVANS knew that death would claim her soon. She knew from the way the doctor had looked at her that morning and had evaded her request to speak up frankly. She raised her head slightly from the pillow and stared in a puzzled manner at her husband. There was something she wanted to ask him, but . . . what? After a great effort she remembered.

'Robert, have the children been sent for?'

'Yes, Christiana. That is, Marian and Isaac. Chrissey is at home nursing you.'

'Marian? Ah, yes, you mean Mary Ann. I particularly want to see Mary Ann. I admit that I have not always been kind to her.'

'Kind and loving, in your own fashion,' Robert Evans said, a trifle hoarsely.

'As you wish.'

Marian reached Griff House before Isaac. It was close on Christmas. Marian, now sixteen, paused before entering the house to admire the scene about her. The trees and shrubs in the garden were laced with the pure white of a first fall of snow. The stillness and the tranquillity stirred her deeply. Almost reluctantly she rapped the door-knocker. A solemn-faced, whispering maid admitted her, her attitude suggesting vividly to Marian that she had entered the presence of death. Robert Evans greeted her in the hall, helped her to remove her cloak, her bonnet and her muff, then led her up to her mother's room. Christiana forced herself into a sitting position and indicated with a weak gesture of her hand that she wished to be left alone wtih Marian. Robert Evans tiptoed from the room and closed the door softly behind him.

'Come and sit by the bed,' Christiana said, when Marian remained hesitantly at a distance.

Marian obeyed but felt at a loss for words.

'I need you more than I need Isaac and Chrissey, *now,*' Christiana said broodingly. 'It must be because I have treated you harshly at times. Conscience is a strange thing. I have lived long enough to realise that it surges strongly in one's breast when one is close to death.'

A lump rose agonisingly in Marian's throat. 'Dear Mother, please say no more about it.'

Christiana laughed dryly. 'You are learning compassion, Mary Ann.'

'I pray constantly for the blessing of compassion, Mother.'

'Not sanctimoniously, I hope.'

'I—I don't think so,' Marian stammered.

'You still feel uncertain of yourself. Insecure. You have always felt like that. The reason is obvious. You have been affected from the first by your father.'

'*My father?*' Marian's eyes widened in amazement. '*In that* way, Mother?'

'Your father is a fine man, a strong man—beyond the confines of Griff House. Here, at home, he has always been in awe of me.'

'In *awe* of you, Mother?'

'His father was a peasant. He has never been able to forget it, but I have always looked up to him, a fact which he has always failed to recognise. I love him dearly. Never forget that, Mary Ann.'

Her thoughts in turmoil, Marian remained silent.

'Now tell me about your new school,' Christiana said, slipping down in the bed and resting her head on the pillow.

'It isn't a *new* school any more, Mother. I've been there for three years.'

'True, child. My memory grows dim. The school is in Coventry. The principals are the two Miss Franklins. Their father is a Baptist minister, one of the lower orders. Despite that they are highly educated, one might even say highly cultured. Have you acquitted yourself well there?'

Pondering on this, Marian said soberly: 'My essays are read to the whole school. I have been given special teachers in German and French. A special music teacher, too. He said only yesterday that he had taught me all he knew himself.'

'You speak without conceit. I hold that to your credit. Do the other girls envy you?'

Still soberly, Marian said: 'Yes, Mother, because Father sends me new-laid eggs every week.'

Christiana looked at her daughter in despair. If only the girl, even in the presence of a fatal illness, would laugh.

27

'The Baptist influence is surely responsible,' Christiana said, speaking to herself rather than to Marian.

'What do you mean by that, Mother?'

'Are all the girls Baptists?'

'Most of them.'

'And ... *you*?'

'I think so, yes.'

'You write often to Miss Lewis. Does *she* approve?'

Marian considered this.

'Miss Lewis approves of my sincere search for true religion. It would be correct, I think, to say that I am not sure, yet, of any creed.'

'I suspect that there is something of the chameleon in you,' her mother commented. 'Are prayer meetings held at school?'

'Frequently.'

A flash of memory caused Christiana to smile. '*You* lead the prayer meetings, Mary Ann.'

'As often as I am permitted,' Marian said proudly.

'Well, there is nothing wrong with praying. Pray for me, I need your prayers. And pray for yourself. Pray, child, for the blessing of at least a little laughter.'

'The world is too wicked a place for laughter,' Marian said staunchly.

Growing very tired, Christiana said weakly: 'Possibly you're right, according to your present point of view. Possibly, to some people, the world has always been too wicked a place for laughter. Jesus wept but I can't recall that he ever laughed. What a pity. Laughter, I'm sure, is capable of casting out wickedness, whatever you might mean by wickedness. Promise me one thing, Mary Ann ...'

'Yes, Mother?'

'That you will try and try again to laugh, if only at yourself.'

Marian was shaken by this—how grim her mother must think her!—but she remained unconvinced that to laugh, even at herself, would solve any problems. After all, there were so many kinds of laughter. If she was unable to laugh freely and joyously, she would rather not laugh at all than laugh cynically or ironically or unkindly.

'I promise,' she said politely.

Surprising everybody, Christiana Evans rallied the next day but remained critically ill for several months before the end came. There was no more school for Marian. She stayed on at Griff House and with Chrissey helped to nurse their mother. She felt, day by day, that she was growing closer to her mother, learning to accept and love her wholeheartedly. Robert Evans himself fell ill, reducing Marian to a state of fevered anxiety. She prayed as never before, telling herself and God, almost as if issuing a threat, that she would take a vow of silence if she lost her father too. His recovery coincided with the last days of his wife. She died towards the end of the summer, but grief-stricken as Robert Evans was he urged his children not to fret.

'It is a merciful release. We must think of it as that and that only.'

Instead of going back to school Marian remained at home after the funeral and with her sister shared the responsibility of running Griff House,

'I, the official housekeeper,' Chrissey joked, 'you my rather clumsy apprentice. Still, you'll learn, Mary Ann. The sooner you are able to become sole housekeeper the better.'

'What do you mean by that, Chrissey?'

Chrissey smiled archly. 'Had you not noticed that I am being courted? I shall marry quite soon. You, of course, will remain a maiden lady all your life.'

Six months after Marian's seventeenth birthday Chrissey married a doctor. Marian suffered a fit of depression during the wedding festivities and wept bitterly when bidding her sister goodbye. It was true, she tried to reason with herself, that she and Chrissey had never been very close, but her marriage meant that the family, to which Marian clung, even though she was an oddity at Griff House, was breaking up. Her mother dead, her sister married—how long, she wondered, before her brother decided to marry? It gave her a feeling of desolation, even of impending doom.

Robert Evans held what he lightly termed a family conference the day after Chrissey's departure.

'Isaac tells me,' he said, smiling fondly on his daughter, 'that you have never wanted to be a housekeeper. What I seek for you, Marian, is the best, as you see it yourself.'

'Mary Ann could become a school mistress,' Isaac ventured.

'You would like that?' Robert Evans asked.

Marian considered this. It was a tempting suggestion, to follow, as it were, in Miss Lewis's footsteps. It would provide a way of escape, yet in her present mood the last thing she wanted was an escape from Griff House.

'No, Father,' she said, shaking her head.

'But are you capable of running Griff House alone?' he asked, and added in a flat voice: 'I could, of course, engage a house-keeper of mature years and experience.'

Marian looked at her father searchingly. He had failed fully to recover his health and strength since the death of her mother and his illness which had preceded it. At sixty-three he had aged noticeably and was leaving more and more of his work to Isaac. He would hate the presence of a stranger in the house, and so would she.

'Father,' she said quietly, 'it is my duty to look after you and Isaac.'

Robert Evans's face brightened. 'Your decision gladdens my heart.'

Isaac laughed cheerfully. 'There'll be no complaints from me, however many mistakes our young housekeeper may make.'

Marian tried to smile, even to laugh at herself, but dolefully she thought: So there it is, a housekeeper, after all.

8

MARIA LEWIS, making one of her rare visits to Griff House, found Marian in the dairy. She was making butter. It was a task, Maria Lewis knew, which the young woman had never been expected to perform, but she was determined, as she had said, to master all things concerned in the running of a house, especially a country house. It was a determination based on despair and frustration, or so Maria Lewis was inclined to suspect from the contents of Marian's many confiding letters. Still unobserved, the school mistress studied her former pupil covertly. Marian had reached her eighteenth birthday several months ago. She was not as plain as she used to be but nobody would ever be able to call her pretty. Her figure, a not unpleasing one, had filled out; she had the appearance of full womanly maturity. Her hands, Maria Lewis noted admiringly, were fine and slim, the hands, surely, of an artist. There seemed to be something noble (a fanciful thought indeed!) about her countenance as she bent over her humble task.

'Marian . . .' Maria Lewis ventured.

Marian looked up in surprise. 'Miss Lewis!'

'I am as pleased to see you as you are to see me, Marian, but I can spend only an hour with you.'

Marian stripped off her apron, washed her hands and smoothed back her hair. There was something, Maria Lewis decided, not unfeminine about her movements. They were even quite graceful, when she forgot herself. There were times, however, when she moved awkwardly, as if fearful of staring, critical eyes.

'Have you seen Father?' Marian asked.

'For a few moments only, then he went back to his study.'

'Do you think he looks well?' Marian asked anxiously.

'He has aged, certainly, but not too greatly. He tells me that you have become a most proficient housekeeper.'

'It's the only thing I shall ever become proficient at,' Marian said gloomily. 'I feel desperately that I shall never achieve anything worth while.'

'Rubbish, my dear girl! You will become proficient at anything to which you set your mind. I believe it, Marian. Never forget my faith in you.'

Frowning doubtfully Marian led her friend to the drawing-room. Was her life really as dull and unrewarding as she sometimes believed? Apart from keeping house for her father and her brother, she was throwing herself, possibly violently, into what were nicely termed good works, visiting the sick and the poor and contributing to worthy charities. She was continuing her studies too; languages masters came out from Coventry to coach her in Italian and German, and there was a new music master to give her advanced lessons. In addition she was reading more avidly than ever and making an intensive study of the Bible. She sighed heavily. Admirable, no doubt, but where could it all possibly lead her? She saw herself, without regarding the thought as amusing, as an even greater oddity—a housekeeper who had become a veritable bluestocking. Mindful of her friend's comfort she rang for the maid and ordered tea.

'Your father said you had a short holiday recently,' Maria Lewis said presently. 'Your brother took you to London. Did you enjoy your visit to the capital?'

Marian shook her head in quick denial. 'I hated London. I wasn't at all delighted with the stir of the great Babel.'

'A depressing city in many respects, but surely you found something of interest there.'

'I stayed in my hotel room most of the time, reading.'

'Why that, Marian?'

'All Isaac cared about was going to the theatre. The devil's playhouse, Miss Lewis. My religious beliefs prevented me from going with him.'

'That, indeed, was right and proper,' Miss Lewis said approvingly. 'Did you do any shopping?'

Marian looked at her friend askance. 'I needed nothing, except a book. Isaac found it for me, Josephus's *History of the Jews.*' And she added in disgust, '*He* bought two hunting sketches to hang in his room.'

'How very frivolous.'

Marian knew that she and her brother were growing farther and farther apart. Frivolous was indeed the right word to describe his attitude to life, he resisting as he was her every effort to convert him. He called her 'my little saint' and continued shockingly to enjoy his three great, absorbing pleasures: hunting, dancing and theatre-going.

'Isaac,' Marian complained, 'reads only the lightest of novels.'

'Ah yes, all that romantic twaddle.'

'I have nothing against romantic fiction,' Marian pronounced earnestly, 'if it is presented true to life. Or more correctly, true to *history*. I lean largely to historical fiction. I regard it as especiailly beneficial to the discipline of our minds.'

'And, of course, religious fiction is even more beneficial.'

'No,' Marian surprised herself by saying.

Maria Lewis looked aghast. This, in a sense, was revolt.

'Religious novels are becoming more hateful to me than worldly ones,' Marian continued, without having noticed her friend's silent reaction.

'My dear child, what a thing to say!'

'They are a sort of centaur or mermaid,' Marian said, warming to her subject, 'and, like other monsters that we do not know how to class, should be destroyed for the public good as soon as born. The weapons of Christian warfare were never sharpened at the forge of romance. Domestic fiction, as it comes more within the range of imitation, is even more dangerous. For my part I am ready to weep at the impossibility of my understanding, or barely knowing, a fraction of the sum of objects that present themselves for our contemplation in books and in life. Have I, then, any time to spend on things that never existed?'

Maria Lewis laughed weakly. She was being read a lecture, and the extraordinary language of it!

'Your speech is becoming a trifle stilted, Marian,' she contented herself with saying, 'a trifle pedantic, even a trifle pontifical, as if you were writing leading articles for one of the more intellectual journals. Or do I mean psuedo-intellectual? Such language is all very well when it comes to writing, but in general conversation I find it restricting, even disconcerting.'

Marian hung her head. Miss Lewis was making her feel more than ordinarily uncertain of herself.

'I suspect,' Maria Lewis added, 'that you have a masculine mind with the seeds of male genius in it. But note this well, Marian: there are many forms of genius, some good, some evil. Cultivate the good, guard against the evil.'

Marian was shocked tearfully into saying: 'What a dreadful thing to have a masculine mind and yet suffer the slavery of being a girl!'

Maria Lewis sighed heavily. The slavery of being a girl! Such a dreadful statement from one so young! She hoped and prayed that Marian would never become what she herself had become, lonely, when it was too late, for male companionship and male love.

Brightly she said: 'Reverting to the subject of writing, you mentioned in a recent letter that you had written some poetry.'

Marian blushed. 'A few doggerel lines only.'

'Do you know them by heart?'

'Yes, Miss Lewis.'

'Then please recite them for me.'

Marian cleared her throat and began hesitantly:

> 'As o'er the fields by evening's light I stray,
> I hear a still small whisper—"Come away!
> Thou must to this bright, lovely world soon say
> Farewell!"'

'Ah,' Maria Lewis said non-committally.

Marian cleared her throat again and continued:

> 'The mandate I'd obey, my lamp prepare,
> Gird up my garments, give my soul to pray'r,
> And say to earth, and all that breathe earth's air,
> Farewell!'

'How very gloomy,' Maria Lewis commented, 'but the lines are not doggerel. However, they fill me with desolation, a sense of utter loneliness.'

'I was unbearably lonely when I wrote them.'

'Gloomy . . .' Maria Lewis pondered, 'but with one redeeming feature, your reference to "this bright, lovely world".'

'Redeeming,' Marian asked searchingly, 'not sinful?'

'There is nothing sinful in finding the world, by which *I* mean and *you* mean nature, bright and lovely.'

'I'm so glad to hear you say that, Miss Lewis!'

'Then why long to leave it?'

'*Because* . . .' said Marian, sounding and feeling like a little girl.

'I quite understand,' Miss Lewis said heavily. 'Setting aside poetic licence, it is not the earth, and all who breathe earth's air, that you long to leave, but the life which you are forced by circumstances to lead, here at Griff House.'

Marian sprang to her feet instantly, panic in her heart. Miss Lewis, a diabolical but still well-loved Miss Lewis, was trying to force her to recognise the truth of her innermost thoughts and feelings, her emotional response to life as she at present knew it. But . . . escape from Griff House? *That* was neither sought nor wanted.

'The butter!' she cried. 'I must squeeze out the whey. I—I must salt it and shape it into pats, put it in proper shape.'

'Put it in proper shape,' Maria Lewis repeated, and asked gently, 'And your young life also?'

9

ROBERT EVANS was seated near the fire in a deep armchair, listening as Marian played the piano for him with the habitual look of intense concentration on her face. He enjoyed her music, there was something deeply stirring about it, but rarely did he understand it. Presently she would bring yet another evening to a close by reading to him. He was not entirely happy about his much loved daughter and had decided to make a move which might possibly enlarge her present limited horizon. Life had changed in no way for her since her sister's marriage, and that was over four years ago. True, there had been the unexpected and unusual excitement of seeing her first verses in print; the *Christian Observer* had published them. But the chart of ecclesiastical history upon which she had embarked with dedicated enthusiasm had been necessarily set aside when a similar chart had been published in London. It had been, he knew, a bitter disappointment to her. He stared at the glowing embers; Marian at twenty-one, he feared, was in danger of becoming an old maid.

Dissatisfied with her playing, Marian closed the piano. Had she a real soul for music? She was beginning to doubt it. Technical perfection, for which she was always striving, was not and never would be sufficient in itself. She turned from the piano and picked up a book.

'Wordsworth,' she said eagerly. 'I never before met with so many of my own feelings expressed just as I would like to express them.'

Robert Evans smiled up at her. 'No reading tonight, Marian. I want to discuss a number of things with you. I'll begin with Isaac's affairs. I know now the reason for his frequent visits to Birmingham. There was a letter from him today. Has he confided in you at all?'

'No, Father.'

'Isaac will shortly announce his engagement. The young lady is a Miss Sarah Rawlins. Her family, I gather, is eminently respectable.'

'High Church, of course?'

'Presumably,' Robert Evans said, and added with a smile, 'But need you sound so severe about it?'

Marian frowned, yet a small voice, her mother's, surely, seemed to be whispering in her ear: *Laugh, Marian, if only at yourself.* No *not* her mother's, her own; her mother had never called her anything but Mary Ann. It would be worse, Marian reflected, if Isaac had decided to marry a Catholic. To her amazement a strangled sound, laughter of a sort, came from her throat. She coughed to repress it.

'I wish Isaac all happiness,' she said sincerely.

'His marriage,' Robert Evans continued, 'will bring about a radical change in our lives.'

'You mean, Father, that Isaac will bring his bride to Griff House?'

'That is what I have in mind for him.'

Marian digested this. A strange young woman at Griff House, and she Isaac's wife . . . She wanted to love her brother's future wife, but her appearance could lead to many conflicts. It would be worse than employing a housekeeper.

Robert Evans stared at the fire again. 'The new railway is largely responsible.'

'The new railway, Father? I don't follow your train of thought, I don't follow it at all.'

'The London to Birmingham railway has brought about a rapidly expanding progress. Who cares to travel by coach anymore, except a few old diehards like myself? The railway is having an effect on my business and I, at sixty-seven, am too old for new-fangled progress. That is why I have decided to retire and leave the business entirely to Isaac.'

'You mean to move from Griff House, Father?'

'Yes, Marian. I have Coventry in mind, if we can find a suitable house there. You will have the opportunity, in Coventry, to meet people of your own intellectual calibre. You need that and I want it for you.'

Marian wondered whether she should feel happy or sad. Griff House was her world. It gave her a feeling of security, in spite of its restrictions and frustrations. Neither happy nor sad, she decided, but terribly apprehensive. She longed for change yet feared it.

'Who knows,' her father said seriously, 'I may succeed in finding you a husband in Coventry.'

'Please don't try too hard, Father,' Marian begged. 'Please leave the finding of a husband to the will of God.'

'Ah yes, true marriages are made in heaven.'

'That, Father, I firmly believe.'

10

HAVING closed her own gate behind her, Elizabeth Pears walked a few yards along Foleshill Road and paused curiously at the gate of Bird Grove, the adjoining house. A young woman of middle height and slight build was digging purposefully in the garden, a look of utter concentration on her face. It was an interesting if somewhat rugged face, Mrs Pears decided, but the young woman's hair style seemed to her incongruous: the ringlets suggested a contrived femininity at war with the ruggedness.

Elizabeth Pears cleared her throat. 'Miss Evans, I believe?'

Startled, Marian looked up. 'That is correct,' she said guardedly.

'Please let me introduce myself. My name is Elizabeth Pears. My husband Abijah and I, and our young son, live next door. Welcome to Coventry, Miss Evans.'

'Thank you, Mrs Pears,' Marian said formally.

'But how industrious you are! You've been here no time at all and you're already putting the garden in order.'

'It is in a shocking state,' Marian said flatly.

The interruption was by no means welcome, but she had no wish to seem churlish. In any case, despite her native caution, she was beginning to feel drawn to her new neighbour; she had a pleasant smile and a soft, friendly voice. Marian thrust the spade into the ground and rested her hands on the handle, rather in the manner of a labourer taking a much needed rest.

'I already know a lot about you, Miss Evans, and your quite frightening accomplishments,' Elizabeth Pears continued brightly. 'The Miss Franklins often sing your praises. I was a pupil at their school too, but some years before you went there yourself, of course. We have at least that bond in common. Oh yes, and another. We hold the same religious views. I predict that we shall get along very well together, become the best of neighbours.'

'I hope so, Mrs Pears,' Marian said tentatively.

'I expect you are finding Bird Grove a little cramped after Griff House.'

Marian inclined her head in agreement. Bird Grove was small in comparison with Griff House, but large enough for her father and herself and one house-maid, with extra bedrooms for possible visitors. Nevertheless it was rather commonplace, a semi-detached suburban house which had been described as 'modern', a distasteful description to Marian.

'Still, the situation is pleasant enough, for the outskirts of a city,' Elizabeth Pears continued.

Marian considered this not too happily. It was true that from her study window she could see, beyond meadows and a quiet-flowing stream, the three spires of Coventry; from her bedroom window above the view was wider and marred in the near distance by ugly factories, dingy working-class houses and veritable slums.

'Coventry is growing rapidly,' Elizabeth Pears added proudly. 'The population is now over thirty thousand.'

'Rapidly in a commercial sense, Mrs Pears,' Maria pointed out.

'True, Miss Evans, but we are not all commercially minded to the exclusion of higher things. You will find many intellectuals here, much good and lively conversation. Indeed, you will find all the culture you could wish for, at so great a distance from London.'

'That will be pleasing, of course, Mrs Pears, but what distresses me is the poverty. I have already walked through some of the worst slums imaginable.'

'I myself am not impervious to poverty,' Elizabeth Pears said seriously. 'I visit the poor and the sick, just as you did so admirably in the country. And soon I shall set up a clothing club. I need help in that. Why not join me, Miss Evans?'

'Gladly!' Marian said enthusiastically.

11

ROBERT EVANS and his daughter were spending the evening with Abijah and Elizabeth Pears, with whom, during the last few weeks, they had become very friendly. Abijah Pears had made a point from the first of flattering Robert Evans by seeking his advice, even though he himself was a man of substance and importance in the business world of Coventry, a future mayor of the city, or so people said. Marian liked him but held his wife in greater esteem; she was energetic and hard-working and, with Marian's help, had quickly established the clothing club in a poverty-stricken district called Pudding Pits. Also present that night were Mrs Sibree and her adolescent daughter. They, too, lived in Foleshill Road and Mrs Sibree's husband was a Nonconformist minister with whom Marian had already had many earnest, evangelical conversations.

'Did you succeed in meeting the head master of the Grammar School?' Elizabeth Pears asked Marian.

'Yes, and I had a long talk with him. He has agreed to give me private lessons in Latin and Greek.'

'How determined you are to improve your mind,' Mrs Pears said admiringly.

My *masculine* mind, Marian reflected. soberly. She was still studying French and German and Italian and striving for a complete mastery of the piano by having further lessons, now that she was living in Coventry, from the organist of St Michael's Church. She was meeting more and more people, living a fuller life socially than she had ever thought possible or even wise. Why, then, did she feel dissatisfied with herself? Why was she plagued by the fear that she would never find anyone to whom, fully and sincerely, she could pour out her soul? There was Miss Lewis, of course, but Marian and her former teacher, though they exchanged many letters, were growing apart. It was distressing to realise that Miss Lewis's advice and religious exhortations no longer completely contented her. For what, Marian often wondered, was she really searching? Isaac, now settled at Griff House with his young, pretty and quite friendly wife, had said laughingly, 'A husband, my little saint; you can't remain married to books all your life.' Was there, Marian asked herself, any truth in that? One thing she was determined on, she would never marry, as so many young women did, merely for the sake of marrying. *That* would make a mockery of marriage.

There was a knock at the front door.

'My brother Charles,' Elizabeth Pears said, springing to her feet. 'He has a special way of knocking.'

At first glance Marian was not at all sure that she was going to like Charles Bray. He came into the room roaring with laughter, obviously at a joke which he had made himself. Abijah Pears greeted him gruffly, as Marian was quick to notice, and Mrs Sibree and her daughter, inclining their heads, saying nothing, looked at him askance, as if he were some strange animal which they either feared or loathed.

'It interests me very much to meet you, Miss Evans,' he said, when introduced. 'Elizabeth has told me a lot about you. Your cleverness almost terrifies me. Nevertheless, I shall be happy to sit at the feet of the oracle.'

Was he, Marian wondered, making fun of her? She looked at him speculatively, trying to decide whether or not her suspicion was correct. His appearance told her little, except that he had his sister Elizabeth's twinkling eyes. A man of middle height, he wore a black frock-coat carelessly. His hair was rather long and wavy. He was clean-shaven with a face inclined to plumpness. Marian envisaged him, thirty or forty years hence, as a corpulent old gentleman leaning heavily on a walking stick. He was thirty, married and lived at Rosehill, a country house type of residence on the outskirts of Coventry. That was all that Marian knew about him, for Elizabeth Pears had seemed strangely reluctant to say much about the brother whom she so obviously adored.

'Miss Evans,' he said, in a neutral tone, 'your good works are admirable. Elizabeth says so and I have always believed what Elizabeth says.'

'Thank you,' Marian said faintly.

'Since you settled in Coventry,' Charles Bray continued, 'you have come in contact with many Methodists. Tell me, have you found them, without exception, very moral people?'

Marian frowned over this. 'Not without exception,' she admitted grudgingly.

'You have also come in contact with many non-believers, all intent on performing good works. Have you found them, without exception, *immoral* people?'

Marian frowned again. 'I have found many sterling characters among the non-believers.'

'Most interesting,' Charles Bray said enigmatically.

Mrs Sibree and her daughter rose from their chairs, as if at a given signal. Mrs Sibree murmured that unless they made a move immediately they would be late for a prayer meeting. With that she and her daughter withdrew without a further glance at Charles Bray.

'How the Sibrees dislike me,' he said, laughing lightly.

Involuntarily Marian said: 'I thought them most rude, Mr Bray.'

'Rude or not, Miss Evans, they are very charitable people, insofar as I myself am *not* concerned.'

Marian looked at him searchingly. There was something about him which was beginning, strangely, to attract her. She felt, surprisingly, that he represented an intellectual challenge.

'It often seems to me,' he said, his expression solemn, 'that many charitable people, deliberately charitable, relentlessly charitable, never know vinegar from wine until they have swallowed it and got the colic.'

Startling herself, Marian laughed spontaneously. She caught her father's disapproving look—clearly he was thinking that it was a most improper remark to pass in front of ladies—but laughter still got the better of her. Miraculously it made her feel almost reborn. She thought of herself as a flower, if not a pretty one, opening its petals to the morning sun. It was an altogether shattering experience. She would tell Isaac about it the next time she saw him; he would approve wholeheartedly.

Charles Bray turned to his sister. 'A brief visit in passing, Elizabeth. I must hurry home. Cara always grows anxious when I'm late.' He swung round at the door and held Marian's eyes speculatively. 'Miss Evans, have you read Hennel's *Inquiry Concerning the Origin of Christianity*?'

'No, Mr Bray.'

'I advise you to do so. You may well find it very revealing.'

'A dangerous book,' Abijah Pears said heavily.

'All thought-provoking books are considered dangerous by the type of Christian who wears blinkers,' Charles Bray laughed, and humming a Methodist hymn impishly beneath his breath took his leave.

Elizabeth Pears went out to the kitchen to prepare refreshments. Marian followed her to help and asked without preamble why the Sibrees disliked her brother Charles so much.

'It is disapproval rather than dislike, Marian. They regard him as an infidel, and a dangerous one at that.'

'And you yourself, Elizabeth?'

'Dangerous, yes, to some people.'

'Do please tell me more about him.'

Charles Bray, it transpired, was Elizabeth's only brother, the eldest of a family which included seven girls. He was a ribbon manufacturer, quite wealthy, and ran the business which he had inherited from his father so efficiently that he was able to give the greater part of his time to intellectual pursuits. He entertained informally, if lavishly, at Rosehill. His friends and acquaintances were mostly intellectuals; it was his standard joke that anyone who was a little *cracked* eventually found his way to Rosehill and became a member of the ever-widening Rosehill circle of eccentrics. Nevertheless, for all the laughter he indulged in, he was capable of taking himself very seriously indeed.

'But . . . an *infidel*?' Marian questioned. 'I understood that all the members of your family were Evangelicals.'

Elizabeth smiled faintly and explained the change, or changes, which had taken place in her brother's religious thinking. At seventeen he had gone to London as an apprentice, carrying with him an introduction to James Hennell, the brother of another Coventry ribbon manufacturer. The London Hennells were Unitarians and as such, in the eyes of Evangelicals, were very much beyond the pale religiously. The young Charles Bray saw his duty clearly and attempted, disastrously, to convert them.

'Disastrously?' Marian asked.

'He came home to Coventry a Unitarian himself. Possibly love had something to do with it. He fell in love with one of the Hennell girls and eventually married her.'

'Is a Unitarian necessarily an infidel?' Marian asked, a trifle bewildered.

Charles Bray, Elizabeth told her, had gone much further on what some people called the downward path. Much influenced by Shelley's *Queen Mab* and Mirabeau's *System of Nature*, he had argued and quarrelled with the Anglican clergy in Coventry. A lukewarm Unitarian now, he had even argued and quarrelled with his wife's brother, Charles Hennell. As a result the latter, thinking to bring him into line again, had made a deep study of Christianity and finally written his book, *Inquiry Concerning the*

Origin of Christianity. It had turned out to be a highly critical study, with the author becoming a sceptic and with Charles Bray following suit. Neither of them thereafter had thought it right or proper to go to church.

'Charles,' Elizabeth said sadly, 'is now an avowed agnostic.'

'A shocking state of affairs,' Marian said, her voice ringing not too convincingly in her own ears. 'Nevertheless, I should like to meet your brother again. It would be interesting to visit Rosehill and argue the point with him and his agnostic friends.'

'I'm sure he will invite you, but I have certain doubts about allowing you to further the acquaintance.'

'Indeed, Elizabeth?'

'Charles is a persuasive talker. He has an infectious sense of humour, even when he makes the most outrageous remarks. What I really fear is that he might shake your religious beliefs to the point of contamination.'

'Has he shaken yours to that extent?'

'Goodness, no!'

'I myself,' Marian pronounced staunchly, 'have too strong a mind, too deep a faith, ever to be contaminated.'

As it happened, Charles Bray made no move to invite Marian to Rosehill. She felt inordinately piqued and wondered, in one of her moments of uncertainty, if he really had been making fun of her. Yet he had induced her to laugh, and since then laughter had got the better of her many times. She would always be grateful to Charles Bray for that.

Several weeks later Elizabeth Pears suffered a change of mind, or, as she termed it herself, a change of heart.

'I have reached the conclusion,' she told Marian one afternoon, 'that Charles has refrained from inviting you to Rosehill because he is afraid of you.'

'*Afraid* of me?' Marian was completely taken aback.

'Not that he would admit it, but I feel sure he knows instinctively that you could get the better of him in a religious argument.'

'I could at least try,' Marian said thoughtfully.

'What we want, my sisters and I, is to see Charles brought back to true religion. And I myself feel that you are the person to do it.'

Marian began to feel excited, but quickly her face fell. 'How can I possibly break into Rosehill uninvited?'

'I shall take you there myself during one of our walks, ostensibly to meet Charles's wife Cara.'

42

Marian smiled faintly. 'A neat little conspiracy, Elizabeth.'

'And to you, personally, a tremendous challenge.'

Marian found herself burning with missionary zeal. 'A challenge, dear Elizabeth, which I cannot possibly ignore.'

12

MARIAN liked Rosehill the moment she stepped over the threshold with Elizabeth Pears. In part, because it stood majestically in a large, well-cultivated garden, it reminded her of Griff House, except that the whole atmosphere of the place abounded in a sense of freedom which she had never known at her former home. It was an indefinable something which attracted her while at the same time frightening her, as if she had cast off her habitual conventional clothing and become a woman of outrageous fashion.

Charles Bray's wife Caroline, more familiarly known as Cara, greeted her visitors in the spacious hall. She was young and pretty, with fair curly hair and large blue eyes, outgoing and friendly, with a smile which instantly warmed Marian's heart. Caroline Bray had become an agnostic too, but did that, Marian argued with herself, matter so terribly? She was much given to good works, but not relentlessly and humourlessly, Elizabeth Pears had said. She had established a school for young children in the slums of Coventry and was forever trying to teach people that animals, as well as socially handicapped children, were in need of kindness and consideration. In the most natural manner in the world she embraced Marian warmly, then held her at arms' length for a moment. 'I like the look of you, Marian Evans. Not by any means as forbidding as one might have expected.'

Marian blushed. 'Not forbidding at all, I hope, Mrs Bray.'

'Except, perhaps, to yourself.'

'I'm very severe with myself at times,' Marian admitted, with a dry laugh.

'We must change all that,' Caroline Bray commented, her head on one side. 'We have a way of managing people at Rosehill.'

'Is Charles at home, Cara?' Elizabeth Pears asked.

Caroline nodded and smiled. 'He's in the garden sitting on the bearskin, as usual. A sort of English Buddha, but *not* contemplating his navel.'

'The bearskin, Mrs Bray?' Marian asked. 'Your tone suggests a special significance.'

'A sort of prayer mat,' Caroline chuckled, 'except that nobody, least of all Charles, prays on it. Nor do we ever contemplate in brooding silence. We're much too talkative for that and content ourselves with philosophising and arguing and laughing at ourselves and each other.'

She led the way out to the garden through a French window and paused for a moment with Marian and Elizabeth on the flagged terrace which ran along that side of the house. The meticulously kept lawns, the many flowering shrubs and the distant country views gladdened Marian's heart. To live in the country again, or even on the edge of the country, would be sheer heaven.

'There he is,' Caroline Bray said. 'Let's join him.'

The bearskin rug, a large one, had been spread in the shade of an old acacia tree. Charles Bray was lying on it reading a book and in no way resembling any sort of Buddha. He sprang to his feet, kissed his sister and offered Marian his hand.

'Marian Evans! What a singular and unexpected pleasure!'

'I have heard it said,' Marian ventured, 'that anyone who is a little cracked eventually comes to Rosehill.'

'Now that,' he chuckled, 'is stealing my own thunder.' And he added, 'Even a cracked Evangelical?'

'Oh come, Charles,' his wife remonstrated, 'we have not yet had time to discover if Marian is in any way cracked in the head.'

'True,' Bray said, giving his wife an affectionate smile. 'Do sit down, Marian, or lie, or squat, it scarcely matters which so long as you make yourself comfortable and, let me add, at home.'

Marian seated herself on the bearskin, carefully folding her skirt round her ankles, and looked at Charles Bray uncertainly. She had tried to joke with him but of a sudden had been overcome by diffidence, in spite of having written to Maria Lewis confidently on the subject of Bray's forthcoming conversion. She remained silent while the others exchanged a few pleasantries about the weather and family affairs. Then Charles, seated now instead of lying, turned courteously to Marian.

'Have you read the book I recommended, Marian?' he asked seriously.

'Yes, Mr Bray.'

'You must call me Charles and I shall continue to call you Marian. Then, if we quarrel, it will take the sting out of our angry words. What do you think of my brother-in-law's learned little treatise?'

44

Marian hesitated for a moment, wishing that the subject had not been introduced. She had read Hennell's *Inquiry Concerning the Origin of Christianity* only two days ago and after agreeing to come out to Rosehill with Elizabeth. Uneasily she remembered Abijah Pear's remark about it. A dangerous book, but surely not dangerous to her! In it Charles Hennell had drawn a line between historical facts and mythology, and quite correctly Marian could but think. Dangerous because of that? Or dangerous because Hennell had reached the conclusion that Christianity, in its purest form, was no more than a natural phenomenon?

Carefully she said: 'Mr Hennell ought to be one of the happiest of men, he having written such a life's work.'

'I suspect,' Charles Bray said shrewdly, 'that you found it disturbing.'

'To a certain extent, yes.'

'I further suggest that, because of Hennell, you can no longer accept a literal interpretation of the Bible.'

Elizabeth Pears glanced warningly at Marian.

'The thought *had* crossed my mind,' Marian admitted honestly but none too happily.

'Hennell makes it clear that Jesus was a man, not a god,' Bray said warmly, 'but a man, mark you, of moral principles that are difficult, even impossible to equal. Do you agree, Marian?'

'I agree, at all events,' Marian said faintly, 'that the moral principles of Jesus are difficult, even impossible, to equal.'

'Progress of a sort,' Bray said, as if conveying the greatest of compliments. 'But enough for the moment of religious argument. To change the subject ...'

'I have not even *attempted* to argue with you,' Marian interrupted, a trifle indignantly.

'You shall have ample opportunity after you have read my own book. I, too, have written and published a book. It is, I flatter myself, even more thought-provoking and disturbing than Hennell's.'

With that he darted at Marian and, bending over her, removed her bonnet and began to stroke and pummel her head, his strong and purposeful fingers delving into her thick brown hair. Marian, thoroughly alarmed, remained incapable of resistance.

'Be patient with him,' Caroline Bray laughed. 'Charles has a passion for phrenology. But if he demands that you should have your head shaved, resist him manfully.'

Charles Bray laughed reminiscently. 'When phrenology first gripped my imagination I commanded a barber to shave my head until not a single hair remained. Then I had a cast taken and submitted it to an eminent phenologist. However, the drastic lengths I went to were quite unnecessary. An adequate cast can be taken without the removal of one's hair. I shall take a cast of your most interesting cranium one of these days, Marian. Meanwhile, let me give you a brief analysis of your character.'

Feeling petrified, yet finding Bray's deft touches not unpleasant, Marian remained perfectly still.

'An amazingly well-developed bump of curiosity,' he pronounced, 'and developed to such an extent as to suggest a probing, analytical mind, a most superior mind, a mind which will only reach its formidable zenith when set completely free.' Warming to his subject he continued: 'As far as feelings go the animal and moral regions are about equal, the moral being sufficient to keep the animal in order. The social feelings are very active if not fully satisfied. You are of a most affectionate disposition, always requiring someone to lean upon. I would say a man rather than a woman. You are not, I can but read, fitted to stand alone. For the rest . . .'

'Enough, Charles,' his wife interrupted patiently. 'You are only embarrassing poor Marian.'

'Not too distressingly,' he said, and holding Marian's eyes added: 'Come to Rosehill again. Come often, often. I want you to meet all my cracked friends. I want you to become a part of the ritual of the bearskin.'

'Even in winter?'

'In winter the bearskin is spread before a splendid fire. We argue snugly or sleep peacefully. And, let me add, we drink wine, *not* vinegar.'

Elizabeth Pears, who had been squatting uncomfortably, rose to a standing position as if dragged up on invisible strings.

'We must go, Marian,' she said, a look of distress in her eyes.

Marian rose but held back for a moment. 'Mr Bray . . .'

'*Charles*,' he insisted.

'Charles,' she amended, as if hypnotised, 'you mentioned a book of your own.'

'So I did!' Bray rushed indoors with all the enthusiasm of a boy, returned with the book and tucked it under Marian's arm. 'Read it, read it again and again, then tell me exactly what you think of it.'

'I shall spare you in no way,' Marian promised, 'if your ideas conflict with mine.'

'Ah, but will they, Marian, will they?'

Marian and Elizabeth began their homeward walk in silence, Elizabeth clearing her throat significantly from time to time. Marian glanced at her in faint amusement and remarked that it was a lovely, clear evening with the promise of a brilliant sunset.

'The sky looks dull and grey to me,' Elizabeth sighed. 'You failed me, Marian. Forgive me, but you failed me.'

'Possibly I failed even myself,' Marian said soberly. 'Your brother has left me with the feeling that I possess not a thimbleful of brain in my head. I'm more confused than I have ever been, and I dislike being confused.'

Elizabeth took her arm impulsively. 'I love Charles, and I love you. Out of the love I bear both of you I am trying to believe that you will presently get the better of him.'

'Bring him back to Christ, you mean?' Marian asked, surprising and startling herself by the satirical tone of her voice. 'Well, I can but try.'

Elizabeth looked at her doubtfully. 'For your own sake rather than his, I beg you not to read his book.'

Marian shook her head. 'Dear Lizabeth, I am duty bound to read it, if only to arm myself against his agnosticism.'

13

'You were out walking with Charles Bray again this afternoon,' Robert Evans said, his tone unaccustomedly portentous.

Marian had just finished playing Beethoven's sonata in D minor. She swung round on the piano stool.

'Yes, Father.'

'You were seen by the Rev. Mr Sibree.'

'I have never made a secret of the fact that I often go on long country walks with Mr Bray,' Marian said, fearful that she and her father were going to quarrel.

'*Alone* with him, Marian. That is most unwise. People are beginning to gossip.'

'People will always find something to gossip about,' Marian said, as lightly as she could.

'Bray is a married man,' her father said heavily. 'Your behaviour is not only unwise but scandalous.'

'Charles and I are good friends, that and no more,' Marian said hotly.

'I believe you,' Robert Evans sighed, 'naturally I believe you, but others are not so trusting.'

Marian turned back to the keyboard and began, rather automatically, to play the last movement again. During the last two months she had gone often to Rosehill and had quickly become a prominent member of the Rosehill circle. Charles Bray's friends had received her enthusiastically, without reserve. Styling themselves free-thinkers, they discussed every subject under the sun and were always eager to draw Marian out, to encourage her to expound her own views, especially if they conflicted with theirs. Lately they had shown a surprising and quite flattering deference. Not that Marian wanted to be flattered, but it was all very heartening and had inspired in her, particularly when at Rosehill, an undreamed of confidence in herself. Thus her world had changed overnight.

She smiled now at an early memory. She had begun by telling the circle that her mind was an assemblage of disjointed specimens of history, ancient and modern; of scraps of poetry picked up from Shakespeare, Cowper, Wordsworth and Milton; of newspaper topics; of morsels of Addison and Bacon; of Latin verbs, geometry, entomology and chemistry; of reviews and metaphysics—all arrested and petrified in a mind that was still chaotic. Her new friends had laughed disbelievingly at this last statement, and Charles Bray himself had said : 'A vast storehouse of knowledge, Marian; that you should turn it to practical use is all we ask of you.'

Recalling his words she remembered the affectionate twinkle in his eyes and wondered soberly if what she had told her father just now was the exact truth. Good friends, that and no more? Charles had informed her, during one of their country walks, that he could never love any woman but Cara, but that, on the intellectual plane, he could and did love many people, men and women alike. Marian sighed regretfully. If he were single she would allow herself to fall in love with him, but things being as they were she must sternly reject any such impulse. The nobility of rejection! It was very hard to accept; the only consolation was the delight of loving his mind, as he undoubtedly loved hers. And there was the fact, the heart-warming fact, that at Rosehill she always felt as if she had come home after much fruitless and aimless wandering.

'Marian!' Robert Evans said sharply.

She swung round on the stool again. 'Yes, Father?'

'Even if Bray were not a married man I should still disapprove of the friendship.'

'Because you regard him as an infidel?'

'Yes, Marian. I am much troubled by the friendship. I consider it my duty, my stern duty, to forbid you to see Charles Bray again.'

'Father!'

'What I fear most is the influence he may exert over you.'

'Really, Father,' Marian protested indignantly, 'I have a mind of my own.'

'You have already been influenced by his book, *The Philosophy of Necessity*. You admitted as much to Elizabeth Pears.'

'I was impressed by it, Father. *Impressed* was the word I used. Have you read it yourself?'

'Yes. You were careless enough to leave it lying about.'

'It was not my intention to hide it from you.'

'Nor was it your intention, apparently, to ask me to read it.'

'You found it a dangerous book?' Marian challenged.

'Even more dangerous than Charles Hennell's.'

Marian felt saddened. Her father was too old, too hidebound, to accept or even consider ideas other than his own, especially when it came to religious matters. Nevertheless she tried valiantly, if unwisely, to make him feel as she had come to feel, after much soul-searching, about Charles Bray's book.

'My only desire, Father, is to know the truth, and I have found abounding truth in *The Philosophy of Necessity*. Let me state the basic doctrine in the author's own words. He recognised one special truth before he wrote the book, that no part of creation has ever been left to chance, or what is sometimes called free will; that the laws of mind are equally fixed with those of matter, and that all instincts in beasts and calculations in man require that they should be so fixed. He regarded this, as I do, as established fact. He found that *everything* acts necessarily in accordance with its nature, and that there is no freedom of choice beyond this.'

'You are only trying to confuse me,' Robert Evans complained. 'I have always admired your cleverness, been proud of it, but I have never really understood you. Have I, I wonder, been a too indulgent father, a father carried away by sinful pride?'

His confusion was all too evident, all too pitiful, but Marian was still hopeful of enlightening him.

'Consequently,' she said slowly and distinctly, 'if there can be no virtue in the ordinary sense of the term—that is, in action which is determined—neither can there be any sin.'

After a moment of shocked silence her father said: 'There is sin everywhere and sin, most certainly, in Bray's terrible book. As for will, free or otherwise, I recognised only God's will. You, poor Marian, are straying from it.'

'God is Nature, Father.'

'God created Nature. God is all powerful.'

Marian found herself trembling. 'Not powerful enough, Father, to influence me against my better judgment.'

Robert Evans rose shakily from his chair. 'Heresy, rank heresy! Worse than that, *conceited* heresy. I am more convinced than ever that I must forbid you to associate with Charles Bray.'

'Please remember, Father,' Marian begged, 'that I am no longer a child.'

'A daughter is always a child, however old she may grow, until she marries. After that the responsibility for her passes from father to husband. I repeat, I am more determined than ever that I must forbid you to associate with Charles Bray.'

Miserable but determined, Marian said:

'You force me to a decision of my own, one which I have hesitated to make.'

'And ... *that?*'

'I shall never go to church again.'

Robert Evans fell back in his chair, as if struck a mortal, physical blow. At a loss for words, his mind in turmoil, he remained silent for several moments. Then finally, and so incongruously that Marian laughed hysterically, he said:

'You will never find a respectable husband if you turn your back on Christianity.'

'I don't want a husband, Father, respectable or otherwise.'

Robert Evans looked troubled. 'But what is going to happen to you if you remain unmarried?'

'There are more things in life than marriage, even for a woman. As for my turning my back on Christianity, I've done no such thing. Not Christianity as I have come to understand it. The man-made Christianity of organised religion, a sort of business association, is another matter. What I hate, Father, is dogma. That is why I have decided never to go to church again.'

Surprising himself, surprising his daughter even more, Robert Evans said: 'Unless you continue to go to church with me I shall be forced to ask you to leave the shelter of my roof.'

'An ultimatum, Father?' Marian asked dully.

'It is either one thing or the other.'

'Father, we're quarrelling.'

He nodded heavily. 'For the first time in our lives. It hurts me deeply, but I am bound by my religous beliefs, and my deep concern for your spiritual welfare, to make a definite stand.'

'Father,' Marian said earnestly, 'all I seek in this life is tolerance. Tolerance is the greatest lesson of life, and life's greatest blessing.' She feared that she was preaching but hurried on : 'I feel that strongly, Father. Please be tolerant of me and allow me to be tolerant of you.'

Robert Evans looked about him vaguely. 'I must send for Isaac. Isaac is more capable of reasoning with you than I am.'

Marian suffered one of her night terrors during the night and felt barely capable of coping with Isaac when, summoned urgently by his father, he came to Bird Grove just before mid-day the next morning. Isaac sensed at once, from Marian's silent gravity, that something untoward had happened and listened in increasing astonishment to all that his father had to say. Then, giving Marian courage, he smiled and tried to make light of the unprecedented situation.

'How extraordinary that my little saint should have become a sinner so suddenly!'

'Is a free-thinker necessarily a sinner?' Marian asked warmly. 'One must be entirely free in mind if one is to think freely and without prejudice.'

'Come, come,' Isaac said, with brotherly patience, 'free-thinking is nothing but a lack of self-discipline. *Self*-discipline is necessary to a well-ordered, God-fearing life.'

'That one should *fear* God has often seemed odd to me.'

'When one disobeys God, Mary Ann, one should surely fear Him.'

'It's useless to argue with me, Isaac.'

'I'm stating a fact, not arguing.'

'And I, in refusing to go to church again, am stating a fact, not arguing.'

Isaac looked at his sister closely. 'Bray's influence is greater than I would ever have thought possible.'

'It has merely set me free to think for myself, to formulate a doctrine of my own, a doctrine based on the truth of feeling.'

'The truth of feeling—a lofty phrase, that.' But to Marian's surprise her brother spoke gently and accompanied his words with a kindly smile. 'Tell me more about this doctrine of yours,' he invited.

'When the soul is newly freed from the tyranny of dogma,' Marian said breathlessly, 'there is a feeling of exultation and strong hope. But one quickly realises that agreement between intellects seems to be unattainable. That is why we must turn to the truth of feeling as the only universal bond of union.'

'Your truth isn't necessarily my truth, Mary Ann, or Father's, or even Charles Bray's.'

'I'm well aware of that, Isaac,' Marian said woefully, 'and it makes me wonder how we can do much towards the advancement of mankind. Certainly not by holding and cherishing religious superstitions. On the whole, I think that the only way of fulfilling our mission in life is to sow good seed in good ground, well prepared ground, instead of rooting up weeds and flowers with them. That is why we must fight all the time for freedom of thought and freedom of inquiry.'

'You're preaching, not explaining,' Isaac said teasingly. 'As I see it, this doctrine of yours is still ill-formed in your own mind.'

Marian bit her lip. It was true enough, but nothing would stop her from searching and probing and inquiring. She was free now and determined to remain free.

Isaac turned seriously to his father. 'I think we should be patient with Mary Ann and allow her a certain amount of leeway. Heavy-handed opposition will only increase her stubbornness.'

'You are no help, no help at all,' Robert Evans complained.

'Father, what I aim at is an acceptable compromise.'

'You disappoint me, Isaac. Surely you realise that no sort of compromise would be acceptable to me. I see that I must hold firm to my decision without support from you or anyone else.'

Isaac looked troubled. 'You still insist that Mary Ann must either continue to go to church or leave Bird Grove?'

'Indeed I do,' Robert Evans said firmly.

Isaac turned to Marian. 'Mary Ann . . . ?'

Marian tried to still the rapid beating of her heart. 'I—I shall go into lodgings somewhere. Leamington, perhaps.'

Isaac glanced obliquely at his father. 'You will, of course, make Mary Ann an allowance sufficient for her needs?'

'Certainly not.'

'How,' Isaac asked Marian, 'do you propose to support yourself?'

'I have certain qualifications. A—a teaching position at some school or other.'

'You would be required to go to church,' Robert Evans interposed sharply. 'No school of any standing would accept you otherwise.'

'Then I shall teach languages privately.'

'And exist on a miserable pittance in miserable lodgings?' Isaac asked. 'I won't permit it, Mary Ann. I insist, I absolutely insist on your coming to live at Griff House.'

'No!' Marian said stoutly.

'Just for a few weeks, until tempers have cooled. Then we shall have another family conference and reach, I hope, an amicable agreement.'

Marian glanced at her father. Adamant as he was, he looked bewildered and there was a suspicion of tears in his eyes. He held her gaze for a moment and seemed, she thought, to be pleading with her silently. She felt bewildered herself and desperately unhappy, but no sort of compromise, she tried to assure herself, would be acceptable to her either.

'Please go to Griff House with Isaac,' Robert Evans said shakily.

'Very well, Father, if you wish it.'

At Griff House Marian found herself surrounded by every kindness and began, cautiously, to appreciate the company of her sister-in-law, even though she had very little in common with her intellectually. Isaac, no longer the pleasure-seeking young man of his bachelor days, seemed, amazingly, to have grown close to her again. Many childhood memories came flooding back, and now and again brother and sister, as if children again, went fishing together in the round pound. It was a week before Isaac spoke of their father.

'The old man,' he said, almost casually, 'has decided to sell Bird Grove and retire to a small cottage somewhere in the country.'

'No doubt he will be happier in the country.'

'Ah, but he proposes to live alone, to fend entirely for himself.'

'Unthinkable!' Marian exclaimed in alarm. 'He is much too old for that.'

'Bird Grove is far too large for him,' Isaac continued quietly. 'After all, he bought the house chiefly for the purpose of giving you a wider experience, even a place in society.'

'Are you trying to make me feel guilty?' Marian asked uneasily.

'Do you feel guilty, Mary Ann?'

'I feel sorrow rather than guilt, Isaac. It is a great sorrow to me to be separated, and not by my own choice, from Father.'

'In a way it is your own choice.'

'He ordered me to leave, Isaac, but in spite of everything I miss him dreadfully and still love him dearly.'

'Dearly but not dutifully,' Isaac pondered, and left it at that.

The following week Elizabeth Pears called at Griff House with the Rev. Mr Sibree, the latter intent on re-converting Marian. She listened patiently to him for a time, then countered his conventional arguments so thoroughly that he retired defeated and dumbfounded from the verbal conflict. Charles Bray also called and was received courteously by Isaac. Charles agreed with Marian that she must fight continually for freedom of thought and freedom of inquiry, but he expressed the opinion that in respect of her father, if nobody else, she should be prepared to make concessions.

'*He* should be prepared to make concessions too,' she said faintly.

'I'm thinking only of your happiness in the family circle,' Charles said gently. 'Well, now, not only *your* happiness, your father's too. He will never be happy, and nor will you, until this breach is healed.'

Much troubled by Charles Bray's words, Marian went for a long country walk alone. Guilt plagued her now as well as sorrow. Her father had treated her harshly, but only because her new convictions, which he really feared and would never understand, had shocked and horrified him. Her own attitude had been harsh too, she thought miserably, harsh and self-opinionated. It had alienated her father and caused him, out of fear, to take a drastic step, thus depriving him of her companionship and loving care. But concessions! No, *never*!

'I've been thinking about that doctrine of yours,' Isaac said, when joining her on a country walk a few days later. 'The truth of feeling, and all that interesting stuff.' He took her companionably by the arm and continued musingly. 'I've been thinking, in particular, about your wish to do something for the advancement of mankind.'

'A passionate wish, Isaac.'

'Do you regard it in the light of charity?'

'In a sense, yes.'

'Then remember, Mary Ann, that charity, in any sense, begins at home,' Isaac said, thinking himself remarkably cunning. 'Father is stubborn, I admit, as stubborn as you in this instance, but he is also old and frail, and missing you terribly.'

'You are doing your utmost to shake my resolution,' Marian said in tearful reproach.

'Oh, I admit it, but I have already done my utmost to shake

Father's. I saw him again this morning. He is willing, at last, to compromise. Are you willing to compromise also?'

'To compromise, Isaac,' Marian faltered, 'but not to accept defeat.'

'Defeat is inevitable, to a certain extent. That is the essence of compromise. *Mutual* defeat. You must accept defeat and so must Father. To come to the point, he's willing to take you back, providing you promise to go to church with him regularly.'

'That is defeat for me alone, Isaac!'

'No, wait, Mary Ann. All Father wants is to keep up appearances. He, for his part, promises to be tolerant of your new convictions and never reproach you. He promises in addition to allow you to visit the Brays at Rosehill whenever you wish to do so, even to allow you to receive them at Bird Grove.'

'I should feel terribly hypocritical, going to church and not *believing*,' Marian said dully.

'Surely there are times when one is obliged inescapably in this life to feel hypocritical?'

'Perhaps.'

'In this instance, compassion comes into it too.'

'Compassion, yes . . .'

'And . . . so, Mary Ann?'

Tears sprang to Marian's eyes. 'Poor Father, I really am longing to see him again.'

'And . . . so?' Isaac repeated.

Marian had already made up her mind. 'Please take me home to Bird Grove at once, Isaac.'

14

CHARLES HENNELL sprang up from the little group on the bearskin rug and ran forward eagerly to greet Marian as she sauntered across the lawn to the acacia tree.

'My dear Miss Evans, how splendid to see you again!'

Marian blushed with pleasure and shook hands warmly with Hennell, her grip as firm as a man's. This was her second meeting with the author of *Inquiry Concerning the Origin of Christianity*. The first had taken place a year ago, soon after her return to Bird

Grove from Griff House, and the long talk which she had had with him had done much to strengthen her conviction that she had taken the right step when becoming an agnostic.

'I do hope you are in better health, Mr Hennell,' she said solicitously.

'I have nothing whatever to complain about these days, Miss Evans.'

Charles Hennell was over thirty but looked younger. He was slightly built with a shock of wavy fair hair and a country boy's complexion. It was difficult to believe, Marian thought, that he suffered, or had suffered, from a weak chest. He had coughed distressingly at their first meeting but there was no immediate sign of that cough now.

'Come,' he said, 'you must meet Rufa.'

Another figure rose from the bearskin, a lively-looking young woman a few years older than Marian. The latter looked at her guardedly. So this was Elizabeth Rebecca Brabant, called Rufa by everybody, to whom Charles Hennell, according to the Brays, was unofficially engaged. Rufa smiled brightly and offered Marian her hand.

'I hope we shall become good friends, Miss Evans.'

'Allies also,' Charles Bray chuckled, sitting up and clasping his hands round his knees. 'We were discussing you just before you arrived, Marian.'

'In a most complimentary manner,' Caroline Bray added.

Bray chuckled again. 'We have decided to consult the oracle— that is, to seek Marian Evans's always sound advice.'

'You make me feel like an ancient maiden aunt,' Marian said, in mock disapproval.

'We are in something of a quandary, Rufa and I,' Charles Hennell said seriously. 'Domestically speaking, not religiously.'

Marian seated herself on the bearskin and listened attentively while Hennell began, as he put it, at the beginning. Soon after he had published his *Inquiry*, Dr Brabant, Rufa's father, had obtained his address from the publisher and called on him in London to offer his congratulations. Charles Hennell was twenty-nine at that time. Dr Brabant, a biblical scholar himself, had expected to meet an elderly gentleman with many years of scholarship behind him. So impressed was he that he invited Hennell to visit him at Devizes where he had retired after abandoning medical practice in favour of deeper biblical studies. Hennell accepted the invitation and as a result met Rufa. They fell in love. Dr Brabant was delighted, but before giving his consent to the proposed marriage he prudently submitted Hennell to a medical examination.

'He diagnosed tuberculosis,' Charles Hennell told Marian, 'and a London specialist confirmed his diagnosis.'

With that, Dr Brabant's whole attitude had changed. He withheld his consent but based his objection on the fact that Charles Hennell, an unsuccessful silk and drug merchant, lacked the means to support Rufa in reasonable comfort. True, he was rich himself, but he was unprepared to make his daughter an allowance. That was three years ago, and recently Rufa had inherited some family money and Hennell had secured a managerial position in an iron-manufacturing company. They were able now to marry, with or without Dr Brabant's consent.

'What of the tuberculosis, Mr Hennell?' Marian asked carefully.

'The specialist has reported a complete cure.'

'Father is afraid of a recurrence,' Rufa said. 'It is a hard decision to make, to marry without his consent.'

'And you want me, the oracle, to decide for you?' Marian asked, laughing dryly. 'Really, now, would you take the slightest notice of me?'

'Try us and see,' Hennell laughed.

'I think,' Marian said cautiously, 'that you should talk to Dr Brabant again and try to reason with him.'

Charles Bray pounced at once. 'How innocently you have played into our hands, Marian! In our opinion *you* are the best person in the world to reason with Dr Brabant.'

'*I*?' Marian asked in astonishment.

'We feel that you and the good doctor would have much in common if you became friends. For instance, like you he is an eminent German scholar. I could list a number of other things, including biblical studies, but need I waste my breath at this moment?'

Marian began to feel excited. She was flattered and rather touched to think that her friends, especially Charles Hennell to whom she owed so much intellectually, should seek her help.

'There is one difficulty,' she said. 'Dr Brabant lives in Devizes. That is a long way from Coventry.'

Charles Bray swept this aside instantly. 'You're in need of a change, Marian, a little holiday. We shall all go to Devizes and make a jolly touring party of it.'

'My father . . .' Marian began.

Bray laughed gaily. 'With or without his consent, dear girl.'

Much to Marian's surprise her father merely nodded and smiled when, tentatively and a little fearfully, she broached the subject of a touring holiday with the Brays, and later in the day he remarked that a change of scene would be good for her.

'You will be quite all right without me?' she asked doubtfully.

'Quite, Marian. My health has improved during the past year. In any case I can always stay with Chrissey or Isaac. You expected me to object strongly, of course?'

'Yes, Father, I did.'

'That was silly of you. Mrs Bray will be present to preserve your respectability. You may go freely, my dear, though on one condition.'

'And that, Father?' She saw that his eyes were twinkling.

'You must remember to go regularly to church during your holiday.'

'I shall remember,' Marian said, smiling faintly.

15

As if Marian were not present Dr Brabant said to his daughter: 'I am most impressed with Miss Evans. It pleases me to know that you have made at least one sensible friend.'

'Sensible!' Rufa Brabant laughed. 'How can you be so sure? You and Marian have only had time to say "Good evening" to each other.'

'I can tell by the look of her, even by the sound of her voice,' Dr Brabant said gravely. 'My intuition is never at fault. As you well know I have always flattered myself on that.' He turned to Marian and smiled broadly. 'Am I alarming you, Miss Evans?'

'By no means, Dr Brabant,' Marian said, finding his smile irresistible.

'Did you have a pleasant journey from Coventry?'

'Pleasant and interesting, thank you.'

Marian, the Brays, Charles Hennell and Rufa Brabant had reached Devizes during the afternoon. Rufa had, of course, come home, leaving the others to stay at a nearby inn, and had thought it prudent, in the first place, to bring only Marian face to face with her father. Marian had warmed to Rufa during the journey from Coventry. She was gay, she gossiped a lot without malice;

it was as refreshing as a gust of spring air to be with her. They often conversed in German, for Rufa was as fluent in German as Marian was. She also had her serious side; she was intelligent as well as intellectual, a rare combination, and on that score alone, Marian had quickly decided, she was *almost* worthy of the great Charles Hennell.

'How long do you propose to stay in Devizes?' Dr Brabant asked Marian, as if making polite conversation.

'I can't be absolutely sure, Doctor.'

'I quite understand,' he said, smiling in a way which puzzled Marian. 'However, you must call on us every day during your visit and we shall have some long conversations. Unfortunately I have an appointment tonight and must leave immediately.'

He held out his hand. Marian took it and liked the warm firmness of his grip; it gave her a man to man feeling. Rufa had told her that he was sixty-three. He looked much younger and not at all as studious as one might have expected. He was slightly taller than Marian, a rather broad, solid figure of a man, inspiring confidence in his very appearance; there was very little grey in his hair and very few lines on his face; it was obvious that he was proud of his distinguished appearance, his fine physique and his undoubted good health. Marian felt instinctively that she would soon grow to like him as much as she liked his daughter. Her task, she feared, was going to be a difficult one; he was much too charming and probably much too clever to be argued with successfully.

At her second visit to the Brabant house Marian met Mrs Brabant. She was blind. She stumbled against furniture several times when feeling her way about the room and would have fallen near the piano if her husband had failed to take her by the arm and guide her to a chair. Marian felt instantly sorry for Dr Brabant, then chided herself for not having first felt sorry for his poor wife. Rufa herself seemed indifferent, or possibly resigned, after several years, to the inevitable.

During tea Dr Brabant introduced the subject of German literature, Mrs Brabant meanwhile sitting in silence in her chair, apparently uninterested. Had Marian heard of his friend, David Friedrich Strauss, the German philosopher and author? Yes, said Marian, but she had not yet had the opportunity of reading *Leben Jesu*, his latest book.

'Then you shall have a copy at once,' Brabant went on, speaking in German. 'I look forward to your opinion of it. Has Rufa told you that she is translating it into English for me?'

'Yes,' Marian answered, in the same language. 'A labour of love and a tremendous task.'

'I sometimes despair of ever completing it,' Rufa sighed.

Mrs Brabant said suddenly, 'It is rude to converse in a language which not everybody present is capable of understanding.'

Her husband reverted to English. 'Thoughtless of me, my dear,' he said jovially, 'but I wanted to test Miss Evans's skill in German. And, you know, you do understand a little German.'

Mrs Brabant said acidly, 'I prefer English. English for the English, German for the Germans.'

At her third visit, with only Rufa present, Dr Brabant looked at Marian thoughtfully, then chuckled as if at a joke understandable only to he himself.

'Father,' Rufa said, 'you're up to mischief.'

He chuckled again and addressed himself to Marian. 'How clever of Rufa to bring up reinforcements in the guise of a persuasive young woman.'

Marian felt startled. Persuasive? She had not yet attempted to persuade him in any way.

'Reinforcements, Doctor?' she asked guardedly.

'My intuition again, dear Marian. Rufa wants to marry Charles Hennell. You are here to persuade me to give my consent.'

'Frankly, Doctor,' Marian said quietly, 'your consent is unnecessary, but it would indeed be much appreciated.'

'Ah! A most forthright young woman. I admire you for that, Marian.'

Smiling blandly Dr Brabant studied Marian obliquely, as if gazing at the window behind her. His interest in her had grown rapidly, an interest by no means limited to her intellectual qualities. Her fine eyes had attracted him first, then the apparent strength of her features. He wanted to spring to his feet, reach out and stroke her glossy hair. A plain young woman? That mattered not at all. A plain mistress would make a refreshing change. Mere prettiness (and some of the young women with whom he had conducted what he fondly believed to be secret affairs had been extremely pretty) was often disappointingly rapid.

'It would be interesting to argue the point with you, Marian, even exciting,' he said softly, 'but I have already made up my mind.'

'Yes, Father?' Rufa asked eagerly.

'You have my consent, dear child. I give it freely and happily.'

Rufa burst into tears; Marian smiled in relief.

'Presently,' Dr. Brabant said, 'we shall discuss our plans for the wedding.'

He was seeking in his active mind some means of drawing Marian closer to him. Two ideas occurred to him. Trying not to sound in the least cunning he voiced the first one.

'Rufa will have no time, when married, for translation work. I can think of nobody more capable of taking over the task than Marian Evans.'

Flattered as she was Marian said : 'I feel completely unworthy of such a task, Dr Brabant.'

'Nonsense! Your German is better than Rufa's, which means that it is better than mine. You are much too modest. You must guard, in future, against underestimating yourself.'

'Please do as Father wishes,' Rufa urged eagerly.

Dr Brabant laughed playfully. 'I could, of course, have made it a condition to the granting of my consent. Am I not a most generous old fellow?'

'Most,' Marian agreed.

'And . . . your decision?'

'I shall take over the work from Rufa,' Marian said, without further hesitation. 'A new and intellectual occupation will bring some relief from domestic chores at home.'

'Thank you,' Dr Brabant said warmly. 'It will, I feel sure, give you much satisfaction to see your translation in print, as well as a certain standing in literary circles.'

'Publication is anticipated?' Marian asked breathlessly.

'Assuredly. Financial support has already been promised.'

Marian smiled thoughtfully. Yet another new world was opening up before her.

Dr Brabant then voiced his second idea. 'The wedding will be held in London, for your convenience rather than mine, Marian.'

'What do you mean by that, Doctor?'

'It is easier to travel from Coventry to London than from Coventry to Devizes. I want you to be Rufa's bridesmaid. Do you agree?'

'Gladly!' said Marian.

She wondered, not too uneasily, what her father would have to say about a second absence from home, and in the not too distant future. Much to her satisfaction he agreed without argument and asked her when the wedding was to take place.

'On the first day of November. You are very generous, Father.'

Robert Evans smiled and made one of his semi-serious jokes. 'My daughter to go to church, and not unwillingly, in the guise of a bridesmaid—nothing could be more pleasing.'

Marian smiled too. Strangely enough she felt in no way hypocritical about it. A betrayal of her convictions? Certainly not. Rather was it an act of friendship and kindness, a display of the tolerance which she held so dear.

16

THE wedding reception, a modest one, was drawing to a close and Marian, now that the excitement was over, was beginning to feel a marked disinclination to return to Coventry. She had thoroughly enjoyed her few days in London with the Brays. They had made several sightseeing expeditions, pretending to be country cousins up in London for the first time, wide-eyed and open-mouthed, and one evening they had gone to the Theatre Royal in Haymarket, Marian laughing at herself for her former refusal, when in London with Isaac, to enter the devil's playhouse.

'Marian . . .'

She turned to find Dr Brabant at her side. A third idea for drawing Marian closer to him had occurred to him. Something of an actor when necessity called for it, he looked deliberately tearful and spoke as lugubriously as he could.

'A joyous occasion, yes, but I have lost a daughter, my only child. I feel quite bereft, Marian.'

'An understandable feeling, Doctor,' Marian said, her voice vibrating with sympathy.

'I should like to think that I have also gained a daughter,' he added pathetically.

'Indeed?' Marian was momentarily puzzled.

'Who else but you, dear Marian?'

'A kind thought,' Marian said faintly, 'but how could I possibly take Rufa's place?'

In gentle reproach Dr Brabant said: 'Once again you underestimate yourself. At least we have become good friends, you and I.'

'Very good friends, Doctor.'

'Your sincerity warms my heart. It is difficult at my time of life to make new friends, but the difficulty has been overcome in this instance. It would help me and further our friendship if you would join me at Devizes for a week or two before returning to Coventry. Does my suggestion appeal to you at all?'

'My father . . .' Marian said doubtfully.

'He can surely spare you for a little longer. Not that I would be willing to spare you at all, if you really were my daughter. Am I beginning to sound possessive?'

'Flatteringly so, Doctor.'

'In any case,' he pressed, 'I consider it necessary that we should have a thorough discussion of *Leben Jesu* before you embark upon the translation.'

An intellectual appeal, as Dr Brabant suspected, was the surest means of getting one's way with Marian. She flushed; her eyes lit up with enthusiasm. Plain as she was, Brabant thought, she looked really beautiful at that moment and very nearly told her so.

'I shall write to my father and ask his permission,' she said.

Dr Brabant smiled impishly. 'And give your address as care of Dr Brabant of Devizes?'

'Yes, of course!' Marian laughed, and felt like a conspirator.

She hurried across the room to acquaint the Brays with her decision. Much to her surprise they looked doubtful. Charles Bray cleared his throat and said, 'Well, now . . .'

And Caroline Bray said, 'Do you think it wise, Marian?'

Marian looked nonplussed. 'I understand what you mean. I should gain my father's permission before going to Devizes, not after the event. I really am being dishonest.'

Caroline Bray shrugged her shoulders. 'You are old enough to please yourself, and old enough, I hope, to know how to look after yourself.'

'The latter, certainly,' Marian said, with unaccustomed haughtiness.

Charles Bray shrugged his shoulders too, then laughed in his usual joking way. 'Remember to take plenty of warm clothing with you. It can be quite cold in that part of the country at this time of year.'

Marian looked searchingly from Charles to Caroline. Their disapproval was too evident; she could only conclude that they were jealous of her new friend, Dr Brabant. Turning from them she found the new Mrs Hennell and eagerly acquainted her with her decision.

'Father will love it,' Rufa said, an edge to her voice, 'and he will certainly love you.'

Marian sighed in despair. Rufa, too, was jealous.

17

IT was late afternoon. Two hours ago Marian and Dr Brabant had returned from their habitual brisk country walk. Since then, another habit formed during the last two weeks, Marian had been reading aloud to her host, he reclining on the sofa. Yesterday it had been Greek prose, today it was German. Marian came to the end of a chapter and let the book fall on her lap. A fire was burning cheerfully in the grate; the curtains had been drawn across the windows and the lamps lit. There was a cosiness about Dr Brabant's study which made Marian feel very much at home. Coventry—where *was* Coventry? Was there really such a place?

'Tired, Marian?' Dr Brabant asked solicitously.

'My eyes are a little sore, that's all.'

'And you have a slight headache?'

'Only a very slight one.'

'Nevertheless, no more reading today. I ask far too much of you, but you read so beautifully and your voice is so enchanting. I am, of course, a selfish old devil. Would you like to go to your room and rest?'

'I find it very restful here, Doctor.'

Marian closed the book after memorising the page number and relaxed in her chair. If she had gone to her room her host would have sent up refreshments. He petted and pampered her, gratifyingly if shamefully. She would never tire of his company, quite apart from the intellectual aspect of it. He was beautifully sincere, she had decided, conscientious and benevolent. Here at Devizes she had, she felt, discovered a special little heaven of her own. Mrs Brabant herself was hospitable enough, if somewhat withdrawn, and her unmarried sister, Miss Hughes, who kept house for the Brabants, was at least polite. Both harboured a resentment unsuspected by Marian, but in any case she saw little of them except at the dining-table and was scarcely aware of their existence.

'Come and sit with me on the sofa,' Dr Brabant invited. 'I want to talk to you seriously.' He made room for her and continued softly: 'You father gave you permission to spend two weeks here. Do you realise that you should now be on your way home to Coventry?'

'Are you giving me my marching orders, Doctor?' Marian asked, not intending to sound arch.

'Dear Marian, I want to keep you here for months and months, but what of your father?'

'I wrote to him again,' Marian admitted, and rather enjoyed feeling, as once before, like a conspirator. 'I asked his permission to remain here a full month.'

'What if he refuses?'

'I shall be obliged reluctantly to return to Coventry.'

'Well, never mind. By the time you hear from him you will have been here at least an extra week. A precious week to me, Marian.'

'To me also, Doctor. There's so much to talk about, so much we haven't yet had time even to touch on.'

'Do you feel as earnest as you sound?' Dr Brabant asked, laughter in his voice.

'I think so, yes.'

'But not grimly so, I hope?'

'No, not that,' Marian laughed.

'Dear Marian!' He had made it a habit, morning and night, to kiss her paternally on the brow; now he moved closer and kissed her lightly on the cheek. 'It is all very well to talk and talk,' he went on, 'but good friends, *true* friends, can spend many hours together in companionable silence. You agree?'

'Yes, Doctor,' Marian said dreamily, the warm of the room and the resonance of his voice making her feel drowsy.

Cautiously Dr Brabant slipped an arm round her waist. The important things in life, the *deep* things, are far beyond the expression of mere words.'

Marian was inclined to agree. How wise he was! She relaxed against him, confidently and happily. Not since she was a child had she and her father sat together like this in perfect harmony. It was so strangely comforting, she thought emotionally, that she almost wanted to cry. She looked at the leaping red and purple flames of the fire and the dancing, mysterious shadows on the walls. She felt at peace, even with herself, and miraculously protected from the world beyond the four walls of this lovely room.

Dr Brabant drew her closer. '*This* is what I wanted the first moment I saw you,' he murmured. 'My intuition tells me that you wanted it as much as I did.'

His voice had changed subtly and his breathing had quickened.

Marian, suddenly ill-at-ease and bewildered, tried to move away from him but he held her in a firmer grip.

'Does the difference in our ages matter?' he asked. 'You and I together are ageless. Physical love in itself is of no importance, but when it becomes the culmination of friendship and understanding it is a holy expression of everything that two people in mutual accord hold dear.'

Before Marian could struggle to free herself or utter a single word of protest, the door swung slowly open and the blind Mrs Brabant stood hesitantly on the threshold, calling her husband's name. Dr Brabant placed a finger to his lips, indicating clearly if silently that his wife would withdraw if convinced that nobody was in the room. Then, with his free hand, he turned Marian's face to his and kissed her fully and lingeringly on the lips. Outraged and nauseated, Marian submitted dumbly, and still submitted dumbly when he thrust his hand down the neck of her dress. Sickened as she was, she thought coldly and analytically that he was taking advantage of the situation, daring her to cry out in front of his wife in indignant protest.

'I may be blind but my hearing is very acute,' Mrs Brabant said. 'I can hear heavy breathing.'

Marian looked at her in pity and horror. The blind woman had advanced as far as her husband's desk without stumbling. Her hands gripped the outer edge of the desk. They slid along it until she was in reach of the carved head of the sofa. Steadying herself she stretched out her hand and came in contact with Marian's hair. Slowly and searchingly her fingers touched Marian's brow, slid down her nose, lightly touched her lips and came to rest on Dr Brabant's wrist. She tugged at it none too gently; Marian, released and trembling, sprang to her feet.

'This has happened before,' Mrs Brabant said coldly. 'Young women of a certain type can never leave my husband alone, and he himself is weak, very easily flattered. I suspected the worst when he told me that you had asked to be invited to Devizes. Intellectual companionship indeed!'

Marian glanced appealingly at Dr. Brabant. Surely he would tell the truth, exonerate her of all blame. He smiled sheepishly and remained silent. Marian felt sick at heart and deeply humiliated, but pride came uppermost and she remained silent.

'Miss Evans,' Mrs Brabant continued, 'is it necessary for me to ask you to leave this house at once?'

'Oh, come,' Dr Brabant protested faintly, 'Marian can scarcely start out for Coventry at this hour of day.'

'She stayed at an inn before. She can do so again. Either she leaves at once or I do.'

Placatingly the doctor said: 'You're distressing yourself unnecessarily, my love. Marian will do exactly as you wish. I'll make all the arrangements for her myself.'

'No!' Mrs Brabant said sharply. 'Leave that to my sister.'

'I am perfectly capable of looking after myself,' Marian said, as steadily as she could. 'I shall pack immediately and leave as soon as possible.'

Dr Brabant rose from the sofa and looked at Marian uncertainly. '*Leben Jesu* . . . the translation . . . It is, please believe me, of tremendous importance to both of us.'

'I gave my word, Dr Brabant,' Marian said stiffly. 'Rest assured, I shall keep it.' Pride, prompted by disillusionment, came uppermost again. 'Your conceit is regrettable but I was aware of it from the first. I've been laughing at you in my sleeve the whole time.' She hated herself for her vindictiveness but found it impossible not to add: 'If I offered incense to you it was because there was no other deity at hand, and because it was one way of passing the time. Mock reverence, Doctor, *that* and no more.'

She hurried from the room. She could still feel the touch of his hand on her breast. She felt dirty and wondered if she would ever feel clean again.

18

ROBERT EVANS was dozing in his chair by the fire, a rug wrapped round his knees. Isaac, making one of his brief but regular visits to Bird Grove, had placed himself on the hearthrug with his back to the fire. Marian, seated on the piano stool with her back to the keyboard, studied her brother tentatively. He was very much the man in possession, the master of the house: his arms were folded across his chest; his expression, indeed his whole appearance, was grimly portentous. What, Marian wondered, had she done to displease her brother?

'Mary Ann,' he said at length, 'I want to talk to you seriously.'

'Proceed, dear Isaac,' she said, thinking the sternness of his voice slightly laughter-making.

'You will be twenty-six a week from today, Mary Ann.'

'And so, you want to talk to me seriously.'

'Twenty-six and still unmarried.'

Marian laughed lightly. 'Do I see a match-making glint in your eyes?'

Isaac frowned, decided to change the subject for the moment and said: 'You've geen working on the translation of *Leben Jesu* for almost two years. Will it ever be finished?'

'I sometimes wonder that myself,' Marian admitted ruefully.

She had begun by setting herself the steady task of translasting six pages a day of the lengthy, three-volume German edition, but household chores, regular visits to the sick and poor and the absolute necessity of gaining some relief at Rosehill had caused many delays. Nor had the task turned out to be entirely to her liking. She disagreed with Strauss on many points, considered his prose leathery and longed to embark, providing she possessed the talent, on original work of her own. Often she felt tired and frustrated, and had come to believe that she was living and working in a vacuum of unreality.

Isaac returned to the attack. 'Match-making?' he asked. 'I am not alone in that, Mary Ann. Charles Bray, for instance, agrees that we must put our heads together and find you a husband. We don't want to see you on the shelf for the rest of your life.'

'Charles and you putting your heads together?' Marian asked in astonishment.

Isaac shrugged heavily. 'Oh, Bray is not a bad chap. In fact, I've grown to like him. I disapprove of his religious views, or rather the lack of them, but I respect him in many ways. He is a very astute business man, for all his intellectualism.' And Isaac added generously: 'Tolerance, I'm gaining that from you, Mary Ann.'

'I shall never marry for the sake of marrying,' Marian said gently, 'for the sake of achieving the dubious status—respectability, I think you call it—of a married woman. Need we pursue the subject further, Isaac?'

Isaac scowled and ignored his sister's words. 'Mind you,' he said heavily, 'it would please me in no way, and Father agrees with me, to see you married to one of Bray's intellectuals. Since coming to Coventry your social activities have been sadly limited. You have refrained from branching out as I would like to see you branch out. The Bray circle at Rosehill—*that*, my poor Mary Ann, isn't mixing in real society.'

'What are you trying to say, Isaac?' Marian asked patiently.

Her brother smiled brightly. 'Simply, my dear, that it's high time I shook you out of your intellectual lethargy.'

'You're beginning to frighten me, Isaac.'

'Come now, no joking. I propose to give a birthday party for you at Griff House and introduce you to at least a baker's dozen of sound, eligible young bachelors.'

'An ordinary dozen will be sufficient, Isaac,' Marian said solemnly. 'Thirteen, I'm told, is unlucky.'

Robert Evans woke up with a start. 'Marian, you were going to read to me . . .'

'Yes, Father, immediately.'

Isaac kissed her on the cheek. 'Please buy a smart dress for the party. I want you to look fashionable.'

'Fashionable?' Robert Evans chuckled. 'Marian, God bless her, is no more fashionable than Queen Victoria.'

'God bless Her Gracious Majesty also,' Isaac intoned.

Marian bought a new dress, deliberately choosing one which she knew would make her look extremely dowdy and at least ten years older than her actual age. It was cruel of her, she knew, cruel even to herself, but not without just reason. At the last moment her father decided that he was too tired to go to Griff House and face a possibly late night. Accordingly he suggested that John Sibree, who had been invited, should escort Marian there and Marian agreed readily enough. John was a likable young man and had annoyed his father, the Rev. Mr Sibree, by taking an interest in Robert Evans's infidel daughter. Marian, for her part, was toying with the idea of converting him (he seemed more than ordinarily intelligent) to her own way of thinking. Meanwhile she was giving him and his sister German lessons.

The party was a fairly large one with the Brays, for Marian's sake, included among the guests. They were the only intellectuals present; the other guests were well-to-do business men and their wives, town councillors and theirs, a newly created knight and his lady and a sprinkling of clerics. As it turned out Isaac had been able to assemble only four eligible young bachelors, eligible in the sense that like he himself they were politically conservative and High Church. He presented them to his uncooperative sister one by one. The first was the son of a wealthy ribbon manufacturer. He was tall and thin with a massive head, pale blue eyes (quite vacant, Marian thought) and over-moist red lips. His sole interest apart from making money, Marian quickly discovered, was cricket.

Revolted, she turned from him and said to Isaac: 'Not a thimbleful of brain in that large head of his.'

'You are too apt to jump to conclusions,' Isaac said tersely.

69

The second young man was also the son of a wealthy ribbon manufacturer. He was short and plump. Marian liked his rich brown eyes and smooth rosy cheeks, but he quickly antagonised her by remarking that the good works in which she indulged were misguided rather than worthy and certainly a waste of time and money. The poor were only poor, he said categorically, because they lacked the initiative to better themselves.

Marian turned from *him* in disgust and said to her brother: 'Not even a few grains of common sense in an ounce of miserliness.'

Isaac tried again and brought forward a young man who was wealthy in his own right, he having inherited on his father's recent death one of the largest coal mines in the Midlands. He was sturdily built and quite unfashionably dressed. There was a dreamy, other-worldly look in his mild blue eyes. He attracted Marian instantly when he said earnestly that he was going to give his fortune to the poor, but when he added even more earnestly that he had decided to become a Baptist minister she lost all interest in him.

'You've brought him to my notice several years too late,' she told her brother dryly.

Isaac's fourth prospect was the only son of the newly created knight. He was a tall, strapping young man with a ruddy complexion and an over-loud voice. His accent was so exaggeratedly refined that it made Marian shudder. He asked her at once if she had a good seat, but before she could reply he went on to talk about fox-hunting, apparently his only interest in life. His mother, Lady Bingham, joined them, a watchful and, Marian suspected, quite calculating woman. She was solidly built, flat-chested and very horse-like in general appearance. Her accent was even more painful to Marian's ears than her son's. She studied Marian lengthily and critically, as if examining an entomological specimen not yet accurately classified. Then she appeared to make up her mind.

'Plain young women are preferable,' she pronounced. 'That is, when marriage is contemplated. Or so my husband has always claimed. Marry a plain gal, set up a pretty mistress—*that* is Sir Henry's dictum.'

Marian turned from mother and son; Isaac followed her with a frown on his face.

'Mary Ann . . .'

'Such an affliction on the ears, their accent,' she intoned.

'I wonder if you realise how rude you're being tonight, Mary Ann?'

70

'It suits my mood, Isaac. And in any case Lady Bingham herself was rude.'

'Candid rather than rude,' Isaac corrected. 'You have only yourself to blame if she thinks you plain. You've made yourself look positively ugly tonight.'

'I feel ugly. That suits my mood too, but I'm quite enjoying myself.'

'*Enjoying* yourself?'

'Fiendishly.'

'You really are insufferable. You . . .' Isaac broke off and stared at the door. A stout young man with a pale, babyish face had entered jerkily, like a puppet on strings. 'Ah!' said Isaac.

'Not another of your eligible bachelors?' Marian complained.

Isaac nodded eagerly. 'An unexpected honour. When I issued the invitation he regretted that he would not be able to come tonight.'

'Why an unexpected *honour*?' Marian asked suspiciously.

'My dear Mary Ann, he is Roger Standover. You must have heard of the Standovers. His father is a bishop.'

'Standover—a splendid name for a bishop.'

Quite unable to laugh, Isaac said: 'I see that he has brought his music with him. He has a fine baritone voice. You, of course, will play the accompaniments for him.'

Marian murmured, quite untruthfully, that she had sprained her left wrist that morning and fled to her brother's study in search of temporary refuge. There, to her annoyance, she came upon another young man. He was standing on a stool, his back to her, engaged in the task of carefully adjusting a picture on the wall. Satisfied at last, he jumped down from the stool, turned and caught sight of Marian.

'Miss Evans?' he asked nervously.

'True, but unfortunate,' Marian said tartly.

'We have never met but I know you by sight. Forgive me for calling so late.'

'Late? The party has only just begun.'

'Ah yes, the party,' he said uncertainly and wistfully.

Marian looked at him dispassionately. He was slightly built. His features were finely etched, almost girlish. Sensitive features, Marian decided, and the slight stoop of his shoulders might be called scholarly.

'Is your father a wealthy ribbon manufacturer?' she asked severely.

'No, Miss Evans.'

'Does he own a coal mine? Has he been recently knighted? Is he a bishop?'

The young man, having shaken his head at each rapid, scathing question, looked at Marian now in fascinated silence.

'Then what *is* your father?' she demanded.

'Like me, Miss Evans, my father is a picture restorer.' He glanced up at the oil painting which he had just hung on the wall. 'A fine piece of work, Miss Evans, much finer than I thought before restoring it. It must make you very proud to claim such an aristocratic gentleman as one of your ancestors. A Cavalier. The Dutch school, of course. Sad to reflect that he was murdered by the Roundheads.'

'My brother told you all that nonsense?'

'*Nonsense*, Miss Evans?'

'I bought that painting at an auction sale some little time ago and gave it to my brother,' Marian said dryly. 'As far as I know we Evanses have no illustrious ancestors preserved on canvas.'

The young man smiled appealingly. 'A pretty fable, Miss Evans. I give you my word not to betray your confidence.'

'Hypocrisy,' Marian said severely.

'It is sometimes kind to be hypocritical,' the picture restorer dared to say.

'True,' Marian admitted frowningly. Then she smiled secretly. An idea for bringing her brother's match-making efforts to an end had occurred to her, but first she wanted to know more about this quite interesting young man. 'What is your religion?' she asked.

'I used to be a Methodist, Miss Evans, but by conviction I am now an atheist.'

'Splendid! That is even worse than being an agnostic. And your politics?'

'Like my father I am a confirmed radical.'

'Better and better!' Then Marian, having forgotten this important point, asked a shade anxiously: 'Are you by any chance married?'

'No, Miss Evans.'

'Engaged?'

He shook his head, too confused now to speak.

'Do you sing?'

He blushed and nodded.

'A pleasing tenor voice, I should imagine.' Marian held out her arm. 'We shall now join the party.' He hesitated and drew back. 'Come, please take my arm.'

He found his voice at last. 'I—I wasn't invited, Miss Evans. I . . . Your brother would never dream of entertaining me socially.'

'*Please*,' Marian said, begging now rather than commanding. 'It is, after all, *my* birthday party.'

He took her arm gingerly and, with dragging steps, escorted her back to the drawing-room. The Brays saw them first and looked at Marian with laughter in their eyes. Then Isaac saw them and came forward with a look of indignation on his face.

'Tell me your name,' Marian said urgently.

'I—that is . . .' But the young man was speechless again.

'Never mind,' Marian said, thoroughly enjoying herself. 'P for picture, P for Peter; R for Restorer, R for Robinson.' Then she faced her brother with mischief in her eyes and said loudly: 'Isaac, this is Mr Peter Robinson. He is going to sing for us. *I* shall play the accompaniment.'

Isaac stared at her stupidly. 'But—but your wrist . . .'

'A miraculous and fortunate recovery, dear Isaac.'

19

ROBERT EVANS faced his daughter across the dinner table. 'You went to the party last night with John Sibree,' he said, somewhat querulously, 'yet you were brought home by a person who, I believe, is a picture restorer.'

Marian nodded. 'Peter Robinson.'

'No, that is not the name.'

'It's the name I gave him, Father. He was too tongue-tied to tell me his real name.'

Robert Evans, suffering these days from failing memory, made an effort to gather his thoughts together.

'According to Isaac, who called this morning while you were working, you caused considerable consternation at the party by introducing the picture restorer to Isaac's guests and declaring that he was a special friend of yours.'

'The consternation made me laugh, Father.'

Robert Evans looked at his daughter reproachfully. 'You have a peculiar sense of humour at times, Marian.'

'It's better than not having any sort of sense of humour.'

'That I doubt, Marian. You have completely ruined your

chances with any of the young men Isaac brought to your notice last night.'

'How terrible, Father.'

Robert Evans snatched at a thought that had almost eluded him. 'John Sibree, unsuitable as he is, would be preferable to a poverty-stricken picture restorer.'

'Unsuitable—*John*? You're forgetting, Father, that John Sibree is studying for the ministry. That, in your eyes, should make him eminently suitable. Really it should, Father.'

'True, true,' Robert Evans said, his daughter's irony lost on him. 'Why, then, did I think him unsuitable? Bless my soul, *why*?'

'Possibly because it will be some time yet before John can afford to marry.'

'Of course!' Robert Evans took a sip of water. 'What are you going to read to me tonight, Marian?'

'I shall be going out tonight, Father,' Marian said, trying to sound firm.

'Dear me, how inconvenient.'

'I'm sorry, Father.'

'Last night, and again tonight.'

'I have a delicate mission to perform,' Marian said gravely. 'It comes under the heading of good works.'

'Ah, well, in that case . . .'

Quite apart from her daring determination to alarm her father and her brother, Marian had decided that she must take a real interest in her Peter Robinson. She had begun by seeking only to use him; now, because she felt that they might have a lot in common, she wanted to know him better. She had, in fact, made an appointment with him at his workroom, telling him that she would bring him one of her own pictures, a small landscape, which was in need of the picture restorer's art. She felt somewhat abandoned and guilty at the same time; the picture was in almost perfect condition.

Marian found the young man in shirt-sleeves when she reached his workroom with the landscape under her arm. He blushed at the sight of her and bowed her to a chair, his movements appealingly clumsy. She espied at once a canvas on an easel and asked him if the unfinished painting, a river scene, was his own work.

'Yes, Miss Evans,' he replied in confusion. 'I don't want to be just a picture restorer all my life.'

'Your ambition does you credit,' she said, and thought in some dismay that she sounded exactly like a school mistress.

After a moment's silence he got the better of his confusion and said rather hurriedly: 'What I need, what I have always needed to give me confidence in myself is the encouragement of a sympathetic and understanding friend.'

'You will always find *me* sympathetic and understanding,' Marian said earnestly.

He nodded slowly. 'That I am beginning to believe, Miss Evans.'

'I'm so glad.'

'I—I thought last night that you were making fun of me, but it seemed to me on waking this morning that you acted in a most kindly and charitable manner.'

'Charity in itself was not intended.'

'Forgive me.'

'There's nothing to forgive. I acted impulsively, even selfishly, without realising that I might embarrass you. If I did embarrass you, I'm very sorry.'

'I was embarrassed at first,' he confided, 'and very nervous, but the nervousness left me when I began to sing. You kept smiling at me, and that gave me an amazing feeling of release.'

'You sang splendidly.'

'There was no applause, Miss Evans,' he said soberly, 'except from Mr and Mrs Bray.'

'Applause from the others, even polite applause,' Marian commented scathingly, 'would have been a betrayal of their ridiculous, self-created social importance. Not *ridiculous*,' she corrected, '*pathetic*.'

'One should really be sorry for them,' he ventured.

'Now *you* are being charitable.'

'Faith, hope and charity . . .'

'And now abideth faith, hope, charity, these three,' Marian said, voicing the full quotation, 'but the greatest of these is charity.' She smiled faintly. 'The devil, they say, knows how to quote scripture when it suits him.'

The young man laughed softly. 'Of course.'

'Faith in what, Peter?' she asked, trying to draw him out.

'My own convictions.'

'*Hope* in what?'

'That I shall always have the strength never to betray them.'

'You have gone a great deal further than I,' she pondered. 'Never yet have I thought to call myself an atheist. Is that, I wonder, being completely honest?'

His eyes crinkled in a smile. 'It is, at least, being cautious, Miss Evans.'

Marian laughed lightly. He had a gentle, confidence-inspiring smile which robbed his words of any offence. Such words, from anyone else, would have angered her sorely.

He smiled again. 'Please tell me what brought you to the point of rejecting Christianity.'

'It is incorrect to say that I ever rejected Christianity,' Marian said carefully. 'I admire and will always admire the teachings of Christ. I am inspired and always will be inspired by them. To me the way of life expounded by Christ is true Christianity. What I rejected and will never accept again is the *business* of so-called Christianity, the doctrines and beliefs created and furthered by one theological committee after another, long after Christ's death. A *business* has been made of Christianity. The bishops, all the Church leaders, are nothing to me but self-important managing directors. Do I make myself clear?'

'Perfectly clear, Miss Evans. You're telling me that the inspiration of Christ's example means everything to you, that you find, or seek to find, moral progress in it, without the aid or intervention of the managing directors.'

They laughed together for a moment, then Marian grew serious again.

'Moral progress, Peter! So very difficult to attain, but I think it may be measured by the degree in which we sympathise with individual suffering and individual joy.'

'That calls for a certain amount of sacrifice.'

'True! And individual sacrifice seems to me to prove our total inability to find in our own natures the key to the divine mystery.'

'You recognise a divine mystery?'

'Well . . .'

'A sort of immortality?'

'Yes, and no. Confusion attacks me there. I think that too much importance, too much *mystical* importance, is attached to the question of our future existence, if we have one. Let us try to be practical, Peter. My most rooted conviction is that the proper sphere, here on this earth, of all our highest emotions should be centred in our struggling fellow men.'

'And so you call yourself an agnostic.'

'Well, yes. And a free-thinker too.'

'I think, Miss Evans, that you should simply call yourself a humanist. Or do I mean a humanitarian?'

Marian glowed with pleasure. 'Thank you for saying that, Peter.'

He was silent for a few moments, then he said: 'You have given me much food for thought. May we talk again some time?'

'Any time you wish!'

'Nothing gives me more pleasure, nor helps me to think clearly, than a walk in the country. Would you care to come with me some day?'

'Tomorrow afternoon,' Marian promised at once.

There was aloud and peremptory knock on the workroom door. The picture restorer said 'Excuse me, Miss Evans,' opened the door and stood back in evident consternation at the sight of Isaac Evans. Isaac ignored him and strode into the room.

'Isaac!' Marian exclaimed in surprise.

'Father has been taken ill,' he said tersely. 'You must come home at once, Mary Ann.'

Marian hurried out to her brother's carriage and asked him, once he had whipped up the horse, how he had known where to find her. He smiled grimly and said, still tersely, that it had been a shrewd guess on his part, that and the fact that the Rev. Mr Sibree had seen her walking along Foleshill Road with a picture under her arm. He added that he had called at Bird Grove quite by chance that evening which, all in all, was fortunate.

'Father was quite well when I left him,' Marian said.

'These things happen suddenly. A seizure of some sort, or so I imagine. He appeared to be in a coma when I came in search of you.'

Marian began to feel indignant. 'And you left him alone?'

'Of course not. The Rev. Mr Sibree is sitting with him.'

'You sent for the doctor?'

Isaac hesitated but Marian failed to notice it. 'Naturally.'

On reaching Bird Grove, Marian made to hurry up to her father's bedroom, but Isaac laid a restraining hand on her arm.

'I deemed it wiser to leave the old man where he was, in his chair by the fire.'

Marian rushed to the drawing-room. Her father was seated motionless, eyes closed, in his chair. She scarcely noticed the Rev. Mr Sibree and approached her father fearfully.

'Father . . .'

Robert Evans uncrossed his legs, yawned widely and got up to warm his hands at the fire. Then, yawning again, he turned and saw Marian.

'Well, now, how splendid! You have come home in time to read to me before we go to bed.'

'Incredible,' Isaac murmured.

Marian swung round on him. 'If anything it was a deeper sleep than usual. Often enough I have had trouble waking him, *and* you know it, Isaac.' She paused to take a deep, angry breath. 'Your conduct was despicable, *despicable*!'

'Come, come!' Isaac tried to bluster.

'Not only despicable but childish.'

Isaac grinned like a boy caught stealing apples. 'It was a good enough way of getting you out of the clutches of the picture restorer.'

The Rev. Mr Sibree, his eyes alight with curiosity, excused himself and departed with every sign of reluctance. Marian took another deep breath, almost laughed at the thought that her manner was becoming darkly feminine and attacked her brother again as severely as she could.

'Please remember, Isaac, that I am old enough to choose my own friends.'

'But . . . a *picture restorer*!' Isaac said in disgust.

'For all I care he could be a chimney-sweep. I like him very much. He is the most interesting and intelligent young man I have ever met.'

Isaac laughed suddenly. 'Perhaps I should put myself out and find a chimney-sweep for you.'

Marian laughed too. 'One with intellectual leanings, please.'

Isaac kissed her on the cheek. 'Good night, Mary Ann. You really are a sore trial to me.'

'Are you,' she asked brightly, 'going home before the doctor arrives?'

Isaac grinned again. 'Oh, we shall have to wait till doomsday before that happens.'

'What,' Robert Evans asked fretfully, 'are you going to read to me, Marian?'

'Nothing,' Marian said promptly. 'I shall tell you a bedtime story instead. One of my own invention. Isaac may stay and hear it if he wishes.'

'I am all attention,' Isaac said suspiciously.

'My story,' Marian continued, 'concerns an interfering brother who tries, unsuccessfully, to marry his sister to a bishop's son. In many respects the brother has a great soul, but he also possesses a great bladder fit only for dried peas to rattle in. By dried peas I mean any number of bishops and their worthy sons.'

'How very uncomfortable,' Robert Evans said vaguely.

'The end of my story is most romantic,' Marian concluded.

'The sister, bent on pleasing herself, marries a picture restorer, and the said picture restorer, by the wave of a magic wand, turns out to be a great artist in disguise.'

'Marian!' Isaac was absolutely aghast.

'It may well come to that,' Marian said recklessly. 'And thank you, Isaac, for inadvertently calling me Marian.'

Isaac pulled himself together. 'It is my duty, Mary Ann, to issue a warning,' he said heavily. 'The villain in your bedtime story is not your brother but your picture restorer. He has an evil reputation.'

'Of course, he being an atheist.'

'I'm not referring to that.'

'Not only an atheist but a radical.'

'I'm not even referring to his politics.'

'*Evil* in any sort of way?' Marian exclaimed scornfully. 'You must be out of your mind, Isaac.'

'All I can do,' Isaac said enigmatically, 'is leave you to find out for yourself and learn a well deserved lesson.'

Robert Evans had found his way back to his chair. 'A bedtime story or something else from Walter Scott,' he said plaintively. 'It scarcely matters, but hurry, Marian, before I fall asleep again.'

20

'AND what, Miss Evans, are your views on marriage?' the young picture restorer asked quietly.

Marian walked in contemplative silence at his side for several moments. It was a bright clear afternoon, but very cold, with last night's frost still hard on the country road. Both Marian and her companion were muffled up to the ears and walking briskly.

'It is my considered opinion,' Marian said at length, 'that marriage should consist of the blending of two minds as well as two hearts. Am I being trite? I'm sure it isn't an original opinion.'

'Not really trite, Miss Evans. Original opinions aren't easy to come by.'

It was the third time that they had walked together in the country lanes during the last two weeks and Marian was beginning to feel blissfully happy in the young man's company. They had engaged in deeper and more heart-searching conversation than she had ever experienced during her country walks with

Charles Bray. Peter had a more open mind than Charles; he was forever probing through amicable argument for new ideas and wholesome enlightenment, or so she told herself ecstatically.

'What are your own views on marriage?' she asked encouragingly.

'As a matter of fact, Miss Evans, I don't believe in marriage. Not marriage as an institution. Who, I ask you, wants to live in an institution?'

Marian glanced at him quizzically. There was no hint of laughter in his voice; he was utterly serious. Yet he looked so vulnerably young.

'If by "institution",' she said, thinking that he really ought to be made to laugh, 'you're suggesting a lunatic asylum . . .'

But he grew even more serious. 'Marriage to me, *conventional* marriage, *is* like living in a lunatic asylum. As an unconventional person yourself you may possibly agree with me.'

Marian frowned over this. 'Possibly.'

'What, for instance, would you say if I asked you to marry me—that is, to live with me without benefit of clergy? I am, of course, merely posing a point for further argument.'

'An interesting speculation,' Marian said, and wondered why she should of a sudden feel uneasy.

'A marriage of two minds as well as two hearts,' he said rhetorically, 'has nothing whatever to do with the Christian marriage service. Conventional marriage is, of course, a tie, legally as well as religiously, but as I see it, it is less of a tie, less of a responsibility, than what is termed a free-love association.

Grappling with this, Marian maintained a contemplative silence. *Less* of a responsibility?

'As a free-thinker as well as a humanist,' he went on, 'you must believe in the freedom of love—a freedom, mark you, which in its own special way is binding and irrevocable.'

'I don't quite follow you, Peter.'

'I mean, Miss Evans, that it puts one, as it were, on one's honour.'

'True, perhaps,' Marian said, and wondered why she should feel even more uneasy.

Suddenly he took her by the arm, his grip so firm that she felt as if she had been imprisoned behind unbreakable bars. She was bewildered and, for the moment, desperately uncertain of herself and of him. She saw that he was smiling, as if at a secret joke.

'You brought me a picture to restore,' he said softly. 'I know, being honest, and *you* know, being dishonestly honest, that it is in no real need of restoration. You made that picture an excuse.'

'Indeed I did, but not in the way you mean it.'

'Thank you for recognising the way I mean it,' he said politely. 'But that again, on your part, is being dishonestly honest. Or honestly dishonest. Does it really matter? It is useless, if delightfully feminine, to hide your head in the sand, like an ostrich. You were attracted to me at the very beginning, as I was to you. Attracted *physically*.'

'Peter, you're hurting my arm.'

He came to a determined halt and swung her round to face him. 'When all is said and done,' he asked, 'What other more powerful attraction *is* there between a man and a woman?' Holding her in a still firmer grip, both arms round her waist, he kissed her on the lips. Marian almost responded, then reminded strongly of Dr Brabant she felt nauseated. 'For the rest,' he went on, 'what are the intellectual discussions, the deep arguments, but an evasive preparation for the inevitable coming together of a man and a woman? Let us be entirely frank with each other. I feel, Miss Evans, as you do.'

The 'Miss Evans' made Marian laugh hysterically. Would he, she wondered, continue to address her formally if she went to live in sin with him? But once again, as in the case of Dr Brabant, the disillusionment was strong and humiliating. She freed herself with difficulty and stood back from him, her heart palpitating painfully, her eyes full of anguish.

'Why *this*?' he asked, looking bewildered.

'I—I made a terrible mistake about you, and you about me.'

'Mistake?' he asked, rather shrilly. 'Is it a *mistake* that I should find beauty and promise in your plainness?' His voice rose boastfully. 'I've had many women in my short life, and children by two of them, but never before have I wanted to live permanently with any woman.' He broke off suddenly and seemed, as at their first meeting, to have lost his voice. 'I—you . . .'

Marian felt that she was weeping for him in her heart, and for herself also, but the shadow of Dr Brabant hovered between them menacingly, suppressing the tumultuous feeling in her breast.

As firmly as she could she said: 'If you turn left at the next crossroads you'll find your way back to Coventry by the longer route. That should give you time to think clearly and regret your extraordinary conduct this afternoon.' She swung round from him, feeling melodramatic as well as insecure, and said over her shoulder, 'Goodbye, Peter.'

21

ONCE again Robert Evans faced his daughter across the dinner table. There was, he knew, something very serious that he wanted to say to her. Finally he remembered.

'You were seen walking with the picture restorer this afternoon,' he said, his voice expressing sorrow rather than anger. 'Really, Marian, I must ask you not to do such a thing again.'

Marian had already written to the young man telling him that their short acquaintance had come to an end, that they must never see each other again, but she held her peace in that respect.

'Seen by whom, Father?' she asked.

'The Rev. Mr Sibree.'

Marian laughed involuntarily. 'Ah yes, it was he who complained about my country walks with Charles Bray. Our earnest Nonconformist minister could almost be called a Peeping Tom, or perhaps the unwanted but ever-watchful guardian of my morals. Did Mr Sibree see the picture restorer kissing me?'

'*Kissing* you? How very forward of him! No, Mr Sibree made no mention of that.'

'Then obviously he missed what, to him, would have been a grand treat.'

Robert Evans decided to change the subject. 'Speaking of the Sibrees,' he said chirpily, 'I have received from young John an offer for your hand in marriage.'

Astonished and nettled, Marian said: 'Scarcely a large offer— if I happen to be in the market for the highest bidder.'

'John Sibree is the only bidder, and that worries me, Marian,' Robert Evans said soberly. 'I want to see you settled, happily married, before I die.'

'You spoke earlier of John Sibree as unsuitable,' Marian reminded him.

'I *did*? Ah yes, of course I did! But John is a worthy young man, a God-fearing young man. However, I have yet to reach a definite decision. There are pros and cons to be weighed. Meanwhile I have given the young man permission to discuss the—

hum—proposed alliance with you personally. In short, to court you.'

'Most considerate of you, Father,' Marian said dryly.

The next day was Saturday, the day when Marian gave John and his sister Mary their German lessons, but on this occasion John came to Bird Grove alone at eleven in the morning. His manner was extremely grave and he wore his best suit, as if attending a special church service. Marian invited him to sit at the other side of her desk in her study, then looked at him steadily and, she knew, quite disconcertingly. He had a newly scrubbed and over-earnest look about him—a very worthy young man, God-fearing and undoubtedly clean living. An ideal husband, Marian decided, for a pretty young girl not blessed with too much intelligence, but as far as she herself was concerned . . . ! He blushed under her steady gaze and had obviously become tongue-tied. Marian felt compelled to speak up for him, if not for herself.

'I imagine,' she said sedately, 'that a German lesson is very far from your thoughts this morning.'

His Adam's apple worked painfully. 'Mr Evans has spoken to you?'

'Yes, John.'

'I—I've admired you ever since you came to live in Coventry,' he blurted out. 'Please believe me, Marian, that is the truth.'

'And now,' she said gently, not wanting to hurt his feelings by any hint of irony, 'the admiration has turned to what you think is love.'

'What I *think*! It was love the whole time, but I didn't realise it.'

Marian began to feel a certain tenderness but she was determined to discourage him.

'Dear John, I, for my part, have grown to regard you as a brother. Could I possibly marry a brother?'

'Give me the chance,' he said courageously, 'and I'll change your attitude completely. Please walk out with me. I haven't courted a girl before, but I'm sure I shall soon learn how to do so properly.'

A girl! Marian felt old enough to be John Sibrees' grandmother. She snatched quickly at an obvious objection.

'What of your father? What of *his* attitude? I can't believe that he is in the least pleased, I being what he so insultingly terms an infidel.'

'I haven't spoken to Father yet.'

'But you must, you know.'

'I'm old enough to please myself,' John said defiantly. 'Besides, you go to church every Sunday with your father.'

'Merely out of a sense of duty. Your father is well aware of that.'

'Does it make you feel hypocritical?' he asked unexpectedly.

'Often, John, and it would make me feel even more hypocritical to become the wife of a future Nonconformist minister.'

From having been tongue-tied, John Sibree was becoming most eloquent.

'You need have no worry on that score,' he said, with a triumphant laugh.

'You think that love conquers all?' Marian asked, not intending to utter a popular cliché.

'I do, Marian, indeed I do, but what I mean is this: I have decided not to go back to my training college. I don't want to become a minister any more.'

Marian looked at him in surprise. 'Have you told your father?'

'Not yet. You see, I don't want him to blame you for my decision.'

'*Me?*' she asked in astonishment. 'Have I ever argued with you? Have I tried at any time to dissuade you?'

'No,' John said, smiling fondly. 'You are much too nice a person for that. I think you have wanted to, but you have remained tolerant. Your tolerance is an example to everybody. It's just that I've been influenced by my sister, and she, of course, has been influenced by you.'

'By *me?*'

'Mary has asked you many searching questions and you, to your credit, have answered them truthfully from your own point of view. She has been deeply moved. She has decided, and so have I, to follow you into the wilderness.'

'You sound very melodramatic,' Marian said faintly.

John smiled engagingly. 'I'm only saying what Father will say when Mary and I tell him.'

'And tell him you must,' Marian said promptly, aware now that a way of escape had presented itself. 'You must confide in your father fully before we discuss marriage further.' She reached for the exercise books. 'You came for a German lesson, John. Shall we proceed?'

'What,' he asked urgently and unnecessarily, 'is the German word for love?'

Marian smiled affectionately. 'You are absolutely incorrigible, John.'

'I shall win your love soon, Marian.'

'You have it now, as a friend.'

Inevitably Isaac Evans heard of John Sibree's proposal and said at once: 'Impossible! Young Sibree still has his way to make in the world.' Robert Evans sighed and echoed his sons's words. Marian, he added, must be assured of financial security when she married. The Rev. Mr Sibree, who called on Robert Evans early the following week, said heatedly that he would never permit his son to marry an infidel, an infidel, moreover, who had wrecked havoc within his own family. But Marian, though not displeased with the anticipated turn of events, still had John Sibree to deal with.

'We are old enough to marry without our parents' consent,' he told Marian. 'I can think of nothing more romantic than an elopement.'

'What a child you are,' she said gently.

'Is it that you care very much about money?' he asked earnestly.

'I care nothing whatever about money,' she replied, regretting the fact, under the circumstances, that she was forced to be honest.

Encouraged, he said quickly, 'I intend to go to London as a tutor. I have had a quite good offer. It will lead to better things. And looking to the future I propose to establish a tutorial college. You, with your special knowledge of languages, could help me splendidly, Marian. Come with me to London, *please*.'

'As your partner?' Marian asked brightly.

'As my wife, confound you!' he said in youthful exasperation, '*as my wife*!'

'Marriage is a partnership,' she said unwisely, but stalling for time.

'My partner *and* my wife!'

Marian was beginning to feel trapped. She could see no immediate way out of an embarrassing situation. It was flattering, very touching, that John Sibree should have fallen in love with her, and it gave her a tremendous, unthought-of confidence in herself. How different it would be, she thought wryly, if *she* had fallen in love with *him*.

'John,' she said, feeling suddenly inspired, 'I know that we are old enough to marry without parental consent, but one thing I hold dear, and will always hold dear, is dutiful obedience. You, unless I misjudge you sadly, feel the same as I do.'

John Sibree scowled. 'The devil is at your elbow, prompting you.'

Marian inclined her head. 'A woman likes to have the last word. Permit me that privilege, John.'

'The last word, Marian?'

'The devil at my elbow, prompting me—successfully.'

22

'I T'S a tremendous pleasure to have you staying with me in London, Marian,' Sara Hennell said excitedly.

'It's a tremendous pleasure to me to be here,' Marian responded warmly.

She and Sara had first met at Rosehill, Sara being one of Caroline Bray's sisters, and since then they had corresponded frequently and confidingly. Sara was six or seven years older than Marian but they had quickly become friends and discovered much in common, especially music and poetry. Sara was much the same height as Marian. She had wavy brown hair, a rather plump and by no means pretty face, and eyes that sometimes snapped in amused exasperation. She was lively and excitable and apt to wear herself out when in the grip of a new enthusiasm. Being unmarried she lived with her mother in a pleasant, roomy house in Clapton and had often invited Marian to stay with her. A German scholar herself, she had offered to correct Marian's manuscript and Marian, dreading the task herself, had gladly accepted.

'It must be a great relief to you,' Sara said now, 'to have finished that tiresome translation.'

'Yes, indeed. I was beginning to feel utterly Strauss-sick.'

'Nevertheless, a splendid achievement.'

Marian blushed. 'Thank you, Sara.'

'I've asked John Chapman to join the party tonight,' Sara ran on. 'I wonder if you'll like him, or he you, for that matter?'

Marian smiled comically. 'Always providing you're not intent on match-making . . .'

'Dear Marian, Mr Chapman is married, otherwise he might be just right for you.'

Sara Hennell, a critical writer on theological subjects, was giving one of her literary soirées for which she had become mildly celebrated. John Chapman, whom Marian would have been obliged to meet in any case, was a publisher, soon to be *her* publisher : he had agreed, after negotiating with Dr Brabant, to bring out Marian's translation of *Leben Jesu*. He was confident, he had said in a letter to Marian, of its achieving a notable success. Marian herself was doubtful but she was beginning to feel excited at the thought of seeing her work in print.

'I do trust,' Sara said anxiously, 'that your poor father won't have another fall and break another leg while you're in London. It would be terrible if you had to return to Coventry too soon.'

Before finishing her translation Marian had gone to Scotland with Charles and Caroline Bray, they having persuaded Robert Evans that his daughter was very much in need of a change of scene. The holiday had been cut short at Edinburgh by the arrival of a letter from Isaac. She must return home at once; her father had fallen in the garden and broken a leg. Alarmed as she was, Marian was more relieved and sorry at having to hurry back to Coventry. The Brays knew several eligible young bachelors in Scotland and were match-making busily, while Marian was trying just as busily to make herself look and sound as unattractive as possible.

'Any attempt at match-making on your part, Sara,' Marian said severely, 'And I shall invent another broken leg for my-father.'

'I give you my solemn promise,' Sara laughed. 'And talking of match-making, what of John Sibree these days?'

'He came to London. Apparently he's doing quite well. We write to each other frequently.'

'Ah, a nice, steady platonic friendship has been established.'

'As far as *I* am concerned, yes.'

'Poor boy, how that must make him suffer. Weren't you at least a little bit moved by his youthful persistence?'

'Moved?' Marian said reflectively. 'Yes, I think I was. But I wasn't in love with him and never could be.'

'I predict,' Sara said, laughter in her eyes, 'that when you do fall in love it will be a very serious business, and perhaps painful too.'

'We shall see,' Marian said equably.

'To love, to be in love,' Sara pondered, 'do you know the difference?'

'Do *you*?' Marian countered, hiding her uncertainty.

Sara chuckled deep in her throat. 'I met a man some years ago, a married man, whom I desperately wanted to sleep with. Does that answer your question?'

'No,' Marian said faintly.

'Have I shocked you?'

'Deeply.'

'Mind you, I didn't sleep with him.'

'In that case, I see no reason for being shocked.'

'I didn't sleep with him,' Sara said wickedly, 'only because he didn't want me to. You really are a little shocked, Marian.'

'Startled, I think, rather than shocked.'

'Well, never mind. My respectability was fully preserved— through no fault of my own. If it ever happens to you, let me know. Confide in me fully and we shall commiserate with each other. But isn't it a pity, dear Marian, that a respectable woman, however unwillingly so, must either marry or remain a virgin?'

'I set no very great store on conventional respectability,' Marian said carefully.

'Splendid!' Sara laughed. 'I wonder when it will be necessary to remind you of your words of wisdom?'

'I was trying only to be tolerant in respect of other people,' Marian said earnestly. 'As far as I myself am concerned it will never be necessary to remind me of my words.'

Sara's eyes sparkled mischievously. 'Well, we shall see, darling.'

There were a dozen or more people at the soirée, but Marian had little chance, after John Chapman's arrival, of joining in the general conversation. He led her to a sofa immediately after Sara introduced them and completely monopolised her, causing her to be overcome at first by shyness. She knew him to be a year or more younger than herself, but his beard (newly grown, she suspected) gave him the appearance of a much older man. She thought him handsome and liked the rich timbre of his voice. She gained the immediate impression that he possessed great charm and was possibly a more persuasive talker than Charles Bray. She found herself warming to him, but cautiously. His eyes troubled her; they were, she decided, magnetic eyes, quite dangerously so. He had begun by discussing the weather; now he laughed at his own triteness and became disconcertingly personal.

'My dear Miss Evans, you're not in the least the sort of woman I expected to meet.'

'Indeed, Mr Chapman?' Marian faltered.

'I know your age, of course, but I had expected you to look at least fifty, with cold, preoccupied eyes and a severe expression—even a face lined by too much study. But you're young, Miss Evans, amazingly young.'

Marian, though she blushed, began to gain a little confidence. 'Preconceived ideas are often misleading, Mr Chapman.'

He smiled at this and added seriously, 'I have only one complaint, Miss Evans.'

'And that, Mr Chapman?'

'Your obvious aim is to make the worst of yourself. Somebody must take you in hand some day and teach you how to dress to the best possible advantage.'

Marian thought that she ought to feel affronted, tried to and failed.

'You yourself, Mr Chapman?' she asked daringly, then instantly regretted her words, fearing that he might think quite wrongly that she was flirting with him.

John Chapman laughed comically. 'It would be a pleasure, Miss Evans, but my wife would disapprove. She always disapproves bless her, of my interest in other women.'

Why, Marian wondered in alarmed surprise, should she suddenly resent the fact that her publisher was a married man?

'Is Mrs Chapman here tonight?' she asked hastily.

'I'm afraid not. One of the children is ill. Not seriously, but my wife is apt to fuss over them.'

'How many children have you?'

'Two.'

With that John Chapman began to talk about himself, freely and engagingly, his manner as detached at times as if he were discussing a stranger whose life story he had recently heard. He was born in Nottingham. His father was a druggist, but instead of taking his younger son into the family business he had apprenticed him for no apparent reason to a watchmaker.

'Possibly,' Chapman commented, 'because I never cared much about time and was often late for appointments.'

Well before he was out of his apprenticeship he ran away to Edinburgh and set up a watch-making business of his own, the necessary capital being supplied by his elder brother. Quickly dissatisfied, restless and ambitious, he sold the business at a profit and with sufficient funds in hand for his immediate needs migrated to Australia, carrying with him a stock of watches, chronometers and sextants.

'I felt like a pioneer on the point of making a fortune in a new land.'

In Adelaide, South Australia, he established several watch-making businesses in quick succession, made money out of selling them and then, bored with colonial life, returned to England intent on becoming a doctor. He studied medicine in London and Paris and, long before he was within reach of qualifying, decided that a writing career would be more to his taste. Nevertheless, at twenty-one he set himself up as a surgeon in Derby, unqualified as he was.

'It was an exciting challenge, Miss Evans and my female patients adored me. Fortunately I was never called upon to remove a leg or an arm.'

'I think you would have tried, Mr Chapman.'

'Undoubtedly.'

In Derby he met Susanna Brewitt. She was on holiday there and had sprained an ankle. Anyone, of course, could deal with a sprained ankle. Miss Brewitt fell in love with him. *He* fell in love with *her*, even before learning that her father was a lace manufacturer and wealthy. He made a suitably good impression on Mr and Mrs Brewitt, the latter finding him so charming that she absolutely insisted on 'Dr' Chapman becoming her son-in-law. The entranced Susanna received from her father a substantial settlement which immediately became her young husband's to do with as he pleased. John Chapman was twenty-two and no longer interested in a bogus medical practice. He took his wife to London, leased a house in Clapton and began writing enthusiastically. The result was a book with the impressive if over-long title: *A Philosophical Exposition of the Divine Institution of Reward and Punishment*.

'I was very earnest, very sincere, Miss Evans.'

'Surely, Mr Chapman,' Marian said, wondering whether or not to believe him. 'I regret to say that I haven't yet read your book.' And she asked rather timidly, 'Was it ever published?'

'Most certainly it was. I published it myself.'

After several rejections he came upon a publisher who, rejecting the great work also, said wearily that he would gladly sell his unprofitable business for a song. Unhesitatingly John Chapman bought it, with his wife's money. Since then he had succeeded in making his publishing venture pay, chiefly because he had persuaded Emerson to allow him to bring out the British editions of his books.

'I charmed him into it, Miss Evans.'

'That I can well believe,' Marian said feelingly.

'Emerson, like a number of other friends,' Chapman said lightly, 'soon formed the habit of calling me Byron.'

Marian looked at him lengthily, trying to envisage his profile beneath the beard.

'Byron was beardless, Mr Chapman.'

'That was before I grew a beard, but actually they were referring to my charming personality.'

'Byron had an evil reputation,' Marian said, thinking to deflate him.

Chapman laughed gaily and disarmingly. 'So have I, so be warned, Miss Evans.' Seeing the consternation in her eyes, wondering if he had gone too far, he added glibly: 'I'm not referring to Byron's countless love affairs, but to my business acumen. I never sustain the cost of a publication if I can avoid it. Take your translation of *Leben Jesu*, for instance. Dr Brabant, astute and careful, despite his personal wealth, has found somebody else to provide the money, a matter of three hundred pounds. You yourself will receive exactly twenty pounds.'

'Only *twenty*?' Marian asked involuntarily.

'Does the actual fee really matter, Miss Evans? Are you terribly concerned about money?'

'Money doesn't interest me in the least,' she said staunchly.

'As I thought! I see in you the complete artist, and one with enormous promise.'

Marian looked at Chapman uncertainly. 'Thank you, sir.'

'You're not yet completely at ease with me,' he said, a shade reproachfully.

'I—I'm still very much the country cousin,' Marian apologised.

'I wonder,' he said solemnly, but his eyes alight with encouraging amusement, 'if you realise just how you look at this moment?'

'Badly dressed—you have already drawn my attention to that, Mr Chapman.'

'*Why* are you badly dressed? Simply because you regard yourself as inescapably provincial?'

'No,' she said. 'Simply because I want to discourage unwanted suitors.'

'*Unwanted*, Miss Evans?'

'I am heartily sick,' Marian burst out, 'of my friends trying to marry me off.'

'Never mind that! Pause for a moment and tell me how you think you look at this moment, quite apart from your dowdy clothing and your discouraging hair-style.'

Marian stirred herself and wondered if she could make John Chapman laugh. She wondered also if she could move forward in spirit and look back at herself from the other side of the room. She remembered that he had lived for a time in Australia.

'A kangaroo, perhaps?'

Chapman laughed heartily but not unkindly. 'A kangaroo with its little arms crossed! Fetching creatures, kangaroos, but likely to move, I mean jump, in the most unexpected directions. Please don't jump away from me, Marian Evans.' And quickly, judiciously, he added: 'I mean, don't jump away from London. Naturally you must go back to Coventry and your father, but promise me that you will jump back to London, and all the promise it holds out to you, as soon as you possibly can. I want you to settle here and fulfil yourself.' His eyes held hers compellingly for a moment. '*Promise*, Marian.'

He was thinking, Marian suspected, that her father was old, would die soon and release her from family duties. Then she felt instantly guilty. The thought was her own, entirely her own.

'I promise,' she said shakily.

23

'A success, you say?' Robert Evans asked. He was hard of hearing these days and cupped his hand to his ear. '*Success*, Marian?'

'A surprising and pleasing one,' Marian said, and glanced again at John Chapman's letter.

'I am very pleased for your sake. You laboured long and hard. There were times when I feared you might suffer a nervous breakdown.'

Marian smiled ruefully. She had sometimes feared that herself and night terrors had plagued her frequently. She read Chapman's letter again. *Leben Jesu*, entitled *Life of Jesus* in the English edition, had been published last June, six months after Marian's twenty-seventh birthday. Three months had now passed and the publisher had written enthusiastically about its success. The translator, at the author's insistence, had remained anonymous on the title page, but Chapman had spread the word that the translation was the work of Marian Evans, a young woman of great literary promise. Marian, he wrote now, had gained a small but secure place in the world of letters and he predicted that the entire edition would soon be sold out. She remembered her promise to settle in London as soon as possible, but when, she wondered dully, would that be? She longed for London, chiefly as a means of escape, but how could she possibly long for the one thing that would make it possible, her father's death?

Marian looked at the old man with more than her usual anxiety. At seventy-three he had become a demanding child as well as a demanding father. He was very frail and had never fully recovered from the fall which had resulted in a broken leg. He was perky today and quite oblivious of the fact that he had spent the whole of yesterday in bed, crying out from time to time: 'Lord take me now!' Marian had felt unnerved, listening to him, and exasperated too. The last thing her father wanted was to be 'taken'; he was afraid, good Christian that he was, convinced as he was of a life hereafter, of dying.

'How much did you receive for your translation?' he asked.

'Twenty pounds,' Marian said patiently, having answered this question many times.

'You worked for two years and three months.' He began to count on his fingers. 'Twenty-seven months in all. Less than a pound a month. So much for the world of letters. Road-mending would earn you considerably more.' He laughed at his own joke and submitted, as usual when laughing heartily, to a fit of coughing. Once recovered he added: 'Clearly, my poor Marian, you will never make a living out of writing.'

'Translating is scarcely writing, Father, not creative writing.'

Robert Evans frowned over this. 'Charles Bray wants you to write a novel.'

'And Mr Chapman wants me to translate one of Spinoza's books.'

'*Who?*' Robert Evans asked, cupping his hand to his ear again.

'Spinoza,' Marian said, finding herself shouting.

'Well, well, another twenty pounds. But it will give you something to do, something to occupy that restless mind of yours.' He rose from his chair and stretched. 'I feel so well today that I long to travel a little. Where shall we go, Marian?'

'Wherever you wish, Father.'

'Dover,' he decided.

'A long journey, Father. It will wear you out.'

'Nonsense, child! I am perfectly capable of *walking* to Dover, if need be. However, we shall travel by train. You agree, Marian?'

'Yes, Father, of course.'

'How obedient you sound!' Robert Evans laughed again but managed to fight off another fit of coughing. 'Are you beginning to venerate me because of my great age?'

'You're not really very old, Father.'

'*What?*' he demanded. 'I find it difficult at times to hear you. I'm not deaf, Marian. It is only that you have a habit of whispering.'

In a low voice Marian said: 'One must love and cherish the old, but to venerate them is sentimental weakness. Love as far as you can and feel compassion too, but rule out veneration. I have reached the conclusion that one should never seek the advice of anyone over the age of thirty-five. As for anyone who is over seventy . . . ! I find it impossible to believe or imagine that a worn-out, dried-up organisation can be as rich in inspiration as one which is fraught with life and energy.'

'You are still whispering,' Robert Evans accused.

Marian felt ashamed and cowardly; she had lowered her voice deliberately.

'*What* did you say, Marian?' he demanded.

'I said, Father,' she shouted, 'that you are not really very old.'

'Nor am I,' he chuckled. 'Shall we leave for Ryde early next week?'

'Dover, Father.'

'Very well,' he said generously, 'if you prefer Dover, Dover it shall be.'

Father and daughter went to Dover, and the next year they went to Ryde. Robert Evans was frailer than ever but seized by spasmodic and unbelievable spurts of energy. In June 1848, he being seventy-five, they went to St Leonards, the old man firmly convinced that they were visiting Dover again. Meanwhile, Marian had managed to spend a week in London with Sara Hennell, but she saw no more of John Chapman, he being out of town. She had often thought about him with a peculiar sort of longing, as if he were an attractive and at the same time repulsive creature in a zoo that she wanted to gaze at again. His absence from London left her both relieved and disappointed, yet she forgot him entirely when taken by Sara to Exeter Hall to hear *Elijah*, Mendelssohn's new oratorio, with the composer himself conducting. So moved was she that she burst into tears, but they were tears of pure joy, she assured her friend.

When father and daughter returned to Coventry from St Leonards, Robert Evans retired to bed in a very weakened condition and declared that he would never again travel further than Paris or perhaps Berlin. Marian nursed him devotedly and read to him every night, as usual. He interrupted her reading one night and looked at her with a puzzled expression on his grey, lined face.

'Are you reading Spinoza to me, Marian?'

'No, Father, your favourite author, Walter Scott.'

'But *Spinoza* . . . you mentioned the name, surely?'

'I began a translation a long time ago,' she said, wondering where the years had gone, 'but abandoned it.'

'How very wise of you. Much more sensible and enjoyable to translate Walter Scott.'

'Into German,' she said, on a note of hysteria.

'No, no, into *English*.'

Marian had also begun to write a novel, but feeling unsure of herself had abandoned that too, in spite of Charles Bray's enthusiastic encouragement. Her only successful venture in the literary field since the publication of *Life of Jesus* had been a few book reviews for the *Coventry Herald*, now owned by Bray. John Chapman had praised one of them in a letter and had asked how much longer it would be before they could meet again. He had promised to visit the Brays at Rosehill but had not yet done so.

'Continue your reading, please,' Robert Evans said. 'I find Spinoza most interesting.'

By the end of May 1849 it was clear to Marian that her father was close to death. He was almost completely bedridden but quite unaware of his condition, which Marian considered a blessing. He had gone back happily in time, recalling events of long ago, events which seemed to him to have happened only yesterday. And fondly he reverted to calling Marian 'My little wench'. He died before dawn on the last day of the month with only the doctor and Marian at his bedside. Isaac, who had called late the night before, was hastily summoned and busied himself in a practical way making arrangements for the funeral. Charles and Caroline Bray came to Bird Grove later that morning, intent on supporting and comforting Marian. She looked at them with dull eyes, her thoughts unclear.

'You have some good friends left,' Charles assured her.

'Some very good friends,' Caroline insisted gently.

Marian tried to steady herself; her thoughts became clearer. Her father had convinced himself that he had kept her on the path of his undiverting religious beliefs, having forgotten in recent years that she, an unbeliever, went to church with him merely as a means of keeping the peace at home. But perhaps, despite this, he had continued in part to be a strong moral influence. Would she, she wondered, have submitted to the picture restorer if she had not had her father and his religious attitude to consider? She doubted it very much but it was an interesting speculation. She smiled faintly at another thought; no longer need she go to church every Sunday. That in itself was a very special release, a restoration of personal integrity.

'You loved your father dearly, you devoted many years of your life to him,' Charles said, 'but try not to grieve too much.'

'Dearly, yes,' Marian said, feeling now the full force, as if at a single shattering blow, of the many recent sleepless nights. 'It was a mutual love, an abiding love, in spite of our different interests and opinions. I shall be utterly lost without him.'

'What you need is a complete change of scene,' Charles said persuasively. 'A stimulating change never yet experienced. In short, a Continental holiday.'

'Charles and I are planning a trip to Switzerland,' Caroline said. 'Do please come with us, Marian.'

'I must . . .' Marian began, then stopped short.

She had been about to say that she must ask her father's permission but that was no longer necessary. Whose permission then? Isaac's? No, she thought in wonder, her own, solely her own. She felt timid and lost, and at the same time free and reckless. She wanted to weep for her father, yet dance and sing for herself.

'A Continental holiday by all means,' she said, on a note of hysteria. 'I have a vision of myself becoming earthly and sensual and devilish.'

'Devilish?' Charles asked, smiling affectionately but disbelievingly.

'*Utterly* devilish. What, dear Charles and Cara, is there to restrain me now?'

'The Brays,' Charles murmured.

'And Marian Evans's conscience,' Caroline added brightly.

Part Two

1

'I T is, I admit, a quite comfortable *pension*,' Charles Bray said, 'but Cara and I are reluctant to leave you alone in Geneva.'

'*Most* reluctant,' Caroline Bray said feelingly.

'I'm not a child,' Marian protested. 'Soon I shall be thirty. I want to prove that I'm quite capable of living alone among strangers.' She sighed deeply. 'In any case, I've been a gloomy companion so far. It isn't my wish to ruin your journey back to England.'

'Gloomy indeed,' Caroline said, with a sad shake of her head.

'And not in the least devilish,' Charles tried to tease.

Marian and the Brays had left Coventry eleven days after Robert Evans's death. John Chapman had joined them in London, apparently eager to travel with them to Geneva, but Marian had found him strangely aloof at this second meeting and at Calais, after a stormy Channel crossing, he had declared brusquely that he must return to London. Not that Marian really cared. An uncontrollable lethargy had engulfed her, making her feel as unreal, as unalive, as an embalmed corpse. Paris had failed to interest her and her mood had remained unchanged during the rest of the journey which should have been an exciting and colourful experience. She found it impossible to understand herself; all she knew was that she was abysmally ashamed of having upset her friends.

'I shall never go near a friend again,' she said dully, 'until I can bring joy and peace in my heart and in my face.'

For once the Brays were unable to make a bright remark. They looked at her in affectionate but bewildered silence.

'Have I become neurotic?' she asked, not really caring. 'Is that my trouble?'

'I think,' Charles said lightly, 'that you are still suffering from the shock of your father's death.'

Marian frowned over this. 'Whatever it is, I shall remain in Geneva until I have become human again.'

'Can you afford the expense of a protracted holiday?' Charles asked anxiously.

'That I shall soon discover,' Marian said indifferently.

She knew that Bird Grove would have to be sold and that when her father's estate had been wound up she, since his other children must be considered, would have a very small income. Isaac, while giving her no details, had said as much.

'If you find yourself in need of money,' Charles ventured, 'please don't hesitate to let me know.'

'Thank you,' Marian said unemotionally.

'And do remember, dear Marian,' Caroline said warmly, 'that Rosehill will always be your home.'

A lump filled Marian's throat; the lethargy lifted for a moment.

'I shall remember, Cara,' she said shakily. 'You and Charles are the kindest people in the world.'

After the Brays had departed Marian spent most of her time in her room at the *pension* and rarely spoke to any of the other guests. In this self-imposed isolation she felt as if she were submitting herself to some special but nameless sort of penance. Presently she realised the truth of what her father had meant to her. He had been someone, indeed the only person, for her to take care of, to pamper and protect. In a deep and satisfying sense, despite their different temperaments, they had been all in all to each other. Now the main purpose of her life had been removed, leaving her lost and aimless. A habit formed over the years, it had become the greater part of her nature. Or was it more correct, she wondered, to say that it had arisen out of her nature?

Chiding herself for too much introspection, too much concentration on self, she made an effort to take an interest in her fellow guests at the *pension*, searching in her loneliness for someone to take care of, but ironically enough the people she met were either independent or intent on taking care of her. She wrote about them in her many letters to the Brays and Sara Hennell, laughed as she wrote and realised that she would always find release and relief in letter writing.

The atmosphere at the *pension*, she wrote to Sara Hennell, was pleasingly international in flavour. 'The slightly over-powering American widow embroiders slippers day and night, as if her very existence depends on every stitch, and is embroidering a special pair for me.' She took a fancy to the French marquis but was quite unable to draw him out. 'He is very well bred, an avid whist player but a man of few words, possibly because he possesses, or is possessed by, a managing wife: he grants me one sentence a day; it seems a terrible gestation and comes forth *fortissimo.*' The young German baron tended to monopolise her, quite without gallantry, and lectured her sternly, without allowing her to make any comments, on political science. 'I have decided,' she wrote, 'that he is a Communist in disguise.' As for the managing marquise, she tried to take complete control of Marian, warned her that the German baron's intentions were evil and ordered her to change her hair style. 'You would fail to recognise me if you saw me, dear Sara. She took upon herself the office of *femme de chambre.* I submitted helplessly while she abolished all my curls and made two things stick out on each side of my head like those on the head of the Sphinx. Thus, according to the American widow, I have acquired a learned appearance, but to myself, when I dare to look in the mirror, I seem uglier than ever, if possible.'

And then there was Mrs Locke, an elderly English widow of independent means. She had been at the *pension* longer than any of the others and made a determined effort from the first to adopt Marian, whom she thought much too grave, much too withdrawn. 'If I show the slightest sign of a headache she puts me to bed and fusses over me.' Marian liked her and confided in her, saying on one occasion that if she was to remain indefinitely in Geneva the *pension* was rather too expensive for her.

'You have no intention, then, of returning to England before winter sets in?'

Marian hesitated. Yes, or no? She had fallen into a pleasant rut and to make it all the pleasanter had sent for some of her favourite books. Contentment of a sort had descended upon her. She was alive again and fully aware of the beauty of Geneva. The *pension* was a large white house set in trees; from her window she often gazed in wonder at the towering Jura mountains. That she was running short of money and reluctant to ask her brother for more was her only concern.

'I believe one can live quite cheaply in Paris,' she told Mrs Locke. 'Perhaps I shall go there before winter isolates me in Geneva.'

'Paris?' Mrs Locke exclaimed in horror. 'Impossible for an unmarried woman living alone. Paris is most certainly out of the question. You must remain in Geneva, but not at this *pension*, whether or not you can afford it. You, with your intellectual interests, will never find congenial company here.'

'The marquise thinks I should go to Italy.'

'Equally impossible. The Italian men are no better than the

French. Worse, if anything. Leave everything to me. I shall find a small apartment for you, one that is just right for you, and gain introductions that are just right for you also. An apartment close at hand, of course, so that I can continue to keep a motherly eye on you.'

Marian laughed weakly. 'I appear to have no will of my own where you are concerned, Mrs Locke.'

2

M ONSIEUR D'ALBERT DURADE, looking very small while perched on his chair, looked even smaller when he sprang to his feet to welcome Marian. He was hunch-backed and scarcely more than four feet in height. His wife, already standing, towered over him. Marian, taller than Madame d'Albert Durade, felt that she was towering over both of them. It was a not unpleasing feeling; here, perhaps, were two people who, though older than herself, she could to a certain extent mother.

'I do hope, Miss Evans,' d'Albert Durade said in faultless English, 'that you will like our little apartment and find it comfortable.'

'I'm sure I shall,' Marian responded, 'since Mrs Locke recommended it.'

'A recommendation which included myself and my wife, I trust.'

'That, yes, monsieur.'

He bowed gallantly, then led Marian up three flights of narrow steps. They were uncarpeted stone, cold and dark, almost eerie. Marian's heart sank. It seemed to her that Mrs Locke had made a mistake, but on reaching the apartment, which proved to be an attic, she began to feel happier. Ever since her childhood at Griff House she had liked attics; the thought of living in splendid isolation at the top of the house and emerging only when she felt so inclined appealed to her immensely. She glanced round the attic apartment. The carpet was thin but the feather bed looked divinely comfortable. There were shelves on which she could arrange her books, a desk at which she could sit and write and a deep easy chair in which she could meditate or even remain contentedly mindless.

'It meets with your approval, Miss Evans?'

'My full approval. I shall move in at once.'

She was to be, she discovered, the d'Albert Durades' only paying guest. It was agreed after a brief discussion that she should take breakfast alone in her room, her other meals with Monsieur and Madame. Financially she would be better off than at the *pension*. She would be able to live within her limited means, but even so there would be very little to spare for such extras as concerts and the buying of more books. She decided there and then to write to Charles Bray and ask him to sell her *Encyclopaedia Britannica*, which had not been sent to Geneva with her other books, and her globes. They were prized possessions but the sacrifice would have to be made. Nothing would induce her to ask Charles to lend her money.

From the first she found Monsieur d'Albert Durade an intellectual companion after her own heart. He was the curator of the Geneva art gallery, well read and highly musical. His wife, more practical than intellectual, was charming and considerate. But far from being able to mother either of them Marian soon found herself submitting helplessly to their kindly attentions. 'M d'Albert', she wrote to Sara Hennell, 'has become both a father and a brother to me, and Mme d'Albert so anticipates my every need and comfort, so spoils and pampers me, that I am quickly becoming her baby.' But she was happy in a strangely detached way and not in the least homesick for England until winter, a severe one, set in. 'England', she wrote, 'is the most comfortable country to be in in winter; creature comforts, such as coal fires, are more liberally catered for in my own country than in spartan Switzerland.'

With that she began to miss her friends at home, even to fear, quite unreasonably, that they would quickly forget her if she remained away too long. Dolefully she confided in d'Albert Durade and he, shaking his head, assured her gently that nobody could ever forget Marian Evans.

'The roads to the nearest railway at Tonnerre are well-nigh impassable,' he added. 'I cannot permit you to leave Geneva until spring.'

Marian felt trapped but the kindness of her new friends soon consoled her. She went with them to concerts and plays and was always an honoured guest when they gave, as frequently they did, a musical evening. The time passed rapidly and pleasantly and she began to wonder, with her characteristic uncertainty plaguing her, whether or not she should remain in Geneva until

103

the summer. A letter from Isaac resolved the problem for her. Robert Evans's estate had been wound up; her inherited income was smaller than she had expected, a matter of eighty pounds a year from a trust fund.

'I can't afford to stay in Geneva longer than March,' she told d'Albert Durade. 'Whether I like it or not I must return to England and find some way of augmenting my income.'

'Whether you like it or not?'

'I had thought, perhaps, to stay longer.'

'You could augment your income here by teaching English.'

Marian grasped at this tentatively. 'Do you advise it, Monsieur?'

'The decision must be yours, Marian.'

'I—I find it practically impossible to make up my mind.'

'Very well. My advice is this: return to England, if only to discover if you can feel settled there again. There is nothing to prevent you from coming back to Switzerland later on.'

'Sound advice,' Marian said. 'I shall take it gladly.'

'Return to England,' he said smilingly, 'and write a novel. You have the ability, of that I am sure.'

'A novel . . . If only I had the confidence!'

'Confidence will grow if you will permit it. It is a matter, shall we say, of Marian Evans speaking sternly to Marian Evans. And now,' he added decisively, 'our plans for the journey to England.'

'*Our* plans, monsieur?'

'I shall accompany you. Please refrain from arguing with me. It is not fitting that you should travel alone.'

Marian was overcome by gratitude but she wondered if, in a very different sense, she would ever be able to travel alone.

3

'You actually travelled part of the way by sledge!' Charles Bray exclaimed, an envious look in his eyes.

'That was over the mountains, as I was about to explain,' Marian said. 'The roads were icy and too dangerous for any other form of travel.'

'An exciting experience,' Caroline Bray commented, her eyes as envious as her husband's.

Marian shuddered at the memory. 'I found it frightening and exhausting, Cara.'

The rest of the journey had exhausted her too, especially the very stormy Channel crossing which had terrified her and made her violently ill. So tired and dispirited was she on reaching London that, after spending one night at an hotel, she had decided to part company with d'Albert Durade and entrain for Coventry without even calling on Sara Hennell. Then, with Bird Grove no longer her home and thinking only of the Brays, she had come to the refuge of Rosehill. Now, after a meal which had done little to refresh her, she was giving her friends an account of her experiences between Geneva and Coventry.

'I wonder,' Charles said, laughing mischievously, 'What your brother Isaac will have to say about your travelling across the Continent alone with a foreign gentleman.'

'I expect he will be very disapproving,' Marian said, not really caring.

'You must assure him,' Caroline said, laughing mischievously herself, 'that you managed to preserve your truly British virginity.'

Marian frowned, then smiled faintly. The Brays were trying to make her laugh.

'You did, of course, preserve it?' Charles wanted to know.

Marian smiled faintly again. 'I did, Charles, without being called upon to do so.'

Caroline sighed extravagantly. 'What a pity! A splendid and interesting interlude if you had been obliged to *fight* for it.'

'Especially in a sledge,' Charles suggested.

Marian sent word to her brother that she had arrived safely at Rosehill. She expected him to call at once but to her disappointment all he did was invite her, by letter, to join him at Griff House as soon as possible. Apprehensively she went to her old home after resting for several days at Rosehill. Isaac and his wife greeted her as calmly as if she had not been away so long; indeed, as if they had seen her only the other day. They were friendly enough, in a detached sort of way, entirely absorbed in their own family affairs. Politely, without any show of enthusiasm, they invited her to stay at Griff House until she had decided what to do with her life. She felt as if she were a stranger or, at best, a casual acquaintance whom, out of Christian charity, they felt it their duty to help. When she spoke of her journey home and challengingly stressed the fact that she had travelled alone with d'Albert Durade, Isaac merely said, 'How kind of him to look after you.'

A strange feeling of frustration all but got the better of Marian and after only a few days at Griff House she went, in an almost ghost-like manner, to visit her sister Chrissey at Meriden. Chrissey was kinder. She at least simulated an interest in Marian's travels and Marian tried to tell herself that Chrissey really cared for her happiness, but it was clear that she was just as absorbed in her own family affairs as Isaac was in his. It was equally clear that nothing in the way of family responsibility was expected of Marian now that her father was dead. Again the strange feeling of frustration all but got the better of her. She had at times resented the weight of duty in respect of her father, but now that it had been removed and she was free to choose for herself she wondered if the old life had been the easier one.

'What,' Chrissey asked, almost as if reading Marian's thoughts, 'are you going to do with your life, now that you are entirely free?'

Her sister's manner, Marian noted, was just as polite and detached as Isaac's.

'I am determined,' Marian said, suppressing an urge to laugh wildly, 'to sell everything I possess, except a portmanteau and a carpet bag, and the necessary contents, and be a stranger on the earth forever more.'

Chrissey looked at her as if she were crazy. 'You may please yourself, of course.'

Feeling unwanted in the family circle and very sorry for herself, Marian curtailed her visit and hurried back in desperation to Rosehill. The Bray's warmth and sympathy and understanding did much to reconcile her to her position. Friends were far more important to her now than even close relatives, yet she was reluctant to impose on friendship.

'I must strike out on my own, really on my own,' she told Charles Bray petulantly.

'Oh, I quite agree,' he said, humouring her.

'London,' she pondered, 'or Geneva?'

'You don't sound at all sure, Marian.'

'In point of fact, I'm not,' she said miserably.

'The best advice I can give you is this: when a person can't make up his mind what to do he should make no move at all, sit pat just where he is and wait for fate to take a hand.'

'But, Charles . . .'

'Rosehill is your home,' he interrupted, anticipating her objection. 'Cara told you that before we left you in Switzerland. Stay here as long as you wish. Go away, come back again, but always remember that Rosehill *is your home*. Do I make myself clear, Marian?'

'Very clear,' she said tearfully.

She settled down not too uneasily at Rosehill, but as the weeks dragged by she felt that she was drifting aimless, a ship without a rudder. Timidly she suggested that she should pay for her board and lodgings, but the Brays said that even if they suddenly became poor they would never take in paying guests. In any case it was always open house at Rosehill with friends often staying for a weekend, a week or longer. Encouraged by Charles she found escape and some contentment in writing and wrote more reviews and essays for his paper, but she steadfastly refused to accept any payment.

'Ah, your own special idea of fairness,' he commented.

'Yes, Charles.'

She thought often of d'Albert Durade's exhortation but she still lacked confidence in herself when it came to attempting to write a novel. Yet ideas were simmering in her mind, sometimes even boiling over. Far too many ideas, all battling with each other for supremacy, and the result, time and again, utter confusion. She wondered if the atmosphere of Coventry was responsible for her failure to think clearly, to concentrate on anything but a short review or an essay. Coventry, after Geneva, was restricting and provincial. Should she really go back to Geneva? Surely London, the hub of the world, would be a better choice. Geneva, or London? What had Charles said about sitting pat and waiting for fate to take a hand? Fate...

Towards the end of the year, and not long before Marian's thirty-first birthday, Charles Bray announced at breakfast one morning that John Chapman had asked to be invited to Rosehill for a few days.

'His visit,' Caroline commented, 'will give Marian a wider interest in the world of letters.'

4

THOUGH late autumn, it was a warm sunny day and quite windless. Ceremoniously Charles Bray had spread the bearskin rug beneath the acacia tree. He was lying full length on it, his hands lightly clasped behind his head. Grouped round him were Caroline, Marian and John Chapman. The two women were sitting cross-legged, their skirts neatly and becomingly folded about their ankles; Chapman lay on his stomach with his chin cupped in his hands.

'Tell us about your new home, John,' Charles invited.

'If one can call a boarding-house a home!' Chapman laughed.

He had moved, as he explained, from Clapton to the Strand. The house, No. 142, was a large one. He had set up his publishing offices on the ground floor; the rest of the house, with the exception of the rooms not used by himself and his family, were available to boarders, temporary or permanent.

'But not *ordinary* boarders,' he stressed. 'I have a preference for people of literary interests and importance. I am, I think, in an enviable position, augmenting my income and at the same time enlarging my intellectual horizon.' He glanced up at Marian, held her eyes for a moment and smiled. 'Should you decide to visit London again, Miss Evans . . .'

Marian smiled gravely. 'I shall remember your intellectual boarding-house, Mr Chapman.'

He held her eyes again. 'And add lustre to its name.'

Marian averted her eyes. John Chapman had paid her marked attention ever since arriving at Rosehill the night before; now he was setting himself out to flatter her. But why, she wondered, since he had been so strangely aloof and brusque to the point of rudeness at their last meeting?

'Tell us about your latest publishing venture,' Caroline invited. 'The *Westminster Review*?'

'We knew nothing of *that*!' Caroline said excitedly. 'It was just a general question on my part.'

Chapman glanced up at Marian again and addressed her to the exclusion of the others. She remembered that she had once thought his eyes magnetic; they seemed to her to be even more so now. He had, he explained, recently bought the *Westminster Review*. In his opinion it was an important literary journal, despite the fact that it had been in the doldrums since John Stuart Mill had resigned as editor nine or ten years ago.

'I hold the *Westminster Review* in high regard myself,' Marian said.

'So do many other people, Miss Evans. My plan is to give it new life and vigour.'

Chapman was sure that he was gaining Marian's interest. His aim was not only to gain it but to stimulate it and use it to his own advantage. That was why he had come to Coventry. He was fully aware of her talent as a literary journalist, a talent which far exceeded his own. He needed not only a competent writer but an assistant editor and translator, but he was not the man to rush headlong to his goal where a woman as reticent as Marian Evans was concerned. One step at a time, O Lord, he thought wryly, one step at a time. Charles Bray chipped in, helping him considerably.

'Perhaps Marian could write one or two reviews for you,' he suggested.

Chapman rolled over on his back and sat up, hands behind him on the bearskin. 'Such a thought *had* occurred to me,' he admitted. 'Does the suggestion appeal to you, Miss Evans?'

Marian felt herself quivering with excitement. The *Westminster Review* was both philosophical and radical. Nothing would please her more than to write for such a journal.

'Have you any particular book or books in mind?' she asked guardedly.

'Just one to begin with,' Chapman said. 'R. W. Mackay's *The Progress of the Intellect*.' And he added, knowing that it would appeal to her: 'The intellect as exemplified in the religious development of the Greeks and Hebrews.'

'A fascinating subject!' Marian exclaimed, no longer trying to hide her excitement. 'Please send me a copy when you return to London.'

'It so happens that I have a copy in my portmanteau,' Chapman said guilelessly. 'I shall leave it with you.'

Marian began to write her review immediately after Chapman's departure. She rewrote it twice before she was satisfied with it, then she sent it to London and waited anxiously for Chapman's opinion. He replied by return of post that he was absolutely delighted, that he would use it without hesitation in the first issue of the new *Westminster Review*, and he inquired if Marian had any intention of coming to London in an attempt to find her literary feet in that city. He went even further and reminded her that she had once promised to do so as soon as she possibly could. There was also, he concluded, her promise to remember his intellectual boarding-house.

'What shall I do?' Marian asked Charles Bray.

'Ask the question of yourself, dear Marian.'

'I feel I ought to go to London,' she said, a shade uncertainly.

Charles frowned over this. Marian was unaware that the Chapman household was, to say the least, bohemian, and that Chapman himself was something of a philanderer who took it for granted that all women, young or old, pretty or plain, found him irresistible. The last thing Charles wanted was that Marian should be hurt by a too close association with John Chapman. Yet Marian was surely old enough at thirty-one to control her emotions, should she by some mischance become emotional about Chapman. And the thought of her in the guise of Chapman's mistress, temporary or otherwise, was really too ludicrous for serious consideration.

'Go to London for two or three weeks,' he advised. 'That should be long enough for you to decide whether or not you want to live there.'

'Sound advice, thank you, Charles.' And she added cautiously: 'Two weeks at the most.'

5

CARRYING Marian's portmanteau and carpet bag, John Chapman led the way to the back of the house. Marian caught a glimpse through an open office door of a young man seated at a desk, a frown of concentration wrinkling his brow. She saw at once that he was proof-reading and that excited her as much as if she were a child on the point of sampling a freshly baked apple pie. Chapman kicked open a door at the end of the passage and stood aside for Marian to enter. She found herself in a comfortable, not too small sitting-room. Chapman followed her and put down the portmanteau and carpet bag. Then he opened an inner door, revealing a neat if rather dark bedroom.

'Two weeks only, you said, Miss Evans?' He was looking at her quizzically.

'Two weeks only, Mr Chapman.'

'Very well. This is your home for the next two weeks. The communal dining-room is upstairs.'

'I had expected to be given a room upstairs.'

'There are no vacancies. In any case, you will be much more comfortable here and enjoy greater privacy.'

Marian tried to be practical. 'You have yet to tell me your scale of charges. Obviously two rooms will cost more than one.'

Chapman smiled blandly. 'I want you to be my guest for the first two weeks. After that I shall become strictly businesslike.'

He was trying to insist, she thought, that she should stay

longer than two weeks. Indeed, he was taking it for granted that she would. She felt strangely elated, if a sudden weakness of the knees could be ascribed to elation. She steadied herself; she had every intention of proving, when the time came for her departure, that she had a will of her own.

'You are very kind,' she said demurely.

Chapman laughed lightly. 'Kind, Miss Evans, to myself.' He paused for a moment, watching her reaction, and was pleased to see her blush. 'You must be tired after your journey,' he went on smoothly. 'I'll have a meal sent to you here in your rooms, after which you shall be left in peace to go early to bed. Tomorrow you shall meet my wife and the children's governess. Breakfast is served at nine.'

'I see that I am being thoroughly managed,' Marian said, a shade resentfully.

Chapman smiled disarmingly. 'I am very good at managing people, Miss Evans.'

'You must give me lessons in that particular art,' Marian said, and thought in horror that she sounded skittish, even flirtatious. She remembered that he had had that effect on her once before. 'I would prefer to manage rather than be managed,' she added soberly.

Chapman laughed softly. 'I don't for one moment believe you. You may have, as I suspect from your writing, the mind of a man, but in conflict with that is the heart of a woman.'

'You scarcely know me,' Marian faltered.

'Time is of no account,' Chapman said in a level voice. 'I feel that I have known you all my life. It is not unusual, in my experience, for many years to be compressed into a matter of seconds.'

Marian tried to ignore his words and said tersely: 'I am tired of people trying to manage me, Mr Chapman.'

He laughed shortly. 'To me, Miss Evans, that is a special challenge.'

'Then the battle is joined, Mr Chapman,' Marian said daringly, and felt like a young girl face to face with a new and overbearing school mistress.

Chapman bowed. 'The battle is joined, Miss Evans.'

The next morning after breakfast, at which ten boarders were present and served by a harassed-looking little maid-of-all-work, Marian met John Chapman's wife Susanna. She, too, had a harassed look; it transpired that she did most of the cooking. It seemed clear to Marian that Susanna Chapman was by no means an intellectual. She spoke only of household chores and the children's health, but she was uncomplaining and apparently resigned, a woman whose youthful prettiness had not quite faded. Marian began to feel sorry for her.

Chapman also introduced Marian, as he had promised, to the children's governess, Miss Elizabeth Tilley. Elizabeth was younger than Susanna and not in the least careworn. She was fashionably dressed and as pretty as an expensive doll, but with a doll's vacant smile, or so Marian thought until she saw the young woman's eyes flash in contemptuous amusement as they rested upon her. Marian began to feel uneasy and was relieved when Elizabeth turned on her heels after exchanging only a few inconsequential words and disappeared.

'Headstrong and wayward,' Chapman commented, 'and at times hysterical, but my boarders find her amusing.'

'I take it that you have not yet succeeded in managing *her*,' Marian said quietly.

'Not yet,' he admitted, 'but I have every hope of doing so. Meanwhile, she is very good with the children, otherwise I would have dismissed her long ago.'

Chapman gave frequent evening parties. There was one on the second night of Marian's visit. She met a dozen or more literary figures, some of them Chapman's authors. One of them was Eliza Lynn Linton who monopolised Marian as thoroughly as Chapman himself had done at their first meeting. Mrs Lynn Linton was overpowering but genial, with a sharp, penetrating eye. She might well have been a self-assured matron of forty, not a young woman two or three years Marian's junior. She wrote leaders for the *Morning Chronicle* and had already published two lengthy and learned novels. But she was tired, she said, of *heavy* fiction; her third novel, which Chapman had brought to the proof-reading stage, was concerned candidly and lightly, even scandalously, with theatrical life. She drew Marian out, compelling her to talk about herself until she was quite breathless and bewildered.

'I have enjoyed your company very much, Miss Evans,' she boomed at the end of the party. 'I was never so attracted to a woman before. I find you a most lovable creature.'

Marian, though feeling naive, glowed with pleasure. Chapman, having overheard Eliza Lynn Linton's parting words, took Marian lightly by the arm.

'Have no fear,' he said in a stage whisper, 'the dear Eliza, intent as she is on seeking new experiences, isn't *that* sort of female.'

Speechless, Marian blushed richly.

Secretly amused, Chapman went on seriously and confidingly : 'Eliza's new novel is a worry to me, but it's more of a worry to Susanna.'

'Your wife?' Marian asked in surprise.

Susanna, he explained, was a great help to him in editorial work and in dealing with some of his authors, especially the more difficult ones.

'I wonder if you will be a difficult author,' he asked solemnly, 'when you bring me your first novel?'

'I have yet to write it, Mr Chapman.' Marian smiled wryly How easy it was to misjudge people at first sight. Susanna Chapman had intellectual interests after all. 'Why,' she asked, 'is Mrs Chapman worried about Mrs Lynn Linton's book?'

'Some of the passages have upset her. But talk it over with Susanna herself. Help her with the proof-reading. Criticise as much as you like, advise to the best of your ability. A second opinion, yours, will be valuable.'

'I shall be only too happy,' Marian said excitedly.

Chapman smiled his thanks. He was satisfied that steady progress was being made.

Eliza Lynn Linton's new novel was entitled *Realities*. Marian spent the rest of the week reading the proof pages, then she gave special attention to the passages which Susanna had marked and discussed them with her. Susanna said that they were more than sufficient to excite the sensual nature of any reader; Marian contented herself with pronouncing them most improper. After a further discussion Susanna and Marian decided to advise Chapman not to go ahead with the publication of *Realities*.

'There are far too many realities,' Marian told him.

'*Obscene* realities,' Susanna said.

'Are you being prudish, both of you?' Chapman asked smilingly.

Marian shook her head. 'You have a notable reputation as a publisher, Mr Chapman.'

'A reputation that must *not* become tarnished,' Susanna added.

'I had certain doubts when I first read the manuscript,' Chapman admitted, 'but I was carried away by enthusiasm. I was thinking, of course, of Eliza's other two successful novels.'

'*Business* enthusiasm,' Susanna said severely.

'Well now, a publisher *is* a man of business.'

'There are certain limits, even in the world of commerce,' Susanna said warmly.

'*Moral* limits,' Marian said, with equal warmth.

'Is this an attempt to manage me?' Chapman asked mildly, his eyes on Marian, not his wife.

Marian could but smile. 'We urge you not to publish *Realities*, Mr Chapman.'

Chapman glanced from one to the other. 'A compromise is called for. I agree that it is unpublishable in its present form, unpublishable by me with my so far untarnished reputation. I shall ask Eliza to revise and rewrite here and there. Does that satisfy you?'

Marian and Susanna agreed that it did.

Chapman looked solely at Marian. 'Am I right in believing that you are beginning to feel very much at home in my publishing house?'

'Yes,' Marian answered briefly.

'Editorial work appeals to you?'

'I find it stimulating, Mr Chapman.'

He turned to his wife. 'Marian,' he said, using the christian name for the first time, 'would be a valuable addition to my staff.' It was a statement, not a question, but his tone demanded an answer.

'A very valuable one, John.'

He swung round on Marian. 'What if I were to offer you a job?'

'I should give it careful consideration,' she said cautiously.

'An important job, Marian.'

'To what extent important?' Susanna asked.

'I have in mind the assistant editorship,' Chapman said, without glancing at her.

Marian looked at him in astonishment. 'You overwhelm me, Mr Chapman!'

'Nothing delights me more than to overwhelm people.'

'*Nothing*,' Susanna said feelingly.

Chapman looked at her speculatively. 'Am I going too far, Susanna?'

'The business is yours not mine,' she said with a shrug.

'In addition to your editorial duties,' Chapman said, addressing Marian again, 'you would be called upon to write reviews and essays and make translations.' He paused for a moment. 'Well, Marian?'

'I . . .'

He interrupted with a hearty laugh. 'I know what you're going to say! You're going to say "I must sleep on it." '

'Sleep on it I must,' Marian said gravely.

'I shall expect you to give me your decision tomorrow morning.'

'You shall have it, Mr Chapman.'

'If "no" the loss will be yours,' he said lightly. 'If "yes" the gain will be mine. Sleep well, my dear Marian, and wisely.'

She scarcely slept at all. She was too excited to relax, and too fearful also. Just before dawn, after dozing fitfully, she sprang out of bed in the grip of one of her night terrors. Yes, or no? She wanted with all her heart to say yes, yet a strange feeling —it amounted almost to premonition—held her back. In her mind's eye she saw Elizabeth Tilley's contemptuous smile, but what did *that* matter? Why should it affect her decision? Elizabeth Tilley was contemptuous only of her plainness, her dowdy way of dressing. Marian ran to the window, shaking off her terror. If only she could be more definite, more forceful.

'Well?' Chapman asked her, after breakfast.

'I need more time,' Marian apologised. 'I—I shall write to you when I get back to Coventry.'

'I want you to remain in London, Marian.'

They held each other's eyes, Marian sensing that a battle of wills had been joined. She remembered that it had been her intention to prove that she had a will of her own. She found herself trembling and gripped the edge of the table for support.

'I came for two weeks only, Mr Chapman.'

'Very well,' he said brusquely, 'but blame yourself, not me, if I find another assistant editor.'

Shaken by this, Marian nonetheless remained resolute and felt inordinately proud of herself. Then later, when the train was carrying her through the London suburbs on her journey north, she felt foolish and apprehensive. What if John Chapman *did* find another assistant editor? Panic-stricken, she wrote to him from Rosehill that night, accepting his offer. He replied briefly by return of post: 'Splendid! I shall now have a second opportunity of managing you. Or have I succeeded already?'

6

AT John Chapman's invitation Marian was accompanying him, for the first time, on his habitual before-breakfast walk. He walked every morning, whatever the state of the weather, deeming the exercise necessary for two reasons: it stimulated his circulation and whetted his appetite for a hearty breakfast. Marian had already noticed that he was in any case a very hearty eater—good trencherman, he called it himself. They had walked for half an hour, mostly in silence (a companionable silence, Marian told herself) and were now returning to 142 Strand.

'Am I setting too fast a pace for you, Marian?' Chapman asked solicitously.

'No, Mr Chapman.'

'Come, now,' he reproved smilingly, 'you agreed yesterday to call me John.'

'I am well used to brisk country walks, John,' Marian said rather primly.

'Still, you must find the London pavements somewhat hard.'

'I'm getting used to the hardness.'

Chapman glanced at her feet. 'You are at least well equipped with sensible shoes for walking.'

'I always wear sensible shoes,' Marian said, even more primly.

'So I had observed,' Chapman murmured. 'What might be called sensible clothes also.'

Was he, Marian wondered, laughing at her? She remembered that he had once said that somebody must take her in hand some day and teach her how to dress to the best possible advantage. She remembered, too, that she had responded, 'You yourself, Mr Chapman?' She blushed at the memory and drew her cloak more tightly about her body, as if in an attempt to hide her reddened cheeks. It was in any case a bleak and cheerless January morning. A penetrating wind had sprung up, wrapping the skirt of the cloak about her legs and impeding her progress. Chapman took her arm for a moment and slowed down the pace which he had set.

'I must thank you,' he said, 'for working so splendidly during your first week.'

It was January 16th. Marian had returned to London on the 8th after spending Christmas at Rosehill and paying dutiful visits to Isaac at Griff House and Chrissey at Meriden. For some extraordinary reason (or was she merely being fanciful?) Charles Bray had looked at her with a strange, withdrawn expression in his eyes when discussing John Chapman and her decision to join him on a permanent basis, but he had agreed, albeit with seeming reluctance, that she had achieved a measure of independence by accepting the post of assistant editor. Chapman had kept the two rooms on the ground floor vacant for her. Her books had now arrived and she had arranged them to her satisfaction in the sitting-room, a task which had made her feel that she really was making a new home for herself under John Chapman's roof. And she had felt it again when rearranging her few clothes in the bedroom wardrobe and the dressing-table.

'You have worked hard as well as splendidly,' Chapman added.

'I'm enjoying the work. I find it fascinating.'

'Fascinating or not, one would think that you had been engaged on editorial work for many years. I'm proud of you, Marian.'

'Thank you, John,' Marian said, her heart leaping pleasurably.

He glanced at her obliquely. 'However, I have one serious complaint.'

She looked up at him in alarm. 'And that, Mr Chapman?'

'Now, now!' he admonished.

'And that—John?'

'My friends will soon accuse me of being a slave-driver.'

'I shall tell them,' she responded earnestly, 'that I myself am responsible for the driving.'

'Ah, that pride of yours!'

'I deem it better,' Marian said, still earnestly, 'to be one's own slave than somebody else's.'

Chapman laughed lightly, if a shade challengingly. 'I quite agree.' They were in the Strand again and approaching No. 142. Changing the subject he said: 'Do you find it irksome, being obliged to share an office?'

Marian frowned over this. 'Yes, a little. At least, I find it restricting to clear thought, and the scratching of somebody else's pen is sometimes distracting.'

'In that case,' he said promptly, 'I shall have a desk moved into your sitting-room this morning. Privacy for you while you work, greater concentration and the opportunity to work even harder.' There was teasing laughter in his voice as he repeated, '*Even harder.*'

They had reached No. 142 and paused together to inspect a new display of books in the shop window. Frowning, Marian remarked that the books could have been arranged to better advantage; they had the appearance now, she said, of having been thrown together. Chapman smiled and invited her (without any intention of slave-driving, he murmured) to rearrange them herself. They moved to the door but before they could enter it was flung open and Elizabeth Tilley confronted them, her cheeks pale, her eyes flashing angrily. She was dressed for walking, except that she had yet to put on her gloves which she held tightly and almost threateningly in one slim hand.

'You left ten minutes earlier than usual, John,' she said, her voice shrill.

'My watch must be fast,' Chapman said lightly.

'Your watch is never fast. It is always exactly right. You deceived me deliberately, *deliberately*!'

'Control yourself, Elizabeth,' Chapman said, enjoying her anger.

She raised her gloves as if to strike him, thought better of it and swung round on Marian. '*You!*' she said insolently, and turning on her heels retreated, sobbing, into the house.

'Hysterical, as I told you,' Chapman said, facing a startled Marian smilingly. 'Take no notice of her.'

'Does Miss Tilley usually walk with you before breakfast?' Marian asked faintly.

'Usually, but I dislike a hard and fast rule about anything, and her company can scarcely be called intellectual. Her main interests are clothes and gossip.'

'She appeared to be jealous of me,' Marian faltered.

'Ridiculous but true.'

'Ridiculous indeed!'

'She is even jealous of Susanna.'

'That is even more ridiculous.'

'And Susanna of her,' Chapman added.

Marian looked at him in some confusion. 'I find that hard to believe.'

Chapman shrugged and bowed Marian into the house. She was, he decided in amusement, a great deal more naive in some respects than he had first thought. It would be interesting to observe her reactions when, and if, she discovered the truth of his private life at No. 142. Would she be shocked and horrified? She was surely broadminded enough not to be other than surprised. It would all depend on how deeply she had become emotionally involved herself.

The Elizabeth Tilley incident was the start of a bad morning —bad from Marian's point of view, amusing and interesting from

Chapman's. Marian was working at the desk which had been installed in her sitting-room when Chapman, having knocked, came stealthily into the room, his movements exaggeratedly those of a second-rate actor in a melodrama. Trying not to laugh, Marian wondered what it was all about.

'Eliza is here and in a towering rage,' he said portentously.

'Mrs Lynn Linton, you mean?'

'Who else? Susanna is out shopping. Do me the favour, Marian, of dealing with Eliza yourself.'

'If you insist,' Marian said uncertainly.

'I do insist, indeed I do. You have my authority to reach any decision, editorially, which you might think wise and necessary.'

Before more could be said Eliza Lynn Linton marched into the room, her eyes dilated with anger. She wore a walking costume of French design and a poke bonnet slightly awry. In her left hand she swung a fur muff heavily and, Marian thought, quite menacingly.

'Coward!' she cried, glaring at Chapman.

'Pray address yourself to my assistant editor,' he murmured.

Only then did Eliza become aware of Marian's presence. 'But what an unexpected and pleasant surprise! My dear good friend, Marian Evans! Assistant editor? Splendid! An ally! A firm ally, without a doubt. Together we shall drive some sense into the quaking Chapman's head.'

'Please sit down,' Marian invited.

Eliza remained standing, resolutely blocking Chapman's escape from the room.

'Are you aware, dear Marian,' she said, 'that Chapman is trying to insist that I should revise or rewrite certain chapters of *Realities*? In short, that I should emasculate the book?'

'Yes,' Marian admitted, and wished with all her heart that she had not been placed in so difficult a position.

'Have you read the book yourself?'

'Yes, Mrs Linton.'

'Ah! You agree, of course, that his demands are preposterous.'

Marian tried to be courageous. 'No, Mrs Linton.'

Eliza stared at her in astonishment. 'Incredible!'

'I—I consider Mr Chapman's demands judicious, his reputa-ion in the publishing world being what it is.'

Eliza looked at Marian fixedly. 'I made a sad mistake, Miss Evans. You are, after all, nothing but a narrow-minded provin-cial. I refuse, absolutely, to alter one word of *Realities*.'

'I beg you,' Marian said, trying to keep her voice steady, 'to consider deleting at least a few of the, well . . .'

'Purple patches,' Chapman prompted softly.

Marian glanced at him gratefully. 'Purple patches, Mrs Linton, which Mr Chapman and I regard as, well . . .'

'Improper,' Chapman supplied.

Eliza stared at Marian wrathfully. '*You* also, Miss Evans? What insolence! What *provincial* insolence! I absolutely insist on *Realities* appearing exactly as written.'

Marian glanced at Chapman for support; he was staring up at the ceiling with rapt attention.

'In that case,' Marian said faintly, 'the House of Chapman must refuse to publish it. I beg you to reconsider your uncompromising attitude.'

'Never!' Eliza shook her head so violently that the poke bonnet, a smaller and more fashionable one than of two or three years ago, all but fell to the floor. 'I shall consult my legal advisers. I shall take legal action, strong legal action.' She straightened the bonnet, fingering the lace edging so violently that she almost tore it. 'Chapman has bought the rights. He has committed himself to publishing *Realities*—er—*in toto*.'

'There is,' Chapman said absently, 'a large black spider on the ceiling. Are you afraid of spiders, Eliza?'

'*Afraid?* I adore them, except when they happen to be publishers.'

'And you, Marian?'

'I don't adore spiders, but I'm not afraid of them.'

'Then obviously you are not afraid of Eliza Lynn Linton, a very large spider in a poke bonnet. Proceed with the negotiations, my dear.'

Marian had read and studied the publishing agreement which John Chapman had drawn up and which both he and Eliza Lynn Linton had signed.

'Mr Chapman,' she said carefully and more courageously, 'has agreed that *Realities* shall be published, but not, in so many words, that he himself shall publish it.'

'Well?' Chapman asked Eliza, but looking at Marian admiringly.

'Senseless quibbling!' Eliza snorted.

'There is nothing, Mrs Linton,' Marian concluded, 'to prevent Mr Chapman from selling *Realities* to some other publisher.'

'I refuse to permit it!' Eliza shouted.

'You are in no position to do so,' Chapman murmured.

Eliza flung the single epithet 'Bastard!' at him, then smiling unpleasantly turned on Marian. 'Have you become his mistress yet?' she asked, in mock joviality.

Marian blushed richly and gripped the edge of her desk so tightly that her knuckles whitened. Chapman could cheerfully have wrung Eliza's neck; then glancing at Marian's face he thought that Eliza had perhaps done him an unintentional service. It was not, he decided, a blush of embarrassment; there was an inward look in Marian's eyes. Speculation? Fear? Apprehension? It was difficult to be sure, except that it was *not* embarrassment. Perhaps it might be easier than one might expect to make Marian his mistress. He had toyed with the idea as one might toy with a presumably insoluble mathematical problem. Almost instinctively, seeker of new sexual experiences that he was, he had done a little from time to time to prepare the ground, but the last thing he wanted was to frighten her and send her scurrying back to Coventry. She was too useful to him for that, too necessary to him in his business.

Marian was still red in the face when Eliza, gaining no answer to her question, stamped from the room swinging her muff like an agitated pendulum. Marian's prolonged blush fascinated Chapman. It was a blush, he thought, which projected itself, reached out to him and made him feel, hardened though he was, that he was blushing himself. Extraordinary! Never, in that moment, had he desired any woman so deeply.

'That,' he said, steadying himself, 'was a most unfortunate remark. Eliza should be soundly spanked.'

Marian made to speak, then hung her head like a child confronted with an adult statement far beyond her comprehension. Chapman found the gesture vastly appealing. What, he wondered, had Marian been like at the age of ten?

'Embarrassing too,' he added, making his voice shake. 'To me, at all events.'

Marian rose from the desk and turned away from him. 'I was wondering about that.' She knew that she should have said, *Embarrassing to me also.* Agitation made her voice unsteady. 'No doubt she meant no real harm,' she said hurriedly.

'You are far too trusting, Marian. Eliza is a venomous creature when crossed, always has been, always will be. You have made an enemy, my dear.'

'It is impossible to go through life, however innocently, without making enemies.'

'How perceptive you are.'

'I found her charming when I first met her,' Marian tried to argue. 'Nobody is all of a piece. She was angry and frustrated, that is the kindest thing to say.'

Chapman moved round the desk and turned Marian to face him, his hands lightly on her shoulders. It gave him a strange but pleasurable sensation to feel her shoulders stiffen beneath his touch, then relax, as if she had been overcome by helplessness.

'For the rest,' he said, steadying himself again, 'you dealt with Eliza most efficiently. I'm proud of you, Marian. My admiration grows apace.' He smiled—beatifically, he hoped—and kissed her briefly on the brow. The salutation of a friend? A father? A brother? Let her ponder and analyse, and remain uncertain. 'Thank you, Marian,' he said, and released her.

Agitated again, Marian looked up at the ceiling. 'There isn't a spider there.'

'Of course not! And now, to business, Marian. To whom, I wonder, should we offer Eliza's *Realities*?'

Marian tried to be practical. 'It is a matter which calls for serious consideration.'

'That, yes, but bear one thing in mind. We must get a good price for her wretched book. We deserve a handsome profit for all our trouble. Do you think me mercenary?'

Marian frowned, then said, 'No, John, of course not.'

Chapman walked to the door, swinging his arms loosely, a man very pleased with himself and well satisfied with the outcome of the Eliza Lynn Linton incident. Turning, he invited Marian to walk with him again the next morning.

'Is it wise to provoke Miss Tilley further?' she asked quietly.

'Do you want to walk with me, Marian?'

She hesitated for only a moment. 'Yes, John, please.'

'Very well, then! No more need be said.'

Marian waited until he had closed the door behind him, then touched her brow, trying to imagine that his lips were still lingering there. Distractedly she wondered what it would have been like if he had kissed her on the lips. Inconsequently she remembered that she had once resented the fact that he was a married man. She remembered, too, that she had been ready some years ago to fall in love with Charles Bray but had been held back, without really struggling with her emotions, because of his wife Caroline.

Angry with herself, Marian sat down at the desk and read, not very clearly, a review which had been sent in by a German contributor. Presently she spread a sheet of paper in front of her, inked her pen and tried to begin the translation. The first words she wrote were 'John Chapman', then almost frantically she covered several lines with repetitions of 'John'. After a moment's pause she wrote: 'What is happening to you, Marian Evans?' She threw the pen aside; she was, she admonished herself, behaving like a moonstruck girl. Angry again, she screwed the sheet into a tight ball, made to throw it into the waste-basket, then decided furtively that it would be wiser and safer to burn it. Finally she forced herself to work on the translation and, as usually happened when she was intellectually occupied, grew calmer.

Elizabeth Tilley, swinging her gloves in one hand, was waiting on the pavement when Chapman and Marian emerged from No. 142 at eight o'clock the next morning. She began to tug on the gloves and looked at Chapman with hot, furious eyes.

Mildly Chapman said: 'A lady should put on her gloves before leaving the house. It is ill-bred to do it in the street.'

Ignoring this Elizabeth asked: 'Am I to follow like a dog, or may I walk at your side?' Her voice was thinner and higher than usual and exaggeratedly refined. 'Well, *Mr* Chapman?'

Chapman smiled wickedly. 'Unfortunately I don't possess a dog leash.'

Elizabeth screamed with hysterical laughter and began walking ahead mincingly. Chapman took Marian by the arm and led her in the opposite direction before releasing her. Elizabeth glanced over her shoulder, hurried back breathlessly and placed herself on Chapman's other side.

'Do we meditate or do we converse?' she asked him pertly.
'We meditate.'

Marian had already begun to feel uneasy. It was all very petty, if disturbing. Chapman, far from meditating, engaged her instantly in conversation and soon gained her undivided attention in a discussion of Charles Dickens's latest and highly sucessful venture, the weekly magazine, *Household Words*.

'I'm much more interested in Mr Dickens's notorious private life,' Elizabeth chipped in.

Chapman ignored her and asked Marian what she thought of Dickens's last book, *David Copperfield*, published two years ago. Marian said that though it was, and would undoubtedly remain, his most popular book she herself preferred *The Old Curiosity Shop*. With that they began to argue amicably but on a plane far above Elizabeth Tilley's intellectual level. Elizabeth fumed with anger and resentment; they were behaving as if she no longer existed. She took a quick pace ahead and looked back scathingly at Marian. Ridiculous, she thought, to regard this plain, badly dressed and sexless-looking woman as a rival. Even more ridiculous to think of her romping in bed with John Chapman. Not only ridiculous but beyond all belief. In that respect Elizabeth felt eminently secure. What she resented, even feared, was Marian's intellectual superiority. Chapman was clearly fascinated by it. Only last night he had tried to excuse his interest in Marian by saying that he was intent only on bettering himself intellectually. Then he had added something which Elizabeth had failed fully to understand, something about an intellectual climax being more stimulating than a physical one, and that if both could be achieved at the same time the world would be shatteringly conquered. Complete and utter nonsense, Elizabeth thought now, but she was painfully aware that Marian, intellectually, was a formidable rival, especially since Chapman himself was no more than an intellectual snob. He had made a place for himself in the literary world, Elizabeth's native shrewdness told her, simply because through business acumen he, once a watchmaker, had become a successful and much sought-after publisher. Back at his side again she grasped his arm urgently.

'Chapman, we'll be late for breakfast.'

He shook himself free. 'Who cares about breakfast?'

'You do, with that greedy appetite of yours.'

'Hold your tongue,' he said, 'and try not to interrupt again.'

Elizabeth took a deep, angry breath. 'Please understand,' she said shrilly, 'that as far as Miss Evans is concerned you are neither a monkey on a chain nor a parrot in a cage.'

To her intense mortification Marian laughed, but not, as Elizabeth thought, in amusement.

'And nor,' Chapman said smoothly, 'as far as *you* are concerned, Miss Tilley.'

He turned, causing Marian to turn with him. Walking slowly now and still arguing, they retraced their steps to the Strand. Elizabeth followed at a distance and from time to time shouted: 'Monkey! Parrot!' Fully aware of Marian's growing distress, Chapman was relieved when they reached No. 142, the more so since, at the moment of their arrival, three burly men in leather aprons were carrying a piano into the house. He wondered, not too doubtfully, if foresight had served him well on this occasion.

'You've bought a piano!' Marian exclaimed excitedly.

Smiling enigmatically Chapman slipped into the house ahead of the men and issued brisk instructions. Marian followed and in utter amazement watched the piano being placed in her sitting-room.

'*You*,' Chapman said when the men had gone, 'have bought a piano. *I* am only a poor publisher.' He looked at her with an impish smile. 'Would you like me to send it back?'

Almost speechless, she said: 'No, oh no!'

It was, Chapman thought, a cry of anguish.

'It occurred to me,' he said sympathetically, 'that you were somewhat lost without musical expression. That was why I bought this piano in your name.'

'Oh, thank you, John, thank you!' Then a disturbing thought struck her. 'I—I can't really afford it.'

'You shall pay for it gradually out of your salary.'

'How kind and thoughtful you are!'

Elizabeth Tilley had followed them into the room. 'Now,' she said satirically, 'we are going to have concerts. What are you going to play, Miss Evans—Beethoven?' She searched in her mind for another composer's name. 'Or Mozart?' She fumbled over the name and repeated her mispronunciation. 'Mose-art?'

'Mozart,' Chapman said promptly, having ascertained from Charles Bray Marian's current musical preoccupation. 'The Masses in particular.'

'Christ!' Elizabeth exclaimed, 'have we all become Catholics of a sudden?'

Momentarily angry, yet at the same time wanting to laugh, Chapman relaxed when he realised that Marian, now standing lovingly at the piano, had heard not a word.

'The Mozart Masses,' he said loudly.

Marian turned and looked at him gravely. 'My skill is limited but I shall try my best, thank you, John.'

7

'EVERY morning for the last week,' Elizabeth Tilley said angrily. 'Every single morning!'

Susanna Chapman looked at her impatiently. 'What does it matter if John takes his morning walk with Marian instead of you these days?'

'It matters to me, it matters very much!'

'You're making a mountain out of a molehill, Elizabeth. In any case, what can you hope to achieve by complaining to *me?*'

Elizabeth smiled slyly and tried to make her voice sound persuasive. 'I thought perhaps we could put our heads together and do something to drive the intruder away. Two heads are better than one, or so people say.'

Susanna laughed bitterly. 'The mistress and the wife? That's rich, Elizabeth, really rich.'

'We used to be friends,' Elizabeth reminded her.

'Yes, when you first came here, but all *that* is in the past and well you know it.'

Elizabeth tossed her head. 'How difficult you are to understand, Susanna. I find it most unreasonable of you to hate me because I give Chapman something which you're no longer interested in giving him yourself. *Most* unreasonable. A husband can't be expected to live the life of a monk.'

'It would be stupid of me to expect it, in John's case,' Susanna said dryly. 'I know him for what he is. I've known it for quite some time. There were others before you, as you very well know. That is why I withdrew from what is nicely termed the marital bed.'

'How undutiful of you!'

'Oh, I agree.'

'Still, I should be mortified if you *were* dutiful.'

'That I thoroughly understand.'

'Please try not to hate me,' Elizabeth wheedled.

'Hate you?' Susanna said soberly. 'I don't really hate you, Elizabeth. My sole aim is to ignore your existence. In respect of John's adultery, I mean. Indifference at least makes life bearable.'

'*I* can't ignore Marian Evans's existence,' Elizabeth said fretfully. 'You and I should be able to join forces in a common cause. Please help me, Susanna.'

Susanna sighed lightly. 'You're wasting your time and your breath, and you're beginning to bore me. Your jealousy is quite absurd. John is only interested in Marian intellectually. Surely you realise that? I find her intellectually interesting too. Let us say no more about it.'

'I see that I must act entirely on my own,' Elizabeth said furiously. 'Rest assured, I shall do everything in my power, *everything*, to drive Marian Evans away. I shall think of something without any help from you.'

'Please go,' Susanna said wearily. 'I want to rest before the party tonight.'

Petulantly Elizabeth withdrew from Susanna's room and all but tumbled down the stairs. She had already heard the sound of a piano and without hesitation flew along the passage to Marian's rooms. She paused at the door, listening intently. The playing had ceased and a voice, Chapman's, reached her ears. What, she wondered, was he saying to the hated Marian Evans? Was he trying to talk intelligently about music? Unable to restrain herself longer Elizabeth flung open the door without knocking and entered Marian's sitting-room so forcefully that she collided with Chapman who had risen from a chair near the piano. Marian turned on the piano stool, a look of alarm in her eyes.

'Well?' Chapman asked Elizabeth calmly.

'She was playing for you!'

'Indeed she was.'

'Playing for you!' Elizabeth said as accusingly as if she had caught him and Marian in the act of making love. In a sense, to her, it *was* a love scene which she had interrupted. 'Intolerable!' she said, on an even shriller note.

Chapman inclined his head and said mockingly: 'A Mose-art Mass. I found it very soothing. Marian plays beautifully but is far to modest to admit it.'

'Beautifully!' Elizabeth sneered. 'You wouldn't know the difference if she played horribly. You're not really musical. You only pretend to be. You're good, of course, at pretending.' She turned to Marian with a violent twist of her shoulders. 'How well do you understand Chapman? Are you aware that he keeps on flattering you for one reason only? He does it because he wants to keep you here and use you in his business.'

'Hold your tongue, Elizabeth!' Chapman said sharply. 'My admiration of Marian's many talents is completely genuine.' He looked at Marian obliquely, noting her confusion and distress. 'Do you believe me, Marian?'

'I don't know what to believe,' she said miserably.

'You're such a fool,' Elizabeth told her scornfully. 'I thought you were clever, but obviously you're not clever enough to realise that Chapman has a special reason of his own, a most selfish reason, for pretending to see anything in a woman as ugly as you.'

Marian rose shakily from the piano stool, excused herself with a politeness which Chapman found pathetic, and fled to the privacy of her bedroom. For once, and without hesitation, she had reached a firm decision.

'I have half a mind to dismiss you immediately,' Chapman told Elizabeth in a tense, low voice.

'You won't, of course,' she said confidently. 'You value me more highly in bed than you could ever value Marian Evans in an editorial office.'

'Keep your voice low,' Chapman warned.

Elizabeth lowered her voice and said cheerfully: 'No woman has ever been able to satisfy your lust as I do.'

'Nor any man yours, as I do,' he murmured, more in control of himself.

Elizabeth glanced at the closed bedroom door. 'Shall I tell her?'

'She wouldn't believe you, my poor Elizabeth.'

'No,' she admitted. 'She would have to catch us in the act, silly innocent fool that she is.'

'Which will never happen, of course.'

Chapman glanced at the bedroom door himself. He could hear the ominous, suggestive sound of drawers being opened and closed. Quickly he pushed Elizabeth from the sitting-room and slammed the outer door behind her. He listened intently. Another drawer was opened, violently. Softly he opened the bedroom door and found Marian, as he had expected, hurriedly throwing clothes into her portmanteau which lay on the bed.

'Shall I help you with the carpet bag?' he asked cheerfully.

'The carpet bag is reserved for my shoes.'

'One pair, in addition to the pair you're wearing. They'll rattle around quite merrily.'

'Please don't try to make me laugh,' Marian said plaintively. 'My mind is quite made up. The discord here is more than I can bear. I shall spend the night at an hotel and return to Coventry tomorrow.' She paused and looked at him pleadingly. 'Please have my books packed and sent after me.'

'As you wish.' Chapman caught and held her eyes. 'You are wondering, of course, why I hesitate to dismiss Elizabeth and find another governess for the children.'

'The thought had crossed my mind.'

'Dear Marian, the children adore her. It would hurt them terribly if I deprived them of her suddenly. I do beg you to reconsider what I can only regard as a hasty decision.'

'You are trying to appeal to me sentimentally,' Marian faltered.

'Because of your love of children? To that, Marian Evans, I plead guilty.'

Her thoughts beyond her control, Marian said distractedly: 'I should dearly love to have children of my own.'

Prudently ignoring this, Chapman said: 'I have another appeal, an intellectual appeal. Charles Dickens is coming to dinner to-night. Surely you would like to meet him.'

'I have yet to decide,' Marian said, as if defending herself, 'whether or not Mr Dickens is an intellectual.'

Chapman, having long ago taken Dickens's earthy measure, said solemnly: 'Tonight will be a most interesting experience for you, Marian.'

'Most,' she admitted, and felt completely lost.

'Shall I put your extra pair of shoes in the carpet bag?'

Marian shook her head. 'That won't be necessary.'

'Well, there we are!'

'Who,' Marian asked, rallying, 'is managing whom?'

Chapman laughed disarmingly. 'I, for the moment, am man-aging the redoubtable and sometimes frightening Marian Evans.' He looked at her closely. 'Have you a headache?'

'Yes. A bad one. It came on suddenly.'

Chapman led her back to the sitting-room, placed her in the chair which he had previously occupied and standing behind her began to massage her brow and temples with smooth, sure fingers. He noted happily that, as once before, she stiffened at his touch, then relaxed. He was making steady progress, he told himself, and with no great surprise felt a stirring in his loins. He smiled at the thought that Elizabeth Tilley would find him more than ordinarily strong during their next encounter tonight.

'I think you're beginning to feel better already,' he told Marian.

Partly soothed Marian murmured that she was, but she was painfully and at the same time pleasurably aware of the warmth of the padded seat on which John Chapman had sat for the best part of an hour while listening to a Mozart Mass. It was be-coming, she thought, a part of her own warmth, as if he were holding her in a lingering embrace. She wondered whether to be shocked at herself or to giggle: such an improper thought, stem-ming as it did from an unmentionable part of John Chapman's body. Was it sufficient, she asked herself, almost light-heartedly, to create in her a peculiar fetish? Suddenly she recalled a story which Caroline Bray had told her after visiting Paris where she and Charles had met the French writer, d'Aurévilly. He was an amusing conversationalist and had related what he had described as a true incident: a young and innocent girl sitting in an arm-chair vacated by a notorious roué; then, dismayed by the warmth, enveloped and shattered by it, running to her mother to declare that she was going to have a baby. Marian giggled outright.

Fortunately she was not as sexually ignorant as that, and a good thing too, at *her* age.

'I had meant to make you purr like a kitten,' Chapman said, 'not giggle like a child. May I share the joke?'

Marian rose in confusion. 'It would be too embarrassing.'

'Ah, a joke not suitable for mixed company! You surprise me, and quite tantalisingly. How do you feel now? Has the headache gone?'

'Not entirely.'

'Then be a good girl and rest until dinner tonight. I shall place you next to Dickens.'

Charles Dickens, after one penetrating glance at his table companion, was at least polite to her, in spite of the fact that Elizabeth Tilley, who was seated opposite, laughed derisively. He praised the first review which Marian had written for the *Westminster*, but he had nothing to say about her translation of *Leben Jesu* when she mentioned it timidly. Then he began to talk about his own literary affairs, to talk about them in what Marian considered to be a self-satisfied voice. He had in mind a long-range project, the public readings of his books. It was a venture, he thought, which would prove more profitable than the drudgery of writing. Elizabeth constantly interrupted and Dickens seemed not ill-pleased. At thirty-nine a pretty face appealed to him enormously. He called Elizabeth 'My dear' several times and when she remarked that too much culture was as binding to the mind as too much cheese to the bowels he reached across the table to pat her hand.

'Have I said something shocking?' she challenged skittishly.

'This is a bohemian dinner party,' Dickens chuckled, 'not a Sunday-school meeting.'

Marian studied his face, clean-shaven except for a drooping moustache. Much as she admired his work she was beginning to feel quite savage about him. There was a hardness in his eyes, though he laughed easily. Prolonging her study she failed to find any benevolence in his face and decided that there was none in his head either. It was rumoured that he and his wife would soon separate, and this made Marian wonder, her mood being what it was, just how badly he made the poor woman suffer. Nevertheless he interested her and she longed for the opportunity to talk with him more intimately, to assess his character more fully with a view to using him in the novel she had yet to write. But after dinner Elizabeth Tilley monopolised him completely, meanwhile casting defiant and scornful glances at Marian who had become saddled to the point of desperation with one of Chapman's new and inordinately vain authors. She withdrew early from the party and went to bed with a raging headache. How much longer, she asked herself, could she continue to live under the same roof as Elizabeth Tilley?

8

ENTERING softly, Chapman crossed Marian's sitting-room and stood in silence at the open bedroom door. Once again his assistant editor was packing. He was not in the least surprised. Marian had had a difficult week since the party at which she had met Charles Dickens. Elizabeth had made several scenes and this morning, after following them at a distance during their walk, she had created so violent a scene, there in front of the other boarders, that Marian had fled, her shoulders shaking, tears streaming down her cheeks.

'Marian ...' Chapman said quietly.

Without looking round at him she continued to cram clothing into the portmanteau.

'Marian, Emerson is coming to dinner tonight.'

'I didn't know he was in England,' she forced herself to say.

'He arrived yesterday. As a matter of fact, I'm going to do my best to persuade him to stay here. Much cheaper for him than an hotel. You'd like to meet him, wouldn't you, and get to know him really well?'

'Of course,' Marian said tonelessly.

'There are so many literary figures you have yet to meet. Thackeray, for instance, and Tennyson and Ruskin. Why deprive yourself of the pleasure because of Elizabeth Tilley?'

Marian straightened up and said frantically: 'I would deprive myself of any pleasure to gain peace of mind again.' She thought in dismay that it was the wrong thing to say. It was Chapman who had deprived her of peace of mind, not Elizabeth; *she* had merely made her miserable to the point of physical exhaustion. 'I must go this time, John, I really must.'

'I promise you one thing,' Chapman said solemnly, 'Emerson won't make sheep's eyes at Elizabeth the way Dickens did.'

'I scarcely care.'

'Please don't leave, Marian. Stay on for my sake if not your own.'

She hesitated for a moment. 'I shall stay until tomorrow but nothing will prevent me from leaving then.'

Partly satisfied, Chapman took her by the arm, made her sit on the stool in front of the dressing-table and commanded her to look at herself in the mirror.

'We must smarten you up for Emerson, my dear, even if he doesn't care much about a woman's appearance. I think we should begin with your hair. These bangs, if bangs they are, sticking out on each side of your head! Why, Marian, *why?* The ringlets were better, even if unsuitable.'

Marian explained about the French marquise at Geneva. Chapman laughed and said that he had a greater understanding than any marquise when it came to dictating the right hair style for Marian Evans. With that he began to unpin her hair, Marian watching him weakly and helplessly in the mirror. He worked slowly and carefully until it fell about her shoulders in a rich and glossy cascade.

'You wore your hair long when you were young,' he said, not asking a question. 'You must have been an attractive child.'

'My mother called me an ugly duckling.' Marian fought back quick tears at the memory.

'A singularly unperceptive mother. There was surely something special about you, even then.'

'So somebody else told me.' Marian remembered the maid whom she had questioned anxiously. 'Please don't flatter me, John. I know, none better, how plain I am.'

'The plainness is only evident in certain moods. Then, indeed, it becomes outright, even deliberate, ugliness. In any case a plain woman owes it to herself to make the best of her appearance, to turn plainness into something vastly interesting. You have that power, Marian. Rest assured, I am *not* flattering you.'

He took up a brush from the dressing-table and brushed her hair until it shone and gleamed all the more richly, as if little golden lights had appeared magically. Next he took up a comb and parted it down the centre and then, after a moment's consideration, he drew it back and by aid of a few pins arranged it in a large, full loop at the back of her head.

'The latest style,' he said, 'but created especially for you. Well? What do you think of my handiwork?'

Marian stared at herself in the mirror. 'If that is Marian Evans I scarcely recognise her.'

Chapman readjusted the loop and stood back, his head on one side, his eyes critical. Marian felt a wild desire to seize his hand. She wanted him to go on caressing her hair, and caressing it he surely had been, for a few moments longer. She sought to hold his eyes in the mirror, then turned to face him. His eyes had a preoccupied look now; she feared that to him she had ceased to exist as an individual woman.

'John . . .'

'Madame,' he said formally, 'is almost a new woman. Permit me to kiss your hand.' Having done so, his manner still formal, he repeated, '*Almost* a new woman. Now we must do something about your clothes. Your dress, dowdy no doubt when you bought it, is at least ten years out of date, even in dowdiness.'

'I've had it for seven years,' Marian confessed.

'And taken good care of it, obviously.'

'I'm really quite attached to it.'

He smiled briefly. 'A Chapman dinner party is something quite different from a country walk. Do you possess a tape-measure?' Marian shook her head. 'Some string?' Marian found a ball of string and handed it to him. 'Scissors?' She found a pair of scissors and waited for his next move which was not entirely unexpected. He encircled her waist with the string, knotted it and clipped off a length. Then he encircled her bust and clipped off another length. Finally, after measuring her dress from the shoulders to the waist, he measured it from the waist down to the hem. 'Unpack your portmanteau,' he said briskly, 'while I embark on a little shopping expedition.'

Trembling not unpleasurably Marian watched him go, then she turned to look at the almost new Marian Evans in the mirror. Her cheeks were burning; there was a wild look in her eyes. To what, she asked herself, had she submitted? If seduction was in John Chapman's mind, and surely it was, he was taking his time about it.

Chapman was away for an hour, an agonising hour to Marian, during which she unpacked, repacked and unpacked again her somewhat battered portmanteau. He returned trundling before him a wicker basket which looked like a very large picnic hamper. He placed it on the piano stool and opened it, his manner suggestive of revealing a secret vice. Thrusting aside a layer of tissue paper he lifted out a velvet dress, dark green in colour.

'Try it on,' he said, placing it lovingly in her arms.

Unable to think of anything to say, Marian retreated to her

bedroom and carefully closed the door behind her. After a moment's hesitation she removed her serviceable everyday dress as furtively as if Chapman were watching her and slipped the new garment over her head. The bodice, which fastened down the front, had a rounded neckline trimmed with lace; the waist was close-fitting but not too tight and held in place at the left side by an ornamental buckle. Yards of skirt flowed out beneath it down to the toes of her shoes. She turned this way and that in front of the mirror, swishing out the skirt, and felt ridiculously girlish. Presently she heard Chapman's voice asking her to come out and let him see how she looked. Gripped by stage-fright she patted her hair into place and slowly rejoined him.

'An amazing transformation,' Chapman exclaimed admiringly. He studied her for a moment, his head on one side. 'The waist should be a little tighter. Let me adjust it for you.' She protested that she could do it herself but he took not the slightest notice and manipulated the buckle, turning the tong unseen by Marian and bending it. Then he stood back. 'Well? Is it to your liking?'

Marian nodded and felt as if she ought to curtsy.

'I'm sure it is much too expensive,' she said.

'Possibly, but you must learn to spoil yourself a little, Marian. In any case, this dress and the other are on approval. You may send them back if you wish.'

'The *other*?'

Chapman strode to the wicker basket, rustled more tissue paper and lifted out a second dress. Marian gasped at the sight of it. Was it Chapman's intention, she wondered, to present her at Court?

'It's known as a *basque*,' he said, shaking out the folds. 'It is of course intended for evening wear.'

'I can scarcely envisage myself wearing anything so elaborate,' Marian protested.

'Nevertheless, wear it you shall. Please try it on.'

Chapman watched her retreat to the bedroom again. She carried the *basque* as gingerly as if it were a very young baby that she was afraid of dropping. After a few moments her voice floated out to him, a mixture of plaintiveness and agitation.

'The buckle has stuck, I can't loosen it.'

Chapman entered the bedroom before she had time to emerge. Standing behind her he took his time loosening the buckle, saying ruefully that his fingers were all thumbs. Then he encircled her with his arms and, prepared for a rebuff but not seriously expecting one, undid the buttons of the bodice slowly and deliberately. Marian stood perfectly still, as if paralysed. Carefully, but still keeping her with her back to him, he removed the dress, threw it without any sign of urgency on the bed and took up the *basque*.

'You need prettier underclothes,' he said teasingly. 'We shall deal with that problem later on.'

Marian repressed a sob of anguish at the thought of Chapman buying new underclothes for her, stripping her and helping her to put them on. Was that what he had in mind? It was impossible to say from its voice. He adjusted the *basque* to his satisfaction, exclaimed 'Ravishing!' and placed her in front of the mirror.

'Well, madame?'

Marian's cheeks were scarlet, she felt as if she was blushing all over, and the pupils of her eyes were dilated. She tried unavailingly to steady herself. A doctor, she thought, would diagnose a sudden fever.

'You've made me look like a Velásquez painting,' she said shakily—'except for my face.'

'Nonsense! Even your face has taken on a Spanish appearance.'

'My poor nose looks even larger.'

'A pleasing Spanish protuberance.'

She could but laugh. 'Is the *basque* inspired by Velásquez?'

'It is. The seventeenth century but brought up to date.'

Impulsively Marian said: 'Thank you, John, even if you *have* made me look like a sheep in lamb's clothing.'

'They breed some very fine sheep in Spain.'

'Even so . . .'

'Nonsense! A woman of distinction looking exactly how she ought to look.' And slyly he added: 'Coventry society will be shaken to its provincial foundations.'

'Coventry?' Marian had momentarily forgotten her decision. 'I still intend to return to Coventry tomorrow,' she said, so soberly that Chapman was obliged to believe her. 'Please understand that in at least one respect I still have a will of my own.'

'You sound exactly like a drowning woman refusing to be rescued,' he laughed, 'but as I often say, one step at a time, O Lord, one step at a time. The next step is our party tonight. Emerson, unobservant as he generally is, will be absolutely entranced.'

'I value my brain more than my appearance,' she said, as severely as she could, but glancing at herself again in the mirror, trying to imagine what life was like in the seventeenth century, she was anything but sure. '*Much* more,' she insisted.

Afterwards Marian's impressions of the dinner party and the important writers present were vague. If Elizabeth Tilley was there she failed to notice her; she was too preoccupied with thoughts, the most tumultuous thoughts, of John Chapman, and kept glancing in his direction, feeling like a dog (as she wrote in her diary and later tore out the page) begging for a kindly, even a loving, pat on the head. She did, however, make an effort to converse intelligently with Ralph Waldo Emerson, and for a moment, if vaguely, she realised that as far as he was concerned she might well be dressed in rags. That was just as well, she thought, for she felt over-dressed in the *basque* and just a bit silly. Nevertheless, it was clear that she had made a certain impression on Emerson; he remarked, on bidding her good-bye, that she had a calm and serious soul. Serious without a doubt, but *calm*! What on earth had she discussed with him? Surely not her involvement with John Chapman! *Involvement?* She was ready to admit, if only to herself, that it had indeed become an involvement. She searched her now unreliable memory. Perhaps they had discussed religion. She remembered that Emerson had once been a Unitarian minister. It *must* have been religion.

'Marian . . .'

She turned and found herself face to face with Chapman. He had seen the last of his guests to the door and a harassed Susanna had gone to bed. She was alone with him for the moment.

'Tennyson,' he said, 'wants to have a lengthy talk with you some day.'

Tennyson? Marian had no memory of having met Tennyson.

'Does he think I have a calm and serious soul?' she asked wildly.

'Possibly, but he was mainly impressed by your originality of thought.'

'Fancy that!' She sounded, she thought, like a refined lady's maid over-anxious to come up in the world.

Chapman looked at her obliquely. 'Tennyson will be coming to dinner again one night next week.'

Marian steadied herself. 'Unfortunately I shall be in Coventry by then.'

'Ah yes, I was forgetting that. Your last night here. A great pity, in more ways than one. You will be sadly missed, Marian, very sadly missed. Do you, by the way, lock your door when you go to bed?'

'My—my door?'

'I was thinking of prowlers. The house next door was burgled last night.'

'I am *not* afraid of prowlers,' Marian said, as if taking up a challenge.

'Splendid to hear you say that. Good night, Marian. The hour is late. Have a good rest. Sleep well in preparation for tomorrow's long journey.'

Marian went slowly to her rooms and locked the outer door, which she had never done before. She lit a candle in the bedroom and paced up and down restlessly, as if trying to make up her mind about something or in the midst of writing a difficult review. Finally she undressed, donned a sensible if shapeless nightdress and fell into bed. Coventry tomorrow? The thought kept her awake. After tossing and turning for what seemed a timeless age she sprang out of bed and unlocked the outer door. Then she paused and listened intently, without quite realising that she held the still-burning candle in her hand. Except that she was wide awake, and nervous of the slightest sound, she felt like a sleepwalker. Presently the door swung slowly open and there stood John Chapman. He entered softly, closed and locked the door behind him and took the candle from Marian.

'John . . .'

'Don't talk, Marian.'

'John!'

'*Don't talk!*' he repeated.

In the bedroom he placed the candle on the dressing-table, settled Marian in bed as if he were a nursemaid and thumped the pillows to make them more comfortable. After that he undressed slowly until he was completely naked. Marian wanted to avert her eyes but once again felt paralysed. Finally, he blew out the candle.

'John!'

He got into bed at her side.

'John, I feel terrible. I—I feel as if I don't belong to myself any more.'

'For the third time, don't talk,' he commanded. 'Talk, under certain circumstances, can be most destructive. In any case, Marian, I'm desperately tired.'

'I've never been so wide awake in my life, John.'

He smiled in the darkness and turned away from her, simulating immediate sleep. Finally he did sleep, quite soundly. It was his boast, old watchmaker that he was, that he had a special time clock in his brain and could wake at whatever time suited him. In this instance he woke just before dawn and, much refreshed, took a still sleepless Marian into his arms. Was it to be

Coventry or London? he wondered. The risk of driving her away by this mattered not at all. She had been determined to go, in any case. He kissed her with cautious passion. It all depended, he thought, on how skilful he was when it came to managing *and* satisfying a virgin of thirty-one. As for Marian, she felt that a certain unmentionable part of herself was purring like a recently weaned kitten.

10

THEY were taking their morning walk as usual, stepping out briskly in defiance of a fine, penetrating drizzle. Marian glanced covertly at Chapman's face. There was nothing whatever in his expression to suggest that something of vast importance had happened, something capable of changing his life and hers. She wondered if her own expression betrayed her in any way and continued to walk in silence at Chapman's side. She knew that she ought to feel tired, not having slept, but a quivering exhilaration gripped her; she might well be flying, not merely walking. She felt so exhilarated that the little stabs of guilt at the back of her mind were scarcely noticeable. *Devilish*, that was how she really felt, and that reminded her of what she had said to the Brays when discussing with them a Continental holiday after her father's death: 'I have a vision of myself becoming earthy and sensual and devilish; what is there to restrain me now?' Charles had replied, 'The Brays,' and Caroline had added, 'And Marian Evans's conscience.' This pulled her up sharply, physically as well as mentally. Chapman, still not having spoken, looked back at her quizzically. Hurriedly she caught up with him.

'You must often have wondered,' he said equably, 'why I was so brusque with you during the Channel crossing nearly two years ago.'

'Often, John.'

'Have you arrived at any conclusion?'

'My failure to translate Spinoza for you, perhaps?'

'No, not that.'

'The state of your liver, then?' She laughed gaily.

'I expect I was feeling liverish,' Chapman said gravely, 'as liverish as a man is entitled to feel when resisting a devilish temptation.'

Devilish—that word again!

Marian glanced at him suspiciously. 'Self-righteousness was possibly your complaint.'

'Another form of liverishness. To labour the point, Marian, I was afraid that what happened last night might well happen if I went on to Geneva with you.'

'This morning, not last night,' Marian said, finding a modicum of security in correctness.

'I wasted a lot of time,' Chapman sighed. 'It was inevitable, after all, beyond my control *and* yours.'

'John,' she said, battling now with Marian Evans's conscience, 'I feel terribly guilty.'

As if changing the subject he said: 'The first time isn't always completely enjoyable, for the woman.' He felt reasonably safe in saying this; Marian had cried out in pain at first, then in obvious rapture. Softly he added, 'You'll feel less guilty later on.'

'What a cynical thing to say!'

'I mean it honestly, candidly. If Susanna comes into your feeling of guilt, let me assure you that she is no longer part of my life in that respect. I still love her, of course, but platonically.'

'Poor Susanna.'

Chapman began to feel irritated but went on smoothly: 'Can it be called a religious guilt, you being an agnostic?'

'A moral guilt, John. Religion and morality aren't always one and the same thing, any more than the law and justice are.'

'You're dragging me beyond my depth,' he said wryly. 'Tell me what you mean by morality.'

'That which one believes to be right; that which one's conscience tells one is right.'

'I think,' he said carefully, 'that your early religious training still clings to you. A sort of atavistic clinging. The rules and regulations; the Ten Commandments, especially the one forbidding adultery. But how can you regard our relationship as an adulterous one when I no longer sleep with Susanna?'

'You are still married to her.'

'Only because of the cost of divorce,' he improvised. 'The necessary special act of Parliament is costly and beyond my small resources.'

'You—you would marry me if you could?'

'Without the slightest hesitation,' Chapman said, so convincingly that Marian believed him.

'John, I do love you. It would be heaven to be your wife and conceive your children.'

Prudently he refrained from telling her that she might at least achieve the latter ambition. He grew mildly excited at the thought of it. A child by Marian Evans would surely be something of a prodigy.

'Marian,' he said softly, 'we have so many things in common, and now we have sexual congress.' She flinched, causing him to continue persuasively. 'Mind you, I have never regarded it as important in itself. Indeed, I think it quite horrible as nothing more than a means to its own end, but in our case it has given us fulfilment. Do you see it as I do?'

'Well . . . Oh, John, I don't know what to think!'

'*Try* to see it as I do, please.'

'I—I shall try,' she promised.

'Thank you.'

They turned and began to retrace their steps. Chapman was not yet sure that he had bound her completely to him and decided to take a calculated risk.

'I shall help you with your packing after breakfast,' he said lightly, 'and see you safely to the railway station.'

Marian looked straight ahead of her. 'John, I'm not going back to Coventry today.'

'Tomorrow, perhaps?'

'No.'

'Next week?'

Marian still looked straight ahead of her. 'If Mr Emerson is going to be one of your boarders it would be a pity to deny myself the opportunity of getting to know him better.' She smiled wryly at her wilful duplicity and tried, in another respect, to be practical. 'Tell me what the new dresses cost. I want to pay for them immediately. I don't like having debts hanging over my head.'

Mercenary as Chapman was, he said gaily, 'I want to make you a present of them.'

'The last thing *I* want,' Marian said in alarm, 'is to think of myself as a kept woman.'

'Kept?' Chapman chuckled.

'Please don't laugh at me, John.'

'I'm not really laughing at you, Marian. You work for your living, don't you, and pay for your board and lodgings? A *present*, my dear, otherwise I shall feel insulted.'

'Well, in that case . . . Oh, but I must give you a present in return.'

Chapman laughed gaily. He would get his money back after

all, or part of it. No, he decided, all of it, if possible. He gave the matter careful thought then suggested a new overcoat.

'They are shorter this year, more form-fitting, and with slightly narrower lapels.'

'Very well, a new overcoat.'

'Also one of the new pleated shirts.'

'A new overcoat, a new pleated shirt. Splendid!'

'You're spoiling me, Marian.'

'That's what I want to do, John.'

At breakfast Elizabeth Tilley stared lengthily at Marian. She remembered the amazing transformation which she had observed at the party last night—Marian Evans wearing a *basque*, her eyes excited, her face flushed. Her eyes looked even more excited this morning and her colour, fluctuating as it did, was high whenever she looked at Chapman. Elizabeth grew instantly suspicious but contented herself with making a scathing remark.

'New clothes, *fashionable* clothes, but not even our clever Chapman can turn a sow's ear into a silk purse.'

'On the other hand,' Marian retorted, holding Elizabeth's eyes steadily, 'a silk purse sometimes contains a sow's ear. I can see one protruding from your own silk purse, Miss Tilley. However, I shall ignore it henceforth, and you also.'

Elizabeth was left speechless. Not only the excited eyes and the high colour, but an incredible new self-confidence. Her suspicions grew apace. Could she possibly be right? She controlled herself by dint of a great effort and decided to wait and watch, and not run hurriedly to Susanna again until completely sure of gaining her support.

9

'YES,' Susanna Chapman said slowly, 'I agree this time that something must be done to drive Marian Evans away.' She frowned over this. 'That is, if you're not jumping to conclusions, Elizabeth. You often do, you know. It is a failing of yours. What real proof have you?'

'The evidence of my eyes and ears.'

'You actually *saw* as well as heard?'

'We-ell . . .'

'You say you hid behind the piano in Marian's sitting-room.

How could you possibly see if you were hiding?'

'I saw them when they went into the bedroom. Neither of them looked back. They were much too eager to fall into bed.'

'But *before* that...?'

Elizabeth related the scene, as made known to her through intent listening. Chapman had brought Marian a new set of under-clothes—an embroidered chemise, a pair of long pantalettes, a corset, which he said was scarcely needed, two embroidered petti-coats, *everything*. He had undressed the wretched woman, re-marking on her neat breasts, her slender waist, her rounded, flow-ing thighs, and had then dressed her in the new, fashionable underclothes. The thought of Chapman strategically placed be-tween those same rounded, flowing thighs had nearly driven Elizabeth crazy with jealousy and longing.

'There in the sitting-room,' she gasped. 'In broad daylight too. Shameless, quite shameless!'

'How long has the affair been going on?'

'Obviously since the party a month ago for Mr Emerson. If you want further evidence, Chapman was with her last night from eleven o'clock. He didn't go back to his own room until six in the morning. Twice in one day—shameless!'

'That has never happened in your case?' Susanna asked dryly.

Elizabeth smiled reminiscently. 'Three times, before Marian came to live here. Chapman had been drinking. I have a note of the occasion in my diary.'

'It must be a most interesting diary. However, I agree that something must be done, but ... what? My joining forces with you and being disagreeable obviously won't help at all.' Susanna had second thoughts and said wearily: 'Why should I object to his sleeping with her when I don't object any more to his sleeping with you?' She frowned thoughtfully. 'He still does, I suppose?'

'Oh, yes! Chapman is a very virile man. But it isn't just the sleeping part that matters—with her, I mean. It's all the rest, especially as far as you are concerned.'

Susanna nodded slowly. 'Yes, all the rest. She has become every-thing to him, in all other respects. Or so it seems. John is no longer even my platonic husband. We used to have long and interesting discussions, but not any more. I have been reduced completely to the lowly status of a domestic drudge. Marian Evans is even dealing with the authors I used to deal with. A domestic drudge,' she repeated resentfully. Her brows puckered, then her eyes brightened. 'I think I have an idea,' she said slowly. 'She must be disillusioned. Knowing her as I do, I feel sure she experiences many moments of self-reproach at having become John's mistress.'

'Disillusioned, Susanna?'

'I think the best thing to do is contrive some way for her to catch you in bed with him.'

Elizabeth laughed gleefully and admiringly. 'What a splendid idea!'

'Splendid, yes, or so I imagine.'

'How much cleverer you are than I, Susanna!'

But she ought, Elizabeth realised, to have been just as clever. After all, she had once told Chapman that Marian would have to catch them in the act before believing. 'Which of course,' he had replied, 'will never happen.' And now, despite his words, it was certainly going to happen. Elizabeth took a deep breath in pleasurable anticipation. She felt like a playwright who had decided to take over the production of his new play himself. It would be an easy scene to write and produce, Chapman coming to her bed before going on to Marian's. How many times had that happened? Once, certainly, and that last night. He had even said, she being too stupid at the time to understand his true meaning, that the first encounter on any given night was sufficient to stimulate a man and prepare him for a second and lengthier encounter later on. She almost spat in exasperation— she being used like a whore to make it all the better for his other mistress.

Elizabeth was particularly sweet to Chapman during the rest of the day, making as sure as she could, through every feminine wile at her disposal, that he would first come to her room that night, and to egg him on she warned him that probably the next day her menstrual period would be upon her.

'Or perhaps you feel in need of a rest tonight?' she challenged.

'I never feel in need of a rest that way,' he boasted.

In private later Elizabeth apologised quite abjectly to Marian.

'I've been very rude to you at times, Miss Evans. Can you ever bring yourself to forgive me?'

Marian's heart melted. 'I was never an unforgiving woman, Miss Tilley.'

'I have a lot of private troubles,' Elizabeth said woefully, 'and private troubles always make me cranky. I'm cursed, too, by a bad temper. I need somebody to confide in, somebody to help and advise me. Could we, please, have a long quiet talk sometime?'

'Of course,' Marian said eagerly.

'Tonight?'

'Tonight, if you wish.'

'In your room or mine?'

'Yours,' Marian said somewhat hurriedly, as Elizabeth had expected.

'Very well, then, eleven o'clock. Or soon after, if Chapman keeps us up later.'

Elizabeth was in bed and Chapman with her a few minutes before eleven. She had left a candle burning. It was, in any case, her normal practice; she liked, and found it stimulating, to open her eyes and see Chapman's face at the moment of climax. It was irritating, though only slightly so in this instance, the circumstances being what they were, to have the climax cut short by a light tap on the door.

'Come in,' she invited brightly.

Chapman was amazed and appalled. He remembered that he had not thought to lock Elizabeth's door and immediately dived beneath the bed-covers. The door opened and Marian entered with her usual quiet tread.

'Ah, but you've gone to bed, Miss Tilley.'

'I have a headache,' Elizabeth said, and flung back the bed-clothes with a dramatic flourish. 'That is, if one can call John Chapman a headache.'

One startled glance was sufficient for Marian. She turned frantically and fled from the room to stumble down the stairs feeling like a sleepwalker who had been suddenly and violently awakened. Tears were streaming down her cheeks. She locked the outer door of her apartment and began immediately to pack. While she was thus occupied she heard a knock on the door. Resolutely she ignored it. She also heard Chapman's voice beseeching her to admit him but she ignored that too. Hurriedly she completed her packing, carefully leaving the two dresses which Chapman had bought for her hanging in the wardrobe. She also left the new underclothes in the dressing-table drawers, though she was rather regretful about the pantalettes to which she had taken a girlish fancy. Finally when she was satisfied that Chapman had gone, either to his own room or back to Elizabeth Tilley's, she crept from the house, her portmanteau in one hand, her carpet bag in the other. Then she trudged to the nearest hotel where, explaining that she had missed a train connection, she was admitted without suspicion, late as the hour was. And why, she thought without humour, should anyone regard her with suspicion, she dressed in her dowdiest clothes and looking like somebody's maiden aunt returning from or going to a Methodist revival meeting?

She was relieved, yet dolefully disappointed, when she caught the train to Coventry the next morning without being intercepted by John Chapman. She glanced at the portmanteau and the carpet bag on the rack above her. And be a stranger on the earth forever, she thought, a lump in her throat. But she was going to Coventry, to Rosehill, going there as if in search of the shelter of the womb.

11

'You have caused me a great deal of pain and anguish, Marian,' John Chapman said, simulating a bitterness which he by no means felt. 'At first, of course, I was angry with you for running away, but sorrow soon got the better of me.'

'I regret that very much,' Marian said stiffly, but she felt a pang of self-reproach. She still loved Chapman and that made her feel miserable and lost. 'Can you blame me for running away?' she asked defensively. 'You and Miss Tilley, I still find it hard to believe.'

Chapman could think of no immediate answer and maintained a steady pace at Marian's side. Once again they were walking together before breakfast, but along a country road near Rosehill, not a crowded London street. Marian had left London on March 24th, but Chapman had waited for five weeks, meanwhile writing several times and gaining no reply, before following her to Coventry to stay once again with the Brays, just as if nothing had happened. 'I shall leave the moment he arrives,' Marian had told Charles Bray, but her resolution had failed her and here she was, walking with Chapman in the translucent sunshine of a spring morning, the sort of morning which would normally have made Marian feel that life was really worth living.

'Marian,' he said at length, 'after you left London I made a special entry in my diary.'

'Indeed.'

'I don't expect you to be interested, of course.'

'Nor am I.'

'Or perhaps I *do* expect you to be interested. I wrote in my diary : "I accompanied M. to the railway station. She was very sad and hence made me feel very sad too. She pressed me for some intimation of the state of my feelings. I told her that I felt great love for her, but that I loved S. and E. also, though each in a different way. At this avowal she burst into tears. I tried to comfort her but the train whirled her away all too soon, she looking very, very sad indeed." '

A gasp of astonishment had already escaped Marian. 'False, the whole entry! How *dare* you, John?'

'Poetic licence.'

'A diary writer's licence. Henceforth I shall place no faith in diaries. People—you certainly—strive to make a good impression, as if expecting unborn generations to read and study and believe their exaggerations, their deliberate aim to appear saint-like. Henceforth I shall regard diaries as inadmissible evidence.'

'You're beginning to sound quite breathless. Does indignation always do that to you?'

Marian quickened her pace until she was almost running.

'I do love Susanna and Elizabeth,' he said, and repeated, 'though each in a different way. I must be honest with you.'

'Belatedly honest.'

He ignored this. 'Do please believe that it is possible for a man to love more than one woman at the same time.'

'I thought you were all in all to me,' Marian said brokenly, 'and I all in all to you.'

'You still are, when we are alone together.'

'No,' Marian said violently, '*no!*'

'I need Susanna and Elizabeth, but I need you more than I need either of them. You are more important to me, Marian, than anyone else in the world.'

Marian remembered something that Elizabeth Tilley had once said and took him up at once. 'You need me on the *Westminster Review*, John. That is why you flattered me and made love to me. You need me for that reason and no other.'

'I certainly need you for that reason,' Chapman said frankly. 'The *Westminster* is no longer the same without you. I want you to come back and resume your old duties.' He laughed softly, tantalisingly. 'Your old duties in another respect too.'

'Never!'

'Never in both instances?'

'In both.'

'Please walk more slowly,' he said plaintively. 'You're making me quite breathless too.'

Marian slowed down her pace. She was panting slightly and her nostrils were distended as if, she thought without much humour, she was sending forth flames like a legendary dragon.

'To run away is to isolate yourself from life,' Chapman said. 'Why do that when, for the first time, there in London, you really began to live?'

'I *want* to isolate myself. I—I want to feel like an island.'

'But no longer one of the Virgin Islands,' he chuckled.

Marian very nearly laughed but Chapman's aplomb, his self-satisfaction, grated on her too much for laughter. Who did he think he was? God?

'If you won't come back,' he said, 'at least continue to write reviews for me.'

'I shall write reviews for the *Coventry Herald*, no other journal.'

'What about your sense of duty, your sense of *fairness*?'

'You're arguing with me to no avail, John.'

'Before you left London,' he said, 'you agreed to write an analytical catalogue and a prospectus for the *Westminster*.' And stressing the words he added, '*Duty . . . fairness.*'

Marian frowned. 'I shall keep my word, but beyond the catalogue and the prospectus I have severed all connection with the *Westminster*.'

'I am at least grateful for small mercies,' Chapman said, simulating, actor that he was, a deep humility. He came to a halt and glanced up at the sky. 'The weather is splendid today. Do you think it will continue to be mild and sunny during the next few days?'

'More than likely.'

'Then I suggest a little expedition tomorrow. Kenilworth Castle, for instance.'

'Very well, if Charles and Cara are agreeable.'

'To the devil with Charles and Cara! I want to have you as much to myself as possible before I go back to London. Just you and I, Marian, *please*.'

'If you insist,' she said weakly, then added quickly, as if to give herself some much-needed strength of character, 'Shall we walk? It's only six or seven miles.'

'Walk if you must,' he said indulgently.

In the ruins of the Norman castle Chapman expounded on the beauty which had been destroyed when Kenilworth had been dismantled by the Roundheads after the Civil War and went on to say, his voice resonant, his eyes more magnetic than ever, that he thought it shameful that she should insist on reducing to ruins the love which had blossomed between them.

147

'You're trying to make love to me,' she said shakily.

'*And* succeeding.'

Marian evaded his arms and gathered her faltering resolution about her like a cloak of despair. In London she had ceased to be herself; here, in her own country, she was quakingly determined to retrieve at least a little of her pride and self-respect.

'I want you to promise, John, not to make love to me while you remain at Rosehill.'

'Does it matter whether I promise or not? A man can't make love to a lump of granite.'

'I want you to promise, too, that if we ever meet again our relationship will be entirely platonic.'

'You are asking me to perjure my soul.'

'Promise, John, *please*.'

'No,' he said firmly. 'I am a man of my word; therefore, in this instance, I refuse to give my word.'

'Then after you leave Rosehill we shall never meet again.'

'It will break your heart.'

'My heart is already broken.'

'You sound,' Chapman said gaily, 'like a person who has lost a golden sovereign and found a silver sixpence.'

He tried again to take her in his arms but she freed herself and stumbled away from him through the ruins of the castle, the ruins, she thought tragically, of her own life. He caught up with her and asked her in apparent earnestness just what she was reading these days. He would not like to think of her, he said, neglecting her bent for serious reading, for deep and careful study.

'*The Imitation of Christ*,' she replied. 'I'm finding consolation and comfort in it, and some inspiration. I suggest that you should read it yourself.'

'Sarcasm, Marian?'

'I mean it sincerely.'

Chapman spent ten days at Rosehill and tried again, on the eve of his departure, to persuade Marian to return to London, but she remained adamant and still refused to write anything for Chapman other than the analytical catalogue and the prospectus. Nevertheless, immediately after his departure she became vacillatory and suffered torments of indecision. It was the old question of London or Geneva, but with a difference: Coventry or London? Love was natural, she thought, but surely pity and faithfulness and memory, if only directed inwardly, were natural too. What in God's name was she to do? The Brays, suspecting much, informed of nothing, were kinder to her than ever, but she still remained at war with herself. Chapman wrote her lengthy letters; she replied briefly, addressing him (quite pettily, she knew) as 'Dear Mr Chapman', Yet on once occasion she addressed him as 'Dear Friend', decided to tear up the letter, then posted it.

Such was the state of Marian's mind, the state of her self-imposed moral conflict, when Chapman came again to Rosehill and brought Susanna with him. It was September. Six months had passed, six timeless months, since Marian's headlong flight from London. At Susanna's suggestion, an introspective, haggard-looking Susanna, Marian agreed to take a morning walk for the purpose of discussing something of interest and vital importance to both of them.

'How great a part of your life had the *Westminster Review* become before you left London?' Susanna asked.

'I think that it had become almost my whole life,' Marian replied fretfully.

'You regarded it as an important journal?'

'Yes indeed, far superior to the *Edinburgh* and the *Quarterly*.'

'And . . . now?'

'It seems to me to have deteriorated.'

'It *has* deteriorated. Are you aware of the reason?'

'I—well—I think the reason is that your husband is writing some of the reviews himself.'

'Reviews which *you* should have written. You agree, I hope, that John has certain intellectual limitations. He works hard but his talent is a tiny one compared with yours. I am *not* attempting to flatter you, Marian. I'm merely stating a fact. I beg you to come back to London. You are stagnating here in Coventry. I beg you to resume your old duties on the *Westminster*, for my sake if not your own.'

'*Your* sake, Susanna?'

'Mine, yes, but I'm not thinking entirely of myself. I have the children to consider. John has spent all the money I brought him when we married. The *Westminster* must not be allowed to fail. Nor must the publishing business in general. We need you, Marian. *I* need you.'

Marian felt devastated and not a little important.

'Has John put you up to this?' she asked dryly.

Susanna shrugged. 'You know him almost as well as I do.'

Carefully and shyly Marian said: 'Are you aware of the relationship which existed between me and your husband?'

'Fully,' Susanna said, feeling rather sorry for Marian who was blushing richly now. 'And for that reason I have one condition to impose, should you decide to come back. The old relationship must not be resumed.'

'Are you in a position to impose such a condition?' Marian startled herself by asking.

'Not really,' Susanna said wryly.

'Rest assured,' Marian said fervently, 'I am very firm about it myself.'

'You *will* come back, Marian?'

'Yes, Susanna. I realise that I *am* stagnating here in Coventry.'

'Thank you, but please tell John that you will never again be any more to him than an assistant editor.'

Marian did so and was shaken by Chapman's smiling disbelief.

'Never,' she said, quite beside herself, 'never, never, never!'

He bowed ceremoniously. 'Very well, Miss Evans, I shall leave all that to you. I myself, not by a word, not by a single gesture, will ever attempt to persuade you to change your mind.' The actor in him came uppermost; he managed to make his voice sound distraught. 'The *Westminster*, heaven help us both, is all that counts.'

He wondered if he had gone too far and waited expectantly.

'I shall do everything possible, work harder than ever before,' Marian avowed, 'to make the *Westminster* a tremendous success.'

Chapman bowed again. 'In spirit, Miss Evans, I kiss your literary hand.'

12

It was close on midnight and rain, quite heavy for December, was battering at the window of Marian's sitting-room. There was a distant rumble of thunder and for a moment lightning illuminated the room. After that the room seemed even darker; the lamp on the desk had burned low and it was too late to go to the kitchen to refill it. Marian lit four candles and resumed work on the new review which she was writing for the *Westminster*. Dissatisfied, she tried to re-read the last page but the words blurred before her eyes. She had been working, she realised, since nine that morning. Fourteen hours or more, but often enough she worked up to eighteen hours a day. The words danced before her eyes now and crazily took on an outline of Chapman's profile in black relief. The thunder rumbled again and shook the foundations of the house, and in the silence which followed Marian heard the closing of her outer door. She looked up and there stood Chapman shaking his head reprovingly.

'My dear Marian,' he said, 'nobody, least of all I, expects you to work such long hours.'

'I enjoy every minute of it,' she said, and inked her pen again.

'You look forbidding in black velvet,' he remarked teasingly.

'Forbidding or not, black velvet will satisfy me for the rest of my life.'

'Perhaps I should say "impressive", not "forbidding".'

'As you wish, but I shall never wear fancy clothes again.'

Chapman came closer and picked up some proof pages which Marian had corrected earlier. Pretending to read them, he studied the intense expression on her face as she resumed her writing. Her attitude was defensive, he thought, as if she resented his presence at this hour of night but lacked the courage to ask him to leave. Was she close to breaking point, he wondered, either through overwork or repressed desire? He rustled the proofs and smiled to himself. He had kept his word, waiting, not without what Dickens would have called great expectations, for Marian the woman, the passionate woman, to break. There had been certain telltale signs during the past few days when he had caught her unawares: a heightening of her colour, a tenseness of her voice, an inward look in her eyes.

'No work tomorrow night,' he said. 'I shall take you to a concert.'

'Thank you,' Marian said formally, but her voice quivering.

Chapman had taken Marian to concerts and plays several times since her return to London; he had also taken Susanna and Elizabeth, separately in each instance, never the three of them together. Peace of a sort had descended upon the house in the Strand, but both Susanna and Elizabeth were still clearly jealous of Marian. Susanna, for instance, had bought a piano of her own for the drawing-room and was taking lessons, and insisting on Chapman sitting critically nearby while she played *her* piano. Elizabeth for her part, when aware that Chapman was being given German lessons by Marian, had insisted on that same gentleman giving *her* French lessons. As for the morning walks, both women had succeeded from time to time in replacing Marian at Chapman's side. Farcical, Marian thought, but not farcically amusing.

'Marian,' Chapman said, 'there are several mistakes which you have overlooked in these proofs. I absolutely insist on your going to bed at once and resting in the hope of waking tomorrow with a clearer mind.'

Another flash of lightning lit the room and thunder shook the foundations again. Not quite knowing what she was doing Marian sprang up from her chair and flung her arms round Chapman's neck. He held her lightly, almost impersonally.

'Do thunderstorms frighten you, Marian?'

She tightened her grip. 'It's been so long, John, so very long!'

Part Three

1

'SPENCER is at it again,' Thomas Carlyle said, not attempting to hide the disgust he felt.

Marian was sitting on the sofa between Carlyle and Mark Rutherford. She glanced across the room at Herbert Spencer who, having gained everybody's attention, was standing near the piano looking rather shy but quietly determined. It was Friday night, John Chapman's weekly at home night, an occasion which Marian always looked forward to and enjoyed immensely. No specific invitations were ever issued; writers simply drifted in, often a dozen or more, as if calling at a popular public house for drinks and lively argument. Thus Marian had met almost all the people of importance in the world of letters and was gaining a growing reputation as a good and interesting conversationalist. She was particularly successful with the men; they listened to her with respect and argued with her in a thoroughly man-to-man manner, a compliment which filled her heart with a quiet joy.

'Since Chapman introduced the subject of evolution earlier,' Herbert Spencer began, 'and since I am deeply interested in that subject myself, I should like, if you will bear with me, to give you my own definition of the Law of Evolution.'

Carlyle groaned, causing Mark Rutherford to chuckle and Marian to smile tolerantly. Thomas Carlyle was well known for his little bursts of anger when anyone but he himself was permitted to hold the floor. Turning to him Marian whispered in his ear, begging him to control himself and to give serious consideration to her earlier request that he should write an article for the *Westminster*.

'The Law of Evolution,' Spencer continued, 'is, in my opinion, an integration of matter and concomitant dissipation of motion, during which matter passes from an indefinite incoherent homogeneity to a definite coherent heterogeneity, and during which the retained motion undergoes a parallel transformation.'

'I confess to gaining no clear understanding of what Spencer is trying to say,' Mark Rutherford whispered.

'Spencer,' Carlyle said feelingly, 'is the most immeasurable ass in Christendom.'

Marian glanced at Herbert Spencer again, caught his eyes and held them. They twinkled momentarily, then grew exaggeratedly serious as he went on to string together a further series of pompous if obtuse phrases.

'Mr Spencer,' she whispered, 'is merely pulling our legs.'

Marian was beginning to like Herbert Spencer, a new contributor to the *Westminster* with whom she was as yet only slightly acquainted. She had first met him by chance when viewing the Great Exhibition at the Crystal Palace last year with Chapman acting as her guide. She had thought Spencer abrupt to the point of rudeness, but now it seemed to her that the cause, a quite appealing one, had been shyness. Though only thirty-two, a year younger than herself, he had gained an enviable reputation as a philosopher. He wrote for the *Leader* as well as the *Westminster* and his book, *Social Statics*, recently published by Chapman, had impressed her so much that she had recommended it warmly to the Brays and all her other friends. An elderly young man, she decided, studying him afresh, but elderly only in respect of his intellectual qualities; he had the look, despite his thinning hair, of a newly hatched chicken with little bits of the shell still clinging to him. His brow and cheeks were unwrinkled, his fingers long with slightly knotted joints. If he was at all bohemian his dress betrayed it in no way; he was, indeed, a model of sartorial correctitude and looked as if he had just come from one of the Queen's very formal receptions.

'The article we would like you to write . . .' Marian said, addressing herself to Carlyle when Herbert Spencer, with a neat little bow, had withdrawn from his position near the piano.

'An article on the peerage, I believe you said.'

'On the peerage, Mr Carlyle.'

Carlyle glowered at her. 'I'm told that F. O. Ward declined to write such an article. In fact, Ward himself told me. I am not the man, Miss Evans, to take up another man's leavings. And in any case, as Ward himself said, one should devote oneself to improving the physical standard of the people, not eulogising a band of useless if noble lords. Life is a bad business, generally, but we must make the best of it.'

Feeling quite devilish, Marian intoned: 'Amen.' Carlyle's ageing face creased alarmingly but Marian quickly realised that he was smiling. 'I do agree with you,' she said seriously, 'and I assure you that we should expect you to write critically.'

Carlyle shook his head. 'However, my dear persuasive Miss Evans, it would please me to write an article on Robert Browning. There we have an *honest* kind of man with a real enthusiasm, though soft and slobbery, in him.'

'An article on Robert Browning, then,' Marian said promptly.

Carlyle's face creased again. 'Amen, Miss Evans.'

Before more could be said Sara Hennell, who had been talking with David Brewster, the physicist, drifted across to the sofa, pretended to genuflect at the sight of Carlyle and kissed Marian on the cheek. Carlyle and Rutherford rose, excused themselves and bore down on W. R. Greg, the political scientist. Sara flung herself on the sofa at Marian's side and smiled wickedly.

'Chapman,' she said.

'Chapman?' Marian echoed.

'After all this time, my dear, secretive Marian, you have yet to confide in me.'

'What, indeed, is there to confide?' Marian asked shakily.

'The details of your affair with John Chapman. You promised to confide in me fully if you ever became involved with a married man.'

'I made no such promise, Sara.'

'Ah, but I expected it of you.'

'Is the affair common gossip in London?' Marian asked plaintively.

'Actually, no, dear Marian, but I have eyes and ears as far as you are concerned. A fleeting look in your eyes and a tremulous tone in your voice when you speak of Chapman. You can hide nothing from me. You have always tried to be tolerant in respect of other people, myself in particular, but are you now tolerant of yourself?'

'No,' Marian said unhappily.

'I thought as much.'

'There are times when I hate myself.'

'How deeply are you in love with him?'

'Love ... is it really love?'

'That is for you to decide.'

'I feel,' Marian said carefully, 'like a woman in love with love.'

'A good enough explanation for the Chapman fascination. But surely, Marian, you have had plenty of time to learn to know him for what he is.'

'Plenty,' Marian said feelingly.

'Do you enjoy sharing him with Elizabeth Tilley?' Sara asked softly. 'Living, as it were, in a sort of seraglio?'

'There are times when I loathe it. You—you know about Elizabeth Tilley?'

'I do now. A clever guess on my part. What you want, what you need, you being you, Marian, is a man entirely to yourself.'

'A husband,' Marian said, 'and children.'

Sara looked thoughtful. 'Children . . . Surprising, would you say, that Chapman hasn't put you in the family way yet?'

'I think I must be barren,' Marian gasped.

'Barren? I wonder, indeed I do. Elizabeth Tilley barren also? True, Chapman has two children by his wife, but something could have happened to him since then. Virility isn't always sufficient in itself for continued procreation. Take, for example, my own case.'

Marian looked startled. 'You also, with John Chapman? Is that what you mean?'

'Several times,' Sara said cheerfully. 'It may soon get around that Chapman is sterile and therefore completely safe.'

Much to Marian's relief, for the conversation from her point of view was rapidly getting out of hand, she saw that Herbert Spencer was looking in their direction, as if trying to make up his mind to join them. Sara had noticed this too.

'Spencer is admirable,' she said. 'Obviously you have a tremendous amount in common with him intellectually, and he's still a bachelor. Or would Mark Rutherford be more to your liking as a husband?'

Marian considered this soberly. Mark Rutherford was another contributor to the *Westminster*. She had been at pains to put him at his ease when proof-reading with him, he being extraordinarily and touchingly diffident. She was convinced that he had a brilliant future as a writer and had told him so, causing him to blush like a young girl uncertain of herself at her first adult dinner party. He had been educated for the career of a Congregational minister but had abandoned religion, as he had explained stammeringly, on conscientious grounds.

'Rutherford clearly finds you entrancing,' Sara said, wanting to laugh but trying to sound quite solemn. 'How do you feel about him?'

'All I want to do is mother him.'

'Dear Marian, we must establish a special Mothering Sunday for prospective husbands.'

'Mark is much too young for me,' Marian pointed out. 'Do please remember that he is only twenty-two.'

'Age scarcely matters when it comes to love. Has he presumed to kiss your hand passionately yet?'

'You really are incorrigible, Sara. He has offered me his life-long devotion, that and no more.'

'You mean, he is content to worship from a distance?'

'Apparently.'

'Then we are left with the neurotic Spencer.'

'Neurotic, Sara?'

'I leave you to discover that particular trait for yourself.'

Marian looked with renewed interest at Herbert Spencer. He had decided to join them at last. His approach was a slow, sidling movement, this way and that, as if he were a crab searching for the shelter of a rock in the receding waters of a beach. Sara rose and patted her vacated place.

'Be a dear good fellow, Herbert, sit and talk with Marian.'

'Nothing,' he avowed, 'could give me greater pleasure.' He sat down at Marian's side and said explosively, 'The more I see of Carlyle the more I dislike him.'

'His bite is by no means as bad as his bark, Mr Spencer.'

'If you say so, Miss Evans.' He made a vaguely desperate gesture with his hands, giving Marian the impression that he was a not very skilful conjuror striving to produce a rabbit out of a top hat. 'What,' he asked, on the inspiration of the moment, 'did you think of the Great Exhibition?'

'I found it interesting, if confusing. As for greatness, it seemed to me to be "great" only in the sense of quantity.'

'I quite agree, Miss Evans.'

'The Queen was there that evening, if you remember, Mr Spencer.'

'I do indeed remember.' His eyes twinkled but his voice, quite laughter-making, remained solemn. 'The greatest exhibit of them all. Propriety *par excellence*.'

'She was wearing an outdated crinoline, Mr Spencer.'

'Anything her gracious Majesty wears, Miss Evans, is sure to be outdated.'

'That is to say, Mr Spencer, that the Queen is and always will be a leader of *haute couture*—in England.'

'Precisely, Miss Evans.'

'We are being most unkind,' Marian murmured, and wondered what to say next to keep the conversation going on a not too tetchy level. 'I wonder if you agree, Mr Spencer,' she ventured, 'that women should be treated as independent beings and the undoubted equal of men?'

'Agree? Indeed I do, wholeheartedly.'

'I find your attitude most pleasing,' Marian said warmly.

'Every man and, indeed, every woman,' Spencer asserted, 'should have the freedom to do all that he, or she, wills, providing that he, or she, remembers not to infringe the equal freedom of any other man or woman.'

'There is no doubt about it,' Marian said enthusiastically, 'you and I see eye to eye when it comes to the question of sexual equality.'

'I think it evident,' he said gallantly, 'that we shall discover that we see eye to eye in many other respects, yes indeed, many other respects. May I presume on a short acquaintance and address you as Marian?'

Marian inclined her head. 'Please do—Herbert.'

'Thank you, thank you so very much.'

Unobserved by either of them was Elizabeth Tilley. She was standing just behind the sofa and had heard their conversation, a quite promising one, she thought. Pursing her lips she slipped quietly away and sought out Susanna Chapman whom she engaged in earnest conversation, reminding her unnecessarily that the old relationship between Chapman and Marian had been mortifyingly resumed.

'You resent it more than I do,' Susanna pointed out.

Elizabeth ignored this. 'We agreed yesterday that Miss Evans is no longer of tremendous importance to the *Westminster*. There are so many eminent contributors these days that the *Westminster* would suffer very little if deprived of her services.'

'Even so, I see no chance of driving her away a second time.'

'Oh, but I do,' Elizabeth said triumphantly. 'We can contrive to get her married.'

'Married? But to whom?'

'Mr Spencer is clearly interested in her, and Mr Spencer is a bachelor. And she, Susanna, is clearly interested in him. Their conversation just now was sufficient to tell me that.'

'Herbert Spencer is a timid little man where romance is concerned,' Susanna objected.

'He would need a certain amount of prodding, I admit. Or perhaps not as much as we might think, where Marian Evans is concerned. The first step is to do all we can to bring them together, more or less privately.'

'Privately?'

'Chapman is going away on business next week. Invite Mr Spencer to supper on Monday night. Invite Miss Evans also. Make it an intimate occasion by serving supper in your private sitting-room. Just yourself, Mr Spencer and Miss Evans. Then plead a headache at the last moment, leave them alone together and send the maid in with supper.'

Susanna resented being organised by Elizabeth Tilley but she was happy enough to fall in with her plan.

'Very well,' she said.

2

HERBERT SPENCER glanced at the clock and said in surprise that the hour was much later than he had thought. Marian glanced at the clock and was equally surprised. They had conversed earnestly for three hours, touching on mathematics and Western philosophy, and many other divergent subjects. The time had simply flown for both of them and neither of them had missed Susanna Chapman.

Spencer rose reluctantly. 'I have enjoyed our unexpected *tête-à-tête* enormously,' he said gravely.

'I also,' Marian said, just as gravely. 'One of the most stimulating man-to-man talks I have ever experienced. 'Thank you very much, Herbert.'

'Thank *you* very much, Marian.'

'Good night, Herbert.'

'Good night, Marian.'

Elizabeth Tilley's next move was to contrive a walk by the river, another *tête-à-tête* encounter for the unsuspecting Marian and Spencer. Without taking Marian into her confidence she invited Spencer to walk with her and Marian, then at the last moment, when Spencer called for them at No. 142, she grew confused, being no practised intriguer, and told Marian that Spencer himself had issued the invitation.

'I forgot to tell you,' Elizabeth said, 'but you're always ready for a walk at a moment's notice. Unfortunately I have a sudden stomach upset, so you shall have Mr Spencer entirely to yourself.'

'Why,' Marian asked bluntly, 'did he invite you also?'

'Mr Spencer is very fond of me.'

'*That* I can scarcely believe.'

Elizabeth smiled sweetly. 'I expect he felt in need of a chaperon, especially if he is more interested in me than in you.'

'Wherever his interest lies,' Marian said coldly, 'he must be told that if he considers a chaperon necessary in respect of myself I would prefer anyone but you.'

'Miss Evans gains greater confidence in herself every day,' Elizabeth sneered.

'In this instance she has Miss Tilley to thank for it.'

Marian joined Herbert Spencer in the hall and explained that Elizabeth Tilley had become suddenly indisposed. Later, when they were walking in the direction of the river, she thanked him for inviting her to walk with him.

'The invitation came from Miss Tilley,' Spencer said in surprise.

Marian laughed dryly. 'We appear to be in the midst of some small intrigue to throw us together. I no longer believe in Miss Tilley's sudden indisposition, nor in Mrs Chapman's headache of a few nights ago.'

'Dear me, dear me, *dear me!*' Spencer exclaimed, and looked quite frightened.

'I am interested in you, Herbert, as a friend,' Marian said, trying to put him at his ease.

'And I in you as a friend also, Marian.'

But Herbert Spencer was so discomposed that conversation, however general, became difficult. He spoke disjointedly and often left a sentence unfinished. Twice he insisted on sitting and resting during the walk, and three times he came to a halt, anxiously to take his pulse. He suffered, he explained, from palpitations and must always guard against too much physical exertion. Marian tried not to laugh; Spencer, in her opinion, was in splendid physical shape.

However, he was in better, even comic spirits at Chapman's next 'at home' night. He monopolised Marian, seeming to take courage from the immediate presence of other people. With no romantic interest in him whatever, she wondered if, in spite of his shyness, his extreme caution, he was falling in love with her. Friendship, she told herself sternly and perhaps a little too insistently, was all she wanted from Herbert Spencer. On one occasion, when Thomas Carlyle was declaring loudly that Charles Dickens was too intent on pandering to general public appeal, he took a quantity of cotton wool from one of his pockets and stuffed bits of it into either ear.

'Are you suffering from earache?' Marian asked him sympathetically.

'I beg your pardon, Marian?'

She repeated her question loudly and he shook his head.

'When the conversation becomes too exciting or provoking,' he said, just as loudly, 'I often use cotton wool. Thus I am rendered partially deaf. I find it most calming.' Later, when Carlyle had marched off after an inconclusive argument with Thackeray, he removed the cotton wool and grew surprisingly bold. Marian, may I invite you to spend an evening at the theatre with me?'

'But of course you may, Herbert. Have you any particular play in mind?'

'*The Merry Wives of Windsor.*'

'Thank you. I shall look forward to it. I, though not a wife, will contrive to be as merry as possible.'

Spencer looked suddenly alarmed. 'I shall ask Chapman to come with us. It—it would be a pity to waste a box on just two people.'

'Yes, a pity,' Marian said dryly.

She was sure now that Herbert Spencer was falling in love with her. There seemed to be no other explanation for his attitude. She wondered wryly if she should ask for some cotton wool for her own use before the conversation, if only on a tentatively romantic plane, got somewhat out of hand. She decided against it; it was a situation, she told herself, with which she could deal quite adequately. Spencer, however, discussed grand opera during the rest of the evening, that and nothing else.

The performance of *The Merry Wives of Windsor* was not entirely to Marian's liking; there was a certain dolorousness about it which offended her sensibilities. In any case her mood was not a happy one, chiefly because Chapman had evinced disturbing and unnecessary signs of jealousy. 'That silly little rabbit, Spencer,' he had exclaimed, 'what the devil do you see in him?' George Henry Lewes, one of Herbert Spencer's old friends, joined them in their box during the performance. Marian took an instant dislike to him and oddly enough was angry with herself for doing so. He was self-assertive, she decided, and tried too hard to be amusing. The evening, she thought dolefully when going to bed, had not been by any means a raving success.

Herbert Spencer visited Marian the next afternoon and to her surprise brought George Lewes with him. Interrupted in her work, Marian reconciled herself to a later night than usual at her desk and with the co-operation of the Chapmans' maid served her visitors tea. During the conversation which followed she had cautious second thoughts about George Lewes and suspected, as many times before in her life, that first impressions could be wrong. Lewes was more at ease, less self-assertive. He had, she thought, been initially shy in her company the night before. He was the ugliest man she had ever met, and ugliness in a man, when confronted with ugliness in a woman, was not to be set aside as an absolute social handicap. In any case, his slow, thoughtful smile, which she had failed to notice earlier, turned ugliness into an almost heart-rending beauty. It made him look like a boy who, for some reason or other, had lost himself during his childhood experiences of life. She half-smiled to her-self. Was she being ridiculously fanciful?

Suddenly and quite boldly, as if taking courage from the presence of a third person, Spencer began to talk about love and marriage. His approach, however, was so roundabout that Marian wondered if, again taking courage from his friend's presence, he was on the teetering point of asking her to marry him. She listened with increasing interest and curiosity and came close to giggling at the possibility of his saying, 'George, I beg you to ask Marian to marry me,' then turning to her and saying, 'Marian, I beg you to give George your answer.' Finally, after expatiating on the virtues of platonic love, he burst out quite violently:

'Love, that nebulous emotion which springs into being between a man and a woman, is beyond my understanding, if not my imagination. It alarms me when I imagine it, just as marriage alarms me when I go so far as to imagine *it*.'

Marian stared at him frowningly.

'We are forced to agree, Miss Evans and I,' George Lewes said solemnly, 'that you are not what might be called a marrying man, Herbert.'

'Indeed and indeed I am not.' Spencer paused and appeared to be coming to terms with himself. 'Chiefly, no doubt, because I lack ambition. Marriage, in many instances, forces a man to be ambitious, disturbingly so. Or, on the other hand, it forces him to turn himself into a domestic drudge.'

Having prepared herself for the task of rejecting Spencer, Marian was nonetheless taken aback by his words.

'Obviously you prefer a platonic association, Herbert,' she said primly.

'As indeed you do yourself, Marian,' Spencer enthused and looked owlishly at George Lewes. 'Marian and I, my dear George, have agreed that we are not in love and never could be.' Marian was so flabbergasted by his outright lying that she wanted to throw the teapot at his head. 'We are good platonic friends,' he added, still addressing Lewes. 'Our association is a deliciously calm one. Free as it is of what is sometimes, indeed very often, called romance, there is no reason why we, Marian and I, should not have as much of each other's society as we like. Marian is a good and delightful person. I always feel a great deal better for being with her.'

'I feel much the same about you, Herbert,' Marian said faintly and not entirely truthfully.

Spencer beamed on her and rose abruptly. He had drunk three cups of tea, the third rather hurriedly. Now he remembered an appointment for which he was already late.

'George, my dear fellow . . .'

'I myself have no urgent need to rush away,' George Lewes said definitely. 'I would prefer to remain a little longer and chat with Miss Evans.' He gave Marian the benefit of that all-embracing smile of his and added : 'That is, if you have no objection, Miss Evans.'

'None whatever,' Marian said strongly and realised in surprise and gratitude that from George Henry Lewes she was drawing an unthought-of confidence in herself.

'Very well,' Spencer said huffily. 'Goodbye to you both.'

'Goodbye, Herbert,' Marian said. 'Call again soon.'

'Thank you, Marian. You are most kind.'

Lewes smiled again when Spencer had departed. 'A certain amount of disapproval in his attitude, perhaps?'

'Perhaps.'

'Or even a hint of jealousy?'

'Jealousy would be preposterous, Mr Lewes.'

'Nevertheless, I suggest that dear old Herbert is as much in love with you as it is possible for him to be in love, timid soul that he is, with any woman.'

'That is possible,' Marian said frowningly.

'However,' Lewes added, 'I predict that Herbert, timid as he is as far as women are concerned, and neurotic too, as far as health is concerned, will remain a cautious bachelor for the rest of his life.'

'A safe prediction to make, Mr Lewes.'

'I further predict that he will live on, neurotically, to the ripe old age of eighty, or even ninety.'

'Eighty, certainly,' Marian agreed, laughter in her voice.

'A final prediction, Miss Evans. It will not be long before Herbert tells you, good friend though he is of mine, that you must do everything possible to avoid a too close association with me.'

'Why that, Mr Lewes?'

'Because, as Herbert sees it, I have an evil and scandalous reputation.'

Marian looked at him in astonishment. 'An exaggeration, surely.'

'Many people regard it as the sober truth.'

'The reputation one gains is not necessarily a true picture of one's character.'

'That you shall judge for yourself, in my case, when you come to know me better. I warn you, Miss Evans, I have every intention of forming a close, even a very close, association with you. Herbert Spencer, as far as I am concerned, may throw himself into the Thames.'

Lewe's words, bluntly spoken, gave Marian an unaccustomed feeling of excitement, as if she had chanced upon an unexpected discovery of great importance, even of vital importance. In the silence which followed she fell to studying the man closely and boldly. Ugly, yes, and intent, or so it seemed, on making himself look unnecessarily so. Obviously he cared little about his appearance. His hair was untidily long and his moustache and beard were not very well trimmed. Careless of his dress, he wore a mixture of clothing which suggested neither daytime nor evening wear. She remembered that Carlyle, not arousing her interest at the time, had once referred to Lewes as the Ape, but affectionately, and had added that, at thirty-five, he was the Prince of Journalists. This gave her an idea for breaking the continued silence.

'I found the last issue of the *Leader* more than ordinarily interesting,' she ventured.

'By which you mean more than ordinarily radical.'

'True, Mr Lewes.'

'That is praise indeed, you being a Radical yourself.'

'I being entirely *myself*,' Marian corrected. 'I may lean this way and that, I may go to extremes in politics and religion, but I prefer to wear no labels.'

'Truly an individualist.'

'An individual striving to be an individualist.'

Lewes smiled thoughtfully. 'But surely labels are unavoidable in this world. Are you not known, for instance, as an agnostic?'

'True,' Marian admitted ruefully.

They went on to discuss the *Leader* for some time, the radical journal of which George Lewes was literary editor and which he had founded jointly with Thornton Leigh Hunt. Lewes smiled reflectively and remarked that it was a far cry from acting to journalism. It gave him an odd feeling, he said, to remember that he had once been an actor, having been born in a theatrical family. And he added lugubriously that he had never played the hero, almost always the villain.

'Because of my ugliness, Miss Evans.'

'I expect,' Marian laughed, 'that I, if an actress, would play the villainess because of mine.'

'Surely '

Marian knew that she ought to feel affronted by his ready and frank agreement but all she could do was laugh again. What was there about this man that she was beginning to find irresistible? When at last he rose to go she invited him to come and see her again.

'I have every intention of doing so,' he said bluntly.

Still not affronted she added : 'Come often.'

'So often, I warn you, Miss Evans, that tongues will soon start wagging.'

Marian saw no more of Herbert Spencer until Chapman's next 'at home' night. Much to her surprise he kissed her hand, then murmured hastily, 'Merely a friendly salutation.' Taking her by the arm he led her to the sofa, sat at her side and looked at her lengthily and speculatively.

'Is anything the matter, Herbert?'

'It cleared the air, Marian.'

'*What* cleared the air?'

'My declaration of faith.'

Still puzzled, she said : 'I am completely at a loss. Please explain what you mean.'

'I am referring to the views I expressed on marriage. We can now remain the best of good friends without passion rearing its ugly head.'

'It is not your habit, Herbert,' Marian reproved, 'to talk in clichés.'

'Clichés are sometimes useful, Marian, especially when one is otherwise tongue-tied.' He looked at her speculatively again. 'Have you seen any more of George Lewes?'

'Yes, he called on me again yesterday afternoon. We had a long and interesting talk.'

'You actually received him alone?'

'Yes, Herbert.'

He looked at her in absolute dismay. 'Heaven bless me, Marian, that was most unwise!'

She tried not to smile. 'Have you any cotton wool with you tonight?'

'Indeed I have.'

'Then please give me some. A lecture is forming in your mind. I don't want to listen to it.'

'But *I* want you to listen to it, Marian. There are things about George Lewes, *dreadful* things, of which you are regrettably ignorant.'

'The cotton wool, please.'

'*No.*' Spencer said, unaccustomedly firm. 'George is a good friend of mine, and so are you, but since I value your friendship more than George's, and particularly since I am much concerned about your welfare, I must issue a grave, a *very* grave warning. I beg you to bear with me for a few moments, Marian.'

'Very well,' Marian agreed, her curiosity growing apace.

George Lewes, Spencer said portentously, was a married man and the father of three children. There was, of course, nothing scandalous in that; a man, if he was foolish enough, had every right to marry and beget children. The scandal lay in George Lewes's way of life.

'Communal,' Spencer said ominously.

'*Communal*, Herbert?'

It transpired that in 1842, a year after his marriage, Lewes had joined forces with Thornton Leigh Hunt and together they had rented a large house in Bayswater for their two families and, in addition, Hunt's sister and her husband, Mrs Hunt's elder sister and *her* husband and two of Mrs Hunt's younger unmarried and allegedly wayward sisters.

'Free love,' Spencer exclaimed in horror. 'The Hunts and the Leweses were, and still are, very much under the influence of the doctrines of Godwin and Shelley.'

'How dreadful,' Marian said, keeping a straight face.

'*Extremely* free love,' Spencer went on. 'Mrs Lewes became enamoured of Thornton Leigh Hunt and bore him two children.'

'What of Mr Lewes and Mrs Hunt's allegedly wayward sisters? Or Mr Lewes and Mrs Hunt herself, for that matter?'

'Well, now . . .'

Marian began to feel anxious. 'Are you suggesting that Mr Lewes is a philanderer?'

'Indeed no,' Spencer said earnestly. 'Many people believe that he is, *uncharitable* people, but I know them to be absolutely wrong.'

Marian felt vastly relieved. 'Then why this very grave warning, Herbert?'

Before replying Spencer took his pulse anxiously. 'It is simply,' he said at last, 'that it would pain me to see you involved with the Lewes-Hunt communal household. Your reputation would become just as tarnished as George Lewes's if that happened.'

'I have no intention of becoming involved with the whole household,' Marian said dryly.

'What of George himself? That, too, would tarnish your reputation.'

'It might be just as well,' Marian suggested, 'if you stuffed your ears with cotton wool.'

'No, no, I'm most keen to hear your reply.'

'Mr Lewes is the most interesting man I have ever met,' Marian said quietly.

'I feared as much,' Spencer sighed.

'I find your attitude most strange,' Marian objected. 'It was *you*, Herbert, who brought Mr Lewes to see me.'

'My poor Marian,' Spencer wailed, 'I had no choice. He *asked* to be brought.'

Marian digested this, then continued: 'In addition to being the most interesting man I have ever met, Mr Lewes is the most audacious.' She paused contemplatively for a moment. 'A forced audacity, perhaps? I *think* that he feels shame when talking boldly and bluntly but attempts to cover the feeling of shame by, well, attempting to feel no shame whatever. It seems to me that he aims to shock but is somewhat shocked by his own conversation. For instance, he discoursed at our last meeting on the most delicate matters of physiology while pretending not to notice, but fully realising, that he was transgressing the bounds of propriety, just as if he were, well, a learned savage.'

'A learned savage! Did you tell him that?'

'Yes, Herbert.'

'He laughed, of course?'

'On the contrary, he looked embarrassed.'

'Nevertheless,' Spencer said indignantly, 'he succeeded in turning your sitting-room into something resembling a club smoking-room.'

'It has never yet been my privilege to enter a club smoking-room,' Marian said, and tried to sound wistful.

'God forbid that it ever should be!'

'Ah,' Marian exclaimed, 'here comes our learned savage!'

As far as she knew, George Lewes had never appeared before at any of Chapman's literary gatherings. He glanced round the room, caught sight of her and quickly made his way to the sofa. She thought in concern that he looked pale and ill. He greeted Spencer brusquely, then displaying surprising diffidence asked her if she would grant him the favour of a private conversation in her sitting-room. Marian rose at once and led the way, noticing as they left the room together that John Chapman was staring at them in apparent anger. Jealous first of Herbert Spencer; now, or so it seemed, jealous of George Lewes. On reaching her sitting-room she invited Lewes to sit down and asked him if he would care for a glass of wine.

'No,' he said, shaking his head.

'Has something happened to upset you, George?'

'Nothing that I can think of, Marian. I have a rather bad headache, that's all.'

'I called you George,' she said soberly.

'And I called you Marian. Neither of us stopped to think. We spoke naturally and easily, as if we were very old friends.'

'We shall become very old friends, in time,' Marian said carefully.

'Meanwhile your friendship, if a very new one, has done much to save my sanity.'

Startled, Marian said: 'Something *has* happened to upset you.'

Lewes shrugged and smiled faintly. 'A quarrel with my wife, but quarrels with Agnes are no novelty these days.' He looked at Marian seriously. 'If I'm upset at all, it is at the thought of the possibility of losing your friendship.'

'Of losing it because of the scandal of your private life?'

He smiled faintly again. 'I suspect that Herbert Spencer, as I predicted, has already warned you against me.'

Marian smiled faintly herself. 'Yes, and at great length, but no doubt with the best will in the world.'

'You still want to know me?'

'That goes without saying, George.' And she added with a dry laugh, 'After all, Herbert assured me that you are not a philanderer.'

'Handsome of him! Did he also assure you that I ceased to sleep with my wife when she became Hunt's mistress?'

'Not that, no.'

'Why are you smiling in that peculiar way, Marian?'

'Peculiar?'

'A sort of inward, not to say secretive, smile.'

'I think, George, because your words failed to embarrass me,' she said, frowning thoughtfully now. 'I ought to be embarrassed but I'm not. A new Marian Evans is taking shape. I find it amazing, utterly amazing.'

Lewes nodded slowly. 'It seems that I can say anything to you, Marian.'

'Anything!'

'I want you to know,' he continued quietly, 'that I still feel responsible for my wife and her children, even the children fathered by Hunt. I maintain them all to the best of my ability. Do you think me stupid?'

'On the contrary, I admire you for it,' Marian said, warming to him all the more.

'Better to be admired than pitied,' he said bitterly. 'You are wondering, of course, why I continue to live a communal life with the Hunts and tolerate my wife's illicit association with Thornton Leigh Hunt.'

'It would seem, George, that my thoughts are not my own.'

'I doubt if they ever will be again, as far as I am concerned.'

'How strange.'

'Strange?'

'I mean, you don't sound boastful, as one would expect. No, not boastful at all. You are merely stating a fact and—and leaving me more or less at your mercy. Do you find that pleasing?'

Lewes shook his head. 'I am much more at your mercy than you are at mine.'

Marian wondered how true this was and said hurriedly, 'Your reason, then, for continuing the communal and obviously not always comfortable life?'

A look of anguish crossed his face. 'It is a home of a sort and I, believe it or not, am a very homely man. I must make do with what I have and cease to dream of a home with just one person, one beloved person—a settled and tranquil home.'

For all the sympathy she felt, Marian asked quietly, 'Are you feeling sorry for yourself?'

'Men always feel sorry for themselves. Don't you agree?'

'Yes, I think I do. It could be called the special male privilege.'

'However, my main aim is to make *you* feel sorry for me.' He paused and grinned. 'Well, am I meeting with success?'

Marian looked at him with dancing eyes. 'Since my thoughts are not my own you know the answer.'

'It is surely a little out of character,' Lewes said solemnly, 'for Marian Evans to be flirtatious.'

'Flirtatious!' She was absolutely aghast.

Still solemnly Lewes asked: 'Come now, would you say that this is an entirely man-to-man conversation?'

'No,' she replied promptly and candidly, 'a man is talking to a woman, a woman to a man.'

'Two of the plainest-looking creatures on God's earth. At first glance, anyhow. What in the name of heaven do they see in each other?'

'It isn't a matter of *seeing*, not in the physical sense,' Marian said earnestly. 'If I were blind I might think you handsome. If you . . .'

'If *I* were blind,' he interrupted, 'I might think you beautiful. But more than anything else it is a matter of *knowing*. To know Marian Evans is to love her.'

'To know George Lewes,' Marian said, her words beyond her control, 'is to love him.'

'We are dwelling, of course, on the things of the spirit,' he ventured.

'Yes, of course,' Marian agreed faintly.

Before more could be said the outer door swung open and John Chapman strolled into Marian's sitting-room. Marian saw at a glance that he had controlled his anger and remembered that he was, professionally, a man of great charm. He looked from her to George Lewes, a beaming smile on his face.

'Lewes, my dear fellow,' he said genially, 'it was good of you to come tonight. The first time, eh? I much appreciate it. Carlyle has just arrived and wants to see you. The evening will be ruined unless you rejoin the company.'

Lewes scowled but rose from his chair. Chapman bowed him to the door and made to follow him from the room, then hung back with Marian until Lewes was out of earshot.

'I had expected to find you and your latest admirer in the bedroom,' he said viciously. 'Or perhaps I arrived a little too soon?'

Marian flushed in sudden anger. 'That is an unpardonable remark, John!'

'Or did I arrive a little too late?'

'You arrived at exactly the right moment to bring me to my senses. I must at least thank you for that. I've been a complete fool as far as *you* are concerned. Please go, John. I can't tolerate your presence any longer.'

The quiet anger of her voice, the surprisingly controlled anger, made Chapman regret his impulsiveness. What to do or say now? Assuming an expression of weariness which he by no means felt, he flung himself into a chair and spoke to her pleadingly.

'Forgive me, Marian. I'm not myself today.'

'I'm inclined to think that you are indeed yourself. You have allowed the mask to slip for once.'

'Melodrama!'

'If you wish.'

Chapman smiled as charmingly as he could. 'Any moment now you'll utter another cliché. The scales, for instance, have fallen from your eyes.'

'And so they have,' Marian said bitterly. 'I'm sorry, John, but you've become a complete stranger to me.'

He chose to ignore this. 'Marian, I'm not myself today because of certain business worries. My nerves are on edge. It appears that I've been over-optimistic and as a result have over-reached myself financially. Frankly, I don't know what to do for the best. I rely on you to help me, you with that good business brain of yours.'

'I have no help to give or offer.'

Chapman jumped to his feet and took her in his arms. She remained passive, completely unresponsive. How strange, she thought, that she should feel nothing now, nothing whatever.

'Why Lewes?' he asked, releasing her when he found that he could do nothing with her. 'I find it incredible to be replaced by that monstrosity.'

Marian flushed angrily again. 'You have not been replaced by anybody.'

'Marian . . .'

'You have merely, of your own accord, destroyed a relationship which should never have been allowed to exist.'

'All this because of an uncontrollable fit of jealousy on my part?' He flung himself into the chair again. 'You should be flattered, Marian.'

'I'm revolted, not flattered.'

Chapman merely smiled. 'I know you better than you know yourself. Lewes, whether you believe it or not, will very soon be your lover.'

Shaken, Marian said, 'I don't want to listen to you any more. Please go.'

Chapman assumed a pathetic expression and sighed deeply. 'And what now? Are you going to pack your bags and return to Coventry tomorrow?'

'The thought hadn't crossed my mind.'

'Of course it hadn't! You would be leaving Lewes as well as me. But never mind Lewes. Don't you realise that I can't afford to lose you?'

'Your publishing business can't afford to lose me, *that* is what you mean.'

Chapman laughed outright. 'I didn't stop to think and chose my words badly, but that is precisely what I do mean. Even a child would have realised it. Are you, dear Martin, on the point of deserting the House of Chapman?'

'I am on the point,' Marian said quietly, 'of looking for other lodgings in London.'

'And for the rest . . . ?'

'Out of a sense of fairness,' she said, still quietly, 'I shall continue to write for the *Westminster*.'

'And you still refuse to help me with my financial troubles?'

'I shall go through the accounts with you,' Marian conceded, 'but you know very well that I have no real head for business.'

Not ill-pleased with the outcome Chapman rose and walked jauntily to the door. Something at least had been salvaged, something of the utmost importance. For the rest he still had Elizabeth Tilley to console him.

'Thank you, Marian,' he said, turning and looking humble, 'I am not ungrateful for small mercies.'

3

'WELCOME to my new lodgings, George,' Marian said, after answering Lewes's knock.

'Thank you, Polly,' he said gravely.

'*Polly?*' she echoed in surprise.

'My new name for you, my private name. It isn't that I don't like Marian, but I want something of my own, something intimate, when we are alone together.'

'But why *Polly?*'

'Your real name is Mary Ann, which you don't like, or so

Herbert told me, and Polly is a diminutive of Mary. Do you mind my calling you Polly?'

'No, I rather like it,' Marian said indulgently, and fully at ease with him added in gentle reproach, 'It was scarcely necessary for you to ask to be invited.'

Lewes smiled at that. 'So I realise. Let us say that I was merely following the precedent set by the Queen. Whenever she wants to be invited she first asks to be invited.'

'You are surely establishing a royal prerogative for yourself.'

'Surely!'

Marian's new lodgings were at 21 Cambridge Street, Hyde Park Square, and quite handy to the Edgware Road. As at Chapman's she had a sitting-room and a bedroom, but on the first floor not the ground floor. Her landlady was an excellent cook and an accommodating, thoughtful woman apt, as so many people had been in the past, to take special care of Marian. She could either have her meals in her rooms or in a small communal dining-room downstairs. She preferred the former, simply because she could, if she chose, invite guests to dinner and entertain them in a greater privacy than she had enjoyed at 142 Strand. It pleased her to think that George Lewes was her first guest; later she would invite Herbert Spencer, Sara Hennell and all her other literary friends. It excited her to realise that small infrequent dinner parties would be within the scope of her limited income.

George Lewes was glancing slowly round the sitting-room. Marian studied him tentatively and wondered what he thought of her appearance this evening. In an impulsive effort to make herself look femininely appealing she had resurrected the *basque*. After all, had she not once said that it made her look like a Velásquez painting? Nevertheless, she still felt silly and uncomfortable wearing it and half-regretted having brought it with her from the Strand. Then she smiled to herself; she had brought it with her, without quite realising it, for the special purpose of making herself look more attractive in George Lewes's eyes.

'Well?' she asked anxiously, after a few moments of almost intolerable silence.

Lewes nodded approvingly. 'You have turned an otherwise drab sitting-room into a tiny home typical of the Marian Evans I have grown so quickly to admire.' His voice was grave again. 'Your books and globes, your papers stacked neatly on the desk, but not too neatly, even your piano. Intimate and personal, but most of all a homely touch.'

Marian glowed with pleasure. 'Thank you, George.'

Lewes turned and looked at her fully. 'But what, in heaven's name, dear Polly, have you done to yourself?'

She fingered the neck of the *basque*. 'My dress, you—you don't approve of it?'

'Are you trying to look like a high-class courtesan?' he asked angrily.

'As if I could! But I hadn't thought of it like that.'

'Then please don't.'

'I seem to have shocked you, George.'

Lewes laughed suddenly. 'A high-class courtesan! I couldn't possibly afford such an expensive creature, interesting as the experience might be. Whatever induced Marian Evans to buy such an elaborate dress?'

'John Chapman bought it for me.'

Lewes's expression became inscrutable. 'Ah yes, John Chapman.'

'You know about him and me?' Marian asked nervously.

'Understanding Chapman as I do, knowing his reputation as I do, yes.'

'I'm sorry, George,' Marian said abjectly.

'I have no right to expect you to feel sorry, to apologise,' Lewes said roughly.

'It seems to me that you have.'

'Nonsense!'

'John Chapman, in that sense, is a thing of the past,' Marian said pleadingly. 'He's part of a life I should never have led. Please believe me, *please*.'

Lewes smiled faintly. 'I find that hard to believe, Polly, seeing you decked out in the dress he bought for you.'

Encouraged by his faint smile, Marian said: 'I bought him a present in return. However, I shall change at once and never wear this *basque* again.'

Lewes's eyes twinkled. 'Sell it,' he suggested, 'at one of the rag markets.'

Marian retreated to her bedroom and changed hurriedly. When she reappeared she was wearing one of her two black velvet dresses with a little touch of lace at the neck. Did the white lace, she wondered, give her a virginal look? Her hair was slightly dishevelled but as rich and luxuriant as ever. Lewes smiled approvingly.

'The Marian Evans I knew has returned to me. Please don't try to frighten me away again, Polly.'

176

'I shall never want to frighten you away, George,' she said soberly.

They dined for the most part in silence but a companionable silence, they both felt, the sort of silence that arises out of many years of tranquil association and mutual ideas no longer in need of verbal expression. Later, while Marian played a Mozart sonata, Lewes relaxed in an easy chair, listening. She felt fleetingly that she had gone back in time and was playing for her father; but there was one heartening difference, George Lewes was an understanding and appreciative audience. He clapped his hands when she had finished and smiled reflectively when she turned to face him.

'After a trying day I feel very much at peace. Thank you, Polly.'

'A trying day, George?'

'A trying day with *myself*. I spent hours thinking of some of my stupidities of the past and regretting them. Regretting them because of you.'

'Just as I regret John Chapman because of *you*.'

'There's been no female equivalent of Chapman in my life.'

'I'm glad of that.'

'So am I, now that I have found Marian Evans.'

They were talking quietly, as if discussing a problem of no great importance or urgency, a problem which presented no real difficulties. They were like a married couple, Marian thought, with many years of happy marriage behind them and many more years of similar happiness in the future.

'One thing I do not regret, Polly, and that is my friendship with Herbert Spencer. I owe him a deep debt of gratitude, even if he did try to warn you against me. It is through him, whether he likes it or not, that I have learned to know you.'

'Herbert will accept the situation in time,' Marian said confidently. 'But George, the things you do regret?'

'I was lonely when my marriage failed and wasted much of my life. I regret the waste. I gave up all ambition, lived from hand to mouth and thought the evil of each day sufficient in itself. I regret that too. Then I changed a little, or *did* I? I worked harder than ever before but still without ambition. In my spare time, to forget loneliness, I pretended a frivolous interest in worthless pursuits, and I assumed an aggressiveness which secretly appalled me.'

'Poor George.'

'Please don't pity me.'

'I'm merely pitying the person, the *you*, whom you lost for a time,' Marian said softly. 'Loneliness is a terrible thing. I know that only too well.'

'The most terrible loneliness is the loneliness that swamps you when surrounded by friends. Or do I mean acquaintances? A true friend is a very rare person indeed.'

'But . . . you're lonely no more?'

'No more, Polly, thanks to you. I'm ambitious again, at peace again, thanks to you.'

'As for me, I know a peace of mind now such as I've never known before.'

'Not a fleeting one, I hope.'

'I hope not, George.'

Lewes smiled at her gently. 'I think you realise what lies before us.'

Marian smiled gently herself. 'A deep and lasting friendship.'

'Friendship?'

'By friendship I mean everything of human value in this world. Not the evil of each day sufficient in itself, as you just said, but the good, George, the *good*. Light and easily broken associations are the last thing I have ever wanted.'

'The last thing *I* have ever wanted.'

'I think,' Marian pondered, 'that we have both suffered from a lack of security, in the sense of a lack of self-confidence.'

'I can but agree, yet now . . .'

'*Now*, George?'

'I have never felt more sure of myself in my life.'

'Nor I.'

'My whole soul is pervaded by a sense of *rightness*.'

'Mine also.'

Lewes rose and held out his arms; Marian rose also and held out hers. They embraced without hesitation, easily and naturally. They were like old lovers, Marian thought, rediscovering the passion of their youth.

'To me, George, a true marriage, even without the blessing of the church.'

'To me, Polly, a true marriage far above the blessing of any church.'

But later, when they were lying together in the darkness of Marian's bedroom, Lewes stirred uneasily and Marian, feeling very much at one with him, asked him anxiously what was troubling him.

'Nothing,' he evaded.

'*Please*, George.'

'Very well, then, furtiveness.'

'I loathe furtiveness as much as you do. It is as foreign to my nature as it is to yours.'

'To feel a mutual sense of *rightness* is all very well, Polly,' Lewes said sombrely, 'but we must be practical in this world, realistic. I am not accepted freely in society, even bohemian society. I should be a handicap to you. You have friends who would never receive us together or me separately.'

Marian laughed in what she could but regard as a vulgar manner and said: 'We can thumb our noses at any sort of society and live together openly.'

'Here in London?'

'Since furtiveness would destroy us, it is either a matter of living together openly or living apart.'

'Could we sustain the agony of living apart?'

'George, I would rather die.'

Lewes stirred uneasily again and tried once more to be practical. 'This is the position, Polly. A divorce would call for a special act of Parliament and would cost at least a thousand pounds.'

'A lot of money, yes.'

'Far more than I can gather together.' He laughed ruefully. 'I doubt if I shall ever possess a thousand pounds in my life.'

'We can work hard and save.'

'True, but you fail to understand the true position. A thousand pounds would never buy me the freedom to marry you. The fault is mine, stupidly mine. All along I have condoned my wife's adultery.'

'Then there's no more to be said,' Marian said promptly. 'No more except this: since life in London is likely to prove obnoxious, let us live together abroad. We could live cheaply abroad and work well and freely.'

'That thought was already in my mind.'

Marian laughed gaily. 'So the matter is settled!'

Lewes shook his head in the darkness. 'You must be given time to think things out, quietly and logically.'

'It's too late for that, George.'

Lewes tried to sound forceful. 'I insist, Polly, on our not seeing each other again for two or three weeks.'

'It would make not the slightest difference.'

'Polly, I'm thinking only of you, what is best for you.'

'Your voice carries not the slightest conviction,' Marian teased.

Lewes laughed comically at that. 'I was never a very good actor. I am thinking that what is best for you is best for me, in the light that a separation would make not the slightest difference. No separation, then?'

'Yes,' Marian said, surprising him, 'a brief one, but not because either you or I want it *or* need it. I received a letter from my brother Isaac this morning but hesitated to tell you about it. My sister Chrissey's husband, Dr Clarke, died recently. He left poor Chrissey with six children and very little money. Isaac is most concerned and has called a family conference. I must go to Coventry and on to Griff House within the next few days.'

Lewes took Marian in his arms. 'I shall be lonely without you, Polly.'

'And I without you, darling George.'

4

'THE position is a desperate one for Chrissey,' Isaac Evans said gloomily.

'Desperate indeed,' his wife said unemotionally.

'Poor Chrissey,' Marian sighed, 'but surely something can be done to help her. I can contribute a little money from time to time myself.'

'A man,' Isaac said, sounding angry now, 'has no right to beget six children and then die.'

'Most irresponsible of him,' Marian said, wondering if she could make her brother laugh.

'Most!' Isaac agreed violently.

Marian looked at him guardedly. At nearly thirty-eight Isaac had the appearance and manner of a well-preserved, active man of fifty, a man very conscious of the fact that he was a solid, highly respected citizen and family man. Sensitive as ever to atmosphere Marian wondered what she had done to offend him. He had kissed her perfunctorily on the cheek when greeting her a few moments earlier and there had been no warmth in his voice when he had asked her if the journey from London had been a tiring one. It was preposterous, if true, that his coldness towards her had been brought about simply because Chrissey's husband had been inconsiderate enough to die. It was almost, she thought, in dismay, that he blamed her for what he ought to regard, pious Christian that he was, as the will of God.

'What is the exact position, Isaac?' she asked.

Still sounding angry he said : 'Clarke's medical practice is worth twelve hundred pounds, no more, no less. I have, in fact, already sold it for that amount. The money, properly but carefully invested, will yield about a hundred pounds a year, less than two pounds a week.'

'I shall add as much as I can to it,' Marian promised.

'Generous of you!' Isaac sounded as if he wanted to sneer.

'Where is Chrissey to live?' Marian asked.

Isaac assumed a sanctimonious expression. 'As you know, I own several houses. She shall have the use of one of them. Rent free, of course.'

'Generous of *you*,' Marian said quietly. 'What of the children's education?'

'The boys will be sent to a free grammar school.'

'And the girls?'

'Chrissey is quite capable of educating them herself.'

'So everything is settled,' Marian commented carefully. 'It was settled before I came. You could have given me the details in your letter. There was no need to bring me here to what you termed a family conference.'

'I brought you here for a very different sort of family conference,' Isaac said tersely and glanced at his wife. 'Please leave me alone with Mary Ann.'

Mary Ann! How strangely the name rang in Marian's ears. It made her feel like a little girl again, not a woman who had found independence and freedom in London.

'A very different sort of family conference?' she echoed when her sister-in-law, evincing reluctance, had gone.

'It had occurred to me, Mary Ann, that you might regard it as your duty—you always had a strong sense of family duty—to live with Chrissey and help her with the children.'

'We're not discussing a different sort of family conference,' Marian pointed out.

'Be kind enough to answer my question, Mary Ann!'

'A question? You call it that, Isaac? A suggestion at best, but you made it sound like a command.'

'Question, suggestion, command, call it what you will but answer it!'

'I have my own life to lead, Isaac.'

'Exactly the selfish answer I expected. Are you by any chance thinking of marrying Herbert Spencer?'

Marian could but laugh. 'I have no more intention of marrying Herbert than he has of marrying me.'

Isaac's eyes narrowed. 'And you can't, as you must fully realise, marry George Henry Lewes.'

Marian looked at him in astonishment. 'What do you know of my interest in Mr Lewes?'

'Enough, more than enough.'

'I have never mentioned Mr Lewes in my letters to you.'

'You have mentioned him in your letters to the Brays.'

'But of course! I write to them about every point of interest in my life.'

'It is patently clear that Lewes is a bad influence,' Isaac said heavily. 'I won't stand for your continued association with him, by heaven I won't!'

Surprised at the steadiness of her voice, Marian said: 'To what extent are Charles and Caroline Bray implicated in this unwarranted attitude of yours?'

'Unwarranted? Am I not your brother, to a certain extent your guardian?'

'At my age my private life is my own. Please answer my question, Isaac.'

He looked at her wrathfully. 'John Chapman, of whom I do *not* approve, wrote in alarm to the Brays about you and Lewes; *they* confided in me and asked me to exert my influence in an attempt, a brotherly attempt, to break up what they obviously regard as an unwholesome association.'

Marian was shocked and disbelieving. She had written enthusiastically to Charles and Caroline about her new friend and had expected them, always so broadminded, to be sympathetic, even glad, to know that she had at last found somebody who meant everything in life to her.

'Unwholesome!' she exclaimed angrily and unguardedly, 'there is nothing *unwholesome* in my love for Mr Lewes.'

'You have the temerity to tell me,' Isaac raged, 'that you are in love with a married man?'

'I have the further temerity,' Marian said, her voice steady again, 'to tell you this: Mr Lewes and I will shortly go abroad together in search of the freedom we both desire.'

'You must be out of your mind!' Isaac exclaimed in horror.

'No, Isaac. I am perfectly sane. I know what I want, what I need.'

'Poor Father,' Isaac said.

'Why *poor* Father?'

'No,' Isaac said, after a moment's pause, '*happy* Father. He is at least dead and unaware of the shame which you have brought, or are about to bring, on the family.'

'*Have* brought, and will *continue* to bring,' Marian said satirically.

'Perhaps I am wrong about Father,' Isaac mused. 'He must surely be turning over in his grave.'

Marian repressed a wild laugh and asked quietly : 'Have you anything more to say, Isaac?'

'Only this, Mary Ann : go abroad with Lewes, if you must, but remain abroad. If you return to England and continue to live with him I shall turn my back on you forever. *Forever*, you understand? One other thing, never at any time, *at any time*, appeal to me for financial help.'

'I shall not even ask you,' Marian said warmly, 'for the free use of one of your houses.' She held out her hand formally and, she could but think, ludicrously. 'Goodbye, Isaac.'

He ignored her hand. 'Are you going straight back to London?'

'*That* I have yet to decide.'

Marian had promised to spend a few days with the Brays at Rosehill after the family conference at Griff House. Now, so dispirited did she feel, she was in two minds about it. What, she wondered, had happened to her old and good friends, the friends who had always insisted that their home was hers? This sobering thought decided her. She would go as planned to Rosehill. Isaac might well have exaggerated. She owed it to the Brays, and to herself, to discover the exact truth of their attitude.

Charles and Caroline greeted her with a warmth which Marian, suspicious of them now, felt inclined to mistrust. Even so, thus faced with them, she found it difficult to bring up the subject so close to her heart, and they, asking not a single question about George Lewes, made the position even more difficult for her, so difficult that she suffered a return of the old night terrors. They did, however, mention Herbert Spencer several times, Charles saying jovially on one occasion that the excellent Spencer would make *some* woman a very good husband.

'But not *this* woman,' Marian said tartly.

'We regard that as a very great pity,' Caroline ventured.

'Indeed we do,' Charles added, 'you and Spencer having so much in common.'

'Herbert is a good friend,' Marian said impatiently, 'a very good friend, but I'm not in love with him.'

Charles smiled thoughtfully. 'Does the question of being "in love" matter so very much, Marian, where a sensible marriage is concerned?'

Marian thought of Lewes to whom she regarded herself as married, sensibly or otherwise; it mattered very much.

'Or where age is catching up with one?' Caroline said brightly.

'Cara,' Charles interposed, 'isn't reproaching you for being thirty-four.'

'I'm not even reproaching myself,' Marian avowed.

'I'm not *reproaching* you, certainly not,' Caroline said, 'but I think that if you are to marry at all you should do so without too much more delay. I really do think you should have second thoughts about Herbert Spencer. I'm sure he's just right for you.'

'My dear Cara, even if I *were* in love with him, Herbert is not a marrying man.'

Charles smiled impishly. 'Every man is a marrying man— depending on the feminine cleverness of the woman involved.'

'I am *not* involved, Charles,' Marian said, rather crossly.

'Ah, but perhaps you are, without realising it.'

'Have you ever been in love, Marian?' Caroline asked casually.

Marian thought of Chapman and cast him hurriedly from her mind. 'Only once,' she said earnestly. 'Now. And for the rest of my life.'

'I see that you are in the grip of a very deep feeling,' Charles said, as if asking a question.

'Very deep and very sincere, Charles.'

But even then, with the opportunity presented, Marian found it impossible to speak openly of her deep and lasting passion for George Lewes or to question the Brays about their incomprehensible attitude. However, another opportunity presented itself towards the end of her stay at Rosehill. Marian and the Brays were seated, as of old, under the acacia tree discussing, among other literary events, the latest issue of the *Westminster Review*. This led to Charles asking Marian if there was any truth in the rumour that John Chapman was in financial trouble.

'To a certain extent, yes,' Marian replied. 'John is by no means a good business man, though he has always claimed that he is. His business affairs are in something of a muddle and I'm doing my best to create order out of what might be called chaos.' Here she seized the opportunity and added almost breathlessly: 'However, his financial troubles will soon be no concern of mine.'

'Indeed?'

Marian paused to steady herself. 'It so happens that I have made definite plans to go abroad.'

'Alone?' Charles asked quietly.

'No, Charles, not alone.' But she could say no more except, 'I—I'm not fond of travelling alone.'

Charles Bray rose from the bearskin and stretched. 'You and I, Cara too, have behaved rather cowardly since you came to Rosehill.'

'Cowardly, Charles?'

'We have done our cowardly best to avoid a subject which is close to our hearts. And why, dear Marian? Because we hold opposing views, you and I.'

'To what subject are you referring?' Marian asked stiffly.

'George Henry Lewes.'

'Of whom you do not approve!'

'As a journalist I hold him in high esteem, none higher, but as a man, such being his reputation, I disapprove of him roundly.'

'Have you the right to do so?'

Charles shrugged. 'Lewes's private life is no concern of mine. My only concern is that you, Marian, should have become a part of it. It alarms and distresses me far more than I can tell you.'

'Are you angry, Marian,' Caroline asked, 'that we should have asked your brother to intervene?'

'I take it,' Charles interposed, 'that Isaac did intervene?'

'He did.'

'And . . . you *are* angry with us?'

'Not angry so much as shocked.'

'Isaac intervened fruitlessly?'

'Fruitlessly, Charles.'

Charles took Marian by the hands and dragged her to her feet. 'Let's take a walk and discuss the subject fully and frankly.'

'There's nothing to discuss, Charles. Whatever the world may think of Mr Lewes I know him to be good and kind and gentle. I—I've been searching for him, if unconsciously, all my life.'

'Marian Evans, the sentimentalist,' Charles murmured. 'Sentimentality, remember, is blinding.'

'I'm moved by sentiment, not sentimentality,' Marian averred. 'There *is* a difference.'

'Granted, granted,' Charles said airily.

'He is a great deal better than he seems to the world, to the unobservant people who condemn him,' she went on warmly. 'Admittedly he has made a bad impression, made it *deliberately*, but he is, please believe me, Charles, a man of heart and conscience, wearing at times a mask of flippancy.'

'Are you trying to convince me, or yourself?'

'*I* need no convincing.'

'And . . . you propose to elope with him?'

'There's nothing else I *can* do.'

'A momentous and shattering decision,' Caroline said.

'*Shattering?*' Marian questioned.

'We are thinking of the consequences,' Charles said frowningly, 'and the ostracism which will inevitably follow what we can only regard as a very rash and ill-considered action.'

'You, too, will ostracise me?' Marian asked tremulously.

'Marian, what a thing to suggest!' Caroline exclaimed. 'Never forget that you are our dearest friend. Rosehill will remain your home whilever you chose to regard it as such.'

'For that,' Marian said stiffly, 'I am grateful.'

Charles sighed dramatically. 'I never thought the day would come when Marian Evans would be angry with us.'

'I'm angry because of your bringing my brother into it.'

'But behind that our personal disapproval angers you?'

'Yes, Charles.'

'I think it hurts you rather than angers you.'

'That is true,' Marian admitted. 'I had believed you to be broad-minded free-thinkers.'

'I fear,' Caroline murmured, trying to make Marian laugh, 'that Marian Evans has come to regard us as middle-class snobs.'

Charles chuckled richly. 'Or middle-class prudes.'

'The words are your own,' Marian retorted.

Caroline looked genuinely concerned. 'Are we still friends, Marian?'

'Of course.'

'But . . . things are not quite the same?'

'Real friendship,' Marian said desperately, 'can never be changed.'

She left Rosehill the next day and on reaching London sent George Lewes a brief note acquainting him with her return. Later they discussed their plans and reached a mutual decision: they would go to Germany. As a result Marian wrote to the Brays and other close friends. She wanted, she said, to keep in touch with all of them, and begged them to write to her Poste Restante, Weimar, during the next six weeks, thereafter Berlin.

'And after Berlin?' Lewes asked, leaning over her shoulder as she wrote.

'Who knows, who cares?' Marian responded. 'We shall be together. Nothing else matters.'

5

MARIAN paused and turned another page of her manuscript. 'You read splendidly and with deep feeling,' George Lewes commented.

Marian smiled nervously. 'All I want to know is what you think of my first attempt at writing fiction.'

'Continue, please,' Lewes said, trying, despite his twinkling eyes, to sound like a stern schoolmaster.

They were seated, Marian not really at ease in this instance, in their lodgings at Weimar. Marian's cheeks were flushed, her eyes slightly dilated; she would die of shame if George made no favourable comment or if, which would be worse, he only pretended to like what she had written so long ago. She regretted very much that she had brought the old abandoned manuscript with her to Germany, regretted even more that she had been foolish enough to mention it to George. 'Read it to me,' he had said; 'good journalist that you are, I have always fancied that you would make a better novelist.' Herbert Spencer, like Charles Bray before him, had said much the same, but she had never had the courage to read her unfinished first chapter to anyone until now.

'Continue, please,' Lewes repeated.

'Yes, sir!' Marian said, as if springing to attention.

Then she took a deep breath and continued, part of her mind dwelling, as if to give her confidence, on all that had happened since she and George had left England. George had visited Germany often and had many friends in Weimar, all of whom had quickly accepted Marian with a heart-warming enthusiasm. But Marian's greatest joy had been her meeting with Franz Liszt whose work she had always admired. That she should ever meet him, become friendly with him and hear him play his own music had been beyond her wildest dreams. He was to her a bright genius with a tender, loving nature and a face in which this combination was perfectly expressed. It was really because of Liszt and his amiable and hospitable mistress, the Comtesse d'Agoult, that she and George had lingered on in Weimar instead of remaining for only six weeks.

Marian and George's lodgings were comfortable and cheap; they had a bedroom each and a sitting-room of which they had the sole use and in which they worked in harmony at their separate writing tasks. Marian was still writing for the *Westminster*, George for the *Leader* and other journals while working on a long-planned life of Goethe. Free for the moment of money worries, they had ample time to attend concerts, visit friends, entertain on a modest scale and embark, with almost childish delight, on sightseeing tours. 'We are relentless tourists,' they laughed. Growing happier every day and unshakably convinced that she had made the right decision, Marian had never found life so full and satisfying.

'Well, now . . .' Lewes said.

Marian had come to the end of her reading; she looked at him anxiously. 'George . . .'

He frowned thoughtfully. 'I'm not quite sure what to say.'

'You don't like it,' she said miserably. 'I knew you wouldn't. I—I may as well tear it up and forget all about writing fiction.'

'Would you like me to tear it up for you?'

She realised that he was teasing her. 'George, your honest opinion, please.'

Lewes grew even more thoughtful. 'Polly, darling, you have written an unfinished first chapter of a novel, a descriptive chapter, in which I *think* I recognise a touch of genius.'

'Genius!' she scoffed. 'Tease me as much as you like but don't make fun of me.'

'To make fun of you would be to make fun of myself,' he said, smiling fondly, 'and that would never do.'

'Tell me what else you think.'

'You have written an admirable description of a Staffordshire village and life in the neighbouring farm-houses. I could see it all as you read, but . . .'

'*But*, George?'

'I'm convinced of your power to write a novel, but I have yet to be convinced that you possess any dramatic power. You have yet to devise a story, a plot, and for that you need a certain amount of dramatic power.'

'Which patently I do not possess,' Marian said wryly.

'Who can tell until you put your mind to it?'

Marian began to make excuses. 'Dramatic power calls for telling dialogue. I've yet to write a single line of dialogue, dramatic or otherwise.'

' "Otherwise" is a good enough beginning. Form the habit of writing pages and pages of dialogue. Invent a situation between any number of imaginary characters and describe it in dialogue. Form the habit also of *thinking* in dialogue, as if talking to yourself, and listen, listen intently, to the conversation of others, however trivial it might be.'

'Very well, George.'

'And promise, above all else promise to invent a story strong enough, or at least interesting enough to carry this first chapter forward into a real novel. Come, Polly, promise.'

'I promise,' Marian said uncertainly.

6

'I MUST admit to being somewhat disappointed in you,' Arthur Helps remarked, glancing mildly from George to Marian.

'Disappointed in us?' Lewes exclaimed. 'What the devil do you mean, Arthur? You fully approved of our elopement.'

That, Marian reflected, was true. She looked at Arthur Helps curiously, being just as puzzled and surprised as George. Helps was one of George's oldest and most understanding friends. He had come to his aid many times, especially when he was ill and despondent, and on occasion had taken him on recuperative country holidays. Marian had met him a few times in London, had liked him, and with George had discussed their plans with him. He dressed fastidiously, looking most sleek with his close-cropped hair, and, as a rule, had a humorous way of talking, as if he found it impossible to take anything too seriously. Marian wondered now if he were perpetrating some little joke which he alone understood.

'It goes without saying that I am delighted to see you both,' he went on. 'And how well you look, how devastatingly blooming. My one regret is that I can spend only one day in Weimar with you.'

'We regret it too,' Marian said sincerely, 'but you have yet to answer George's question. Why, Mr Helps, are you disappointed in us?'

Helps sighed elaborately. 'I am, perhaps, surprised rather than disappointed. I asked your landlady for Mr and Mrs Lewes. I was told that only a Mr Lewes and a Miss Evans were staying here.' He sighed again, even more elaborately. 'I came to Weimar expecting to find a honeymoon couple. In short, the newly married Mr and Mrs Lewes. Instead, I find Mr Lewes and Miss Evans.' He hunched up his shoulders and smiled slyly. 'I am left to assume, and beat my breast over the assumption, that the association is entirely platonic.'

Marian chuckled involuntarily. 'Not that, Mr Helps.'

'The honeymoon is still proceeding merrily,' Lewes laughed.

'You fill me with a vast relief,' Helps murmured.

'One must be honest,' Marian said seriously. 'It would be dishonest to call myself Mrs Lewes.'

'But my dear Marian, do you not regard yourself as George's wife?'

'With all my heart and soul!'

'In that case your thinking is somewhat confused when it comes to the question of honesty. In all honesty you are Mrs Lewes.'

Shaken, Marian said, 'I—yes, I agree.'

'Apart from that it would be more convenient and give you greater freedom, certainly while travelling abroad, to be known as Mrs Lewes.'

'Henceforth we shall be known as Mr and Mrs Lewes,' George said gaily.

'The landlady will be somewhat startled,' Marian demurred.

The landlady had gained the impression that she and George were literary friends travelling together and working together for English journals. After all, they occupied separate rooms and paid for their board and lodgings separately. That they had the sole use of a sitting-room was only because there were no other boarders in the house. In some dismay Marian realised that they were behaving furtively after all; they were not really living openly together, as intended.

'I myself probably startled the good lady when I asked for Mr and Mrs Lewes,' Arthur Helps pointed out. 'Why not inform her that you eloped from England, married secretly in Weimar but have no further wish to keep the secret?'

'That would be lying,' Marian said stubbornly. 'We shall leave Weimar as Mr Lewes and Miss Evans and arrive in Berlin as Mr and Mrs Lewes. Lying,' she added hastily, 'in respect of a secret marriage. That we regard ourselves as man and wife is another matter.'

Helps smiled blandly. 'And when, dear friends, do you leave for Berlin?'

'Immediately, as far as *I* am concerned,' Lewes said boyishly.

During the afternoon of Arthur Helps's visit a letter arrived for Marian from Charles Bray who was visiting London at the time of writing. To Marian's horror he wrote that ugly rumours were being spread among her friends and acquaintances. It was claimed, and in some quarters believed, that George Lewes, deserting his wife, had left the poor creature penniless with no support whatever for the children. And Marian, regarded as a scarlet woman, was blamed for it all. In silence Marian passed the letter to George, then he, flushed and angry, passed it to Arthur Helps.

'A storm in a teacup,' Helps said lightly. 'In circumstances such as yours one must always anticipate malicious gossip and rise above it.'

'It's more than a storm in a teacup to me,' Marian said, flushed and angry herself now. 'George did not desert Mrs Lewes. *She* deserted *him* long before I met him, even if they continued to live under the same roof.'

'I'm well aware of that,' Helps said soothingly.

Marian's anger grew apace. 'Far from leaving Mrs Lewes and the children penniless, George made adequate provision for them before we left England. And is he not working now for their continued support, just as I am working to help my sister Chrissey?'

'Working willingly, both of us,' Lewes said, trying to control his anger.

'I shall do everything I possibly can to contradict the rumours the moment I return to London,' Helps promised.

Marian smiled her thanks and went on more calmly. 'Beyond the simple fact that I am deeply attached to George and living with him, all rumours are false and must be denied. I shall ask Charles Bray to deny them, my other friends too, if I have any left. Not that I mean to sound bitter, Mr Helps. I am quite prepared to take the consequences of a step which I have deliberately taken, and accept them without irritation or bitterness. No doubt I shall lose friends. It will be painful but that cannot be helped. I have set my own course and will follow it to the end.'

Helps grinned at her. 'Through thick and thin?'

'Through thick and thin!'

His grin widened. 'Relentlessly?'

Marian laughed shortly. '*Relentlessly*.'

'There is one rumour which I shall not attempt to deny,' Helps went on, intent on making her laugh fully.

'And that?'

'It is being said in one quarter—by Eliza Lynn Linton, in fact —that Marian Evans is far too plain a woman to find a man brave enough to elope with her; therefore, Marian Evans cannot possibly be living in sin.' Helps gave her a comical look. 'Have I presumed too far in mentioning this?'

Marian tried to look at him sternly but laughter was bubbling up in her throat. She glanced at Lewes; he was smiling broadly. A moment later all three were laughing heartily.

'I insist, dear Mr Helps,' Marian gasped, 'that you deny that particular rumour too.' Then she grew serious. 'Even though, in my own eyes, I am *not* living in sin.'

'Deny it I shall,' he promised.

Soon after Arthur Helps's visit Mr Lewes and Miss Evans left Weimar and Mr and Mrs Lewes reached Berlin. Berlin, after Weimar, was not much to their liking. Marian found the German capital ugly and dirty, and since it was early winter the cold weather was a trial to her. Nevertheless, she was as happy as ever with George Lewes; just to be with him, in any circumstances, was sheer bliss. His health was her constant concern. If he caught a cold she nursed him as diligently and anxiously as if he were dying, and when she feared that he was growing over-tired she insisted on writing some of his *Leader* articles for him. They worked hard every morning until, as she put it in a letter to Charles and Caroline Bray, their heads were hot; they walked about the city during the early afternoon, then dined at three o'clock; and at night, unless they went to a concert or visited some of Lewes's German acquaintances, they read aloud to each other.

'Some people would call it a dull life,' Lewes commented.

Marian shook her head. 'I find it exciting, George. How could it be otherwise when it is impossible for two human beings to be more happy in each other?'

Though she disliked Berlin she enjoyed the company of the Germans to whom Lewes introduced her. She particularly admired their diligence, their simplicity and their lack of social frills. As she said when writing to Sara Hennell, there were no agonies about one's appearance, no grand dinners and suppers, but much heartiness and solid intelligence. In reply Sara wrote that she had a strange sort of feeling that she was writing to somebody in a book, not the Marian Evans whom she had known and loved for many years. She made no reference to George Lewes and addressed her letter to 'Miss Evans', not 'Mrs Lewes', as requested. Marian frowned uncertainly over this. Did the broad-minded Sara approve or disapprove? She shrugged the doubt aside; her sole concern was the welfare of George Henry Lewes.

Time passed pleasantly and rapidly until, after eight months in Germany, Lewes finished his life of Goethe and realised, as Marian did, that it would be wiser to return to London to find a publisher than to send the manuscript from Berlin and risk losing it. It was necessary, too, that Lewes should make some definite arrangement for his children's education.

'If you wish,' he said without conviction, 'you may remain in Berlin.'

'You know I don't like Berlin.'

'Or return to Weimar, leaving me to rejoin you there as soon as possible.'

'A separation would be intolerable!'

'Nevertheless . . .'

'You are thinking,' Marian said candidly, 'that it would be unpleasant for me to face my friends again.'

'That, yes. You have good friends in Weimar and I need not be away too long.'

'Any unpleasantness that may arise will be created by my English friends, not by me.'

'True, true.'

'A separation would be intolerable to you too.'

'That I admit, Polly.'

'Face my friends in England I must, George, whatever the consequences,' Marian said firmly. 'Let us say no more about it.' Then she smiled brightly. 'We shall at least be warmer in England than Germany—roaring coal fires instead of ugly, impersonal-looking stoves.'

Lewes pinched her cheek playfully. 'A heavenly thought, darling Polly.'

7

'Y our rooms are a bit cramped but reasonably comfortable John Chapman remarked, a shade dolefully.

'Cramped conditions distress us in no way,' Marian said untruthfully, 'when we are working well and happily.'

'In no way at all,' George Lewes supported her, the dislike he felt for Chapman strong in his voice.

On their return to England Marian had remained for a short time at Dover until George had found accommodation for them here at East Sheen. Chapman, a most chastened-looking Chapman, was their first visitor. His financial affairs were still in some confusion. He had moved from the Strand to a cheaper house in Dorset Street, thus enabling him, as he had said in a letter, to keep his head above water.

'Welcome back to England,' he said belatedly.

'Thank you,' Marian said primly.

She felt a little sorry for him, though she had not quite forgiven him for writing to the Brays in an attempt to break up her association with George. The old charm, the magnetism of his eyes, the persuasiveness of his voice seemed to have completely disappeared. She found it impossible to believe that he had once been her lover but she was ready, with certain reservations, to accept him as a friend. *He*, at all events, had addressed his letters to 'Mrs Lewes', and on arrival just now he had asked the landlady if Mr and Mrs Lewes were at home.

'You have yet to visit my new premises in Dorset Street,' he said conversationally.

'I shall do so the next time I come to town,' Marian promised.

He looked at her obliquely. 'You are much too isolated here, Marian. The cramped conditions, as well as the isolation, will wear you down eventually. There's plenty of room for you at the Dorset Street house.' He glanced at Lewes. 'Plenty of room for both of you.'

Marian shook her head. 'I'm sorry, John, but no.'

He laughed lightly and with something of the old persuasiveness in his voice said, 'I've got rid of Elizabeth Tilley, if that is any encouragement to you.'

Marian laughed lightly herself. 'It would make living under your roof more congenial, but my answer is still no.'

'What Chapman really wants,' George Lewes said dryly, 'is an extra lodger or two to help him make ends meet.'

'Oh, I admit it,' Chapman said airily, 'but I miss Marian's company, the stimulation of her conversation. I feel sure, too, that you and I could become good friends. You know how much I admire you as a journalist.'

'Flattery will help you in no way,' Lewes said gruffly.

Chapman shrugged and changed the subject. 'Your brother Isaac was in London recently,' he said, looking quizzically at Marian. 'I met him by chance. Did he come to see you?'

Marian shook her head. 'No, nor would I have expected him to come.'

'As I imagined,' Chapman said. 'He pretended not to recognise me, until I reminded him that I had met him two or three times at Rosehill. I asked after you and found his attitude disturbing. He said he had no sister by the name of Marian. I remembered that he still calls you Mary Ann and asked after Mary Ann. He said he had no sister by that name either.'

'I no longer exist as far as Isaac is concerned,' Marian said, striving to keep her voice steady.

'His behaviour is childish,' Chapman said indignantly. 'In fact, I told him so.'

'That was kind of you but I'm sure it did no good.'

'No good at all. He turned rudely on his heels and marched away looking like the wrath of God.'

Marian could but smile. Isaac must indeed have looked like the wrath of God, if one could possibly imagine what God looked like when in a wrathful mood. She had written to him from Germany asking him to pay her income from the trust fund to Charles Bray, again from East Sheen asking him to pay it into a Coventry bank for transfer to her bank in London. She had also asked him, in the latter instance, to address his reply to Mrs Lewes; he had ignored her request and addressed it to Miss Evans, causing Marian some embarrassment with the landlady, until she explained that that was the name under which she wrote. It was a brief, cold letter; she had destroyed it immediately after reading it. Her name, he said, was never mentioned in the family these days. Chrissey felt the same as he did; so did her half-brother and -sister. He would communicate with her only when his handling of the trust fund made it necessary. That Chrissey felt the same as Isaac did was a sore disappointment to Marian—Chrissey who still accepted financial help unhesitatingly.

'I want you to know, Marian,' Chapman said earnestly, 'that you most certainly continue to exist as far as I am concerned.'

George Lewes laughed shortly. 'As far as the *Westminster* is concerned, *that* is what he really means.'

'To a certain extent, yes,' Chapman admitted. 'The *Westminster* needs Marian as much as ever.'

'And I, of course, need the *Westminster*,' Marian said frankly.

'I want you to take over the Belles Lettres section,' Chapman said, voicing now the real purpose of his visit. 'It will bring you in an additional fifty pounds a year.'

'Thank you, John,' Marian said sincerely, 'you really are a great help to me.'

'And you to him,' Lewes said dryly. 'Everybody knows that the Belles Lettres section is in the doldrums.'

Charles Bray, up in London for a few days, was their next visitor. He treated Lewes with forced affability and insisted, for old times' sake, on Marian taking a walk with him.

'With your permission, of course, my dear Lewes?'

'Permission granted,' Lewes chuckled.

Charles chuckled too. 'I like your sense of humour.'

'Yours,' Lewes retorted, 'I have yet to discover.'

East Sheen, still something of a village, delighted Charles Bray. He thought the atmosphere just right for Marian and was sure that here, which was almost 'country', she would work well and hard.

'Certainly hard, Charles.'

'I expect you and Lewes have fallen into a convenient routine,' he said, trying to draw her out.

Marian nodded eagerly. 'We breakfast at half-past eight, read to ourselves till ten, write till half-past one, walk till nearly four and dine at five, regretting each day as it goes.' She paused, then laughed merrily. 'Our most engrossing recreation at the moment will amuse you. We are taking a quite childish delight in rearing tadpoles.'

'Fascinating!'

'Yes, indeed!'

'You are . . . perfectly happy, Marian?'

'Perfectly. That is to say, deliciously and calmly, and very much at peace with ourselves.'

'You don't mind being somewhat cut off?'

Marian smiled at him gravely. Cut off from society, that was what he meant. After all, he had warned her about the ostracism which she was inviting. There was no need to tell him now that she was ostracised by almost all her friends, except those whom she had made through George, and they, as far as society in general was concerned, were beyond the pale.

'We glory in being cut off,' she said, really believing it.

'So you have no regrets at the step you took, no regrets whatever? Oh, I'm not quizzing you, Marian. I want you to know that you will always have our steadfast friendship, mine and Cara's.'

'Thank you, Charles,' she said, suddenly gripped by emotion. 'But . . . regrets? I regret the alienation of certain friends. I particularly regret the alienation of my brother Isaac. That he should regard my association with George as immoral distresses me deeply.'

'You must have known that he would regard it as immoral,' Charles said gently.

'Yes, but I had hoped to bring him round to my own way of thinking, to convince him that George is the right man for me, whatever the irregularity of the circumstances, as far as convention goes. But *immoral*! Ludicrous! Laughable! George and I are pure-hearted and devoted to each other. We are—I insist on this, Charles!—we are man and wife and will forever remain so.'

'You force me to believe you.'

'I'm so glad!'

'So there's no more to be said.'

'No, Charles.'

'Except this: Rosehill will always remain open to you, if ever you need a refuge.'

'I shall remember that, Charles,' Marian said, her voice quivering, 'but I shall never need a refuge while George is at my side.'

On returning from their walk they found that Herbert Spencer had called. Marian saw at once that there was cotton wool in his ears; George had obviously been saying something much too alarming for poor Herbert to listen to. He removed the cotton wool and shook hands with Charles, saying, 'How splendid to see you again, Mr Bray.' This surprised Marian; she was unaware that Herbert and Charles had ever met. Then Spencer turned to her and greeted her warmly. He was newly returned from Paris, he said, and weary of solitary sightseeing.

'I felt badly in need of the company of old friends, Marian.'

'That you still regard George and me as friends is heartening,' she murmured.

'The best friends in the world, dear Marian.' He shrugged, sighed and then smiled slyly. 'One must accommodate oneself to the inevitable. Indeed, one must accommodate oneself to that which has become an accomplished fact.' And he added very sincerely, 'In point of fact, whatever I might have said in the past, I never really disapproved, as Mr Bray is well aware.'

Puzzled, Marian looked at Bray. 'Charles . . . ?'

'Mr Spencer is a better friend than you might imagine,' said Charles Bray. 'He made a special visit to Coventry in an attempt to persuade me that what Marian Evans had done was entirely right for Marian Evans.'

'And . . . he succeeded?'

Charles laughed gaily. 'I, too, must accept that which has become an accomplished fact.'

'Thank you, Herbert,' Marian said, and to hide her embarrassment asked: 'How is your health these days?'

'Indifferent, as ever.' Spencer paused to take his pulse. 'Well, well, it *could* be worse.'

Early the following week there was a visit from Sara Hennell. She wrote first stating the date and time, and addressed her letter to "Miss Evans", not "Mrs Lewes", as requested. On arrival she asked for Miss Evans, upon which the landlady, growing increasingly suspicious, said: 'If you mean Mrs Lewes, then Miss Evans is at home.' George Lewes had gone for a walk, thus allowing Marian to receive Sara alone. Having overheard her brief conversation with the landlady, she faced her reproachfully.

'Sara, why have you set yourself out to embarrass me?'

'I have always preferred to call a spade a spade,' Sara said airily.

'Is that your sole reason?'

Sara looked contrite. 'I was hurt because you eloped with George Lewes without confiding in me. When people are hurt they often become hurtful themselves. Please tell me, dear Marian, that we are still friends.'

'On one condition,' Marian said vehemently. 'You must remember always that I am Mrs Lewes.'

'Gladly, Marian, gladly.' Then consumed with curiosity Sara asked: 'What explanation will you give your landlady?'

'The same that I have already given her. As Mrs Lewes I write under the name of Marian Evans, and am therefore known to many people as Miss Evans.'

'There was a certain look in her eyes,' Sara pondered. 'If she believed you in the first place I doubt if she will continue to do so.'

'In that case,' Marian said, wondering if she was right in suspecting a hint of malice in Sara's voice, 'George and I will be obliged to find other lodgings.'

Sara pouted like a young girl. 'Oh dear, are you going to blame poor me for that?'

'I must learn to take the consequences of my own actions,' Marian said staunchly, 'as well as the actions of others.'

'One thing having led to the other, of course.'

'Of course.'

Sara sighed and looked at Marian lengthily. 'Are you really happy with George Lewes, darling?'

'I have never been happier in my life.'

Sara sighed again. 'If true, then I envy you.'

'*If* true!'

'Please don't be angry with me, Marian,' Sara pleaded. 'Of

course it's true. Not only do I sense it, but I can see it in your eyes. There's a new light in them. The light of adoration, perhaps?'

'That is one way of putting it,' Marian said, wondering if sarcasm was intended.

'I want you to understand,' Sara said, after looking at her lengthily again, 'that I don't disapprove of what you have done, only of the man with whom you have done it. Many people feel the same as I do. In fact, it is the general consensus of opinion. His reputation, Marian, the dreadful things that are said about him . . .'

'You have yet to meet and know my husband!'

Sara laughed archly. 'If George Lewes is as fascinating as you seem to find him, perhaps I had better never meet him. An intriguing situation if I submitted to temptation and tried to take him from you. A more intriguing situation if I really succeeded.'

'You're absolutely incorrigible, Sara!' Marian laughed.

'I should fail miserably?'

Marian laughed again. 'Miserably!'

'How good it is to hear you laugh like that, Marian, so wholeheartedly! Better still to know that we are still friends.'

'Only, dear Sara,' Marian said gravely, 'if you remember always that I am Mrs Lewes.'

'I myself, under similar circumstances,' Sara commented, 'would take a fierce pride in remaining entirely myself. In short, Miss Hennell. You must be a conventional soul at heart, dear Marian.'

Marian frowned over this. 'Perhaps.'

Sara shrugged and changed the subject. 'Tell me about your work. I want to know, in particular, if you are ever going to write a novel.'

Marian smiled secretly. 'I may yet surprise you, Sara, you and everybody else.'

8

'I AM,' George Lewes avowed, 'a very patient man.'

Marian glanced at him obliquely. 'You have made that same remark once a week, with clockwork regularity, ever since we returned from Germany.'

Mr and Mrs Lewes, having left East Sheen, were now occupying rooms at Richmond after a short seaside holiday at Worthing. They liked Richmond better than East Sheen and were walking now, as they did every afternoon, in the park. They were working as hard and enthusiastically as ever and George, greatly heartened, had found a publisher for his life of Goethe.

'And . . . so?' George asked guilelessly.

'Your repeated declaration,' Marian teased, 'could be called nagging.'

'In that case you must find a ducking-stool, regard me as a nagging wife and place me in it.'

Marian linked her arm through his. 'What fun it is to be with you, George!' Then she quickly grew serious. 'Your patience has earned its just reward. At least I hope you will think it just, in the long run.'

'What have you in mind, Polly?'

'Two or three long stories under the general title of *Scenes from Clerical Life*. I propose to base the stories on my own personal observation of the clergy.'

'What a capital idea! But I pity the poor clergy.'

'Save your pity, darling George, for the poor author.'

'To say nothing of her poor readers! You have, I take it, a sound idea for the first story?'

'I have at least a sound idea for the title. It sprang into my mind when I woke this morning: *The Sad Fortunes of the Reverend Amos Barton*. As for the story itself, my mind is full of it but I find it hard at this stage to describe it to you.'

'That you should get it down satisfactorily on paper is all that matters. I suggest that you make a start on *Amos Barton* tonight.'

'I made a start this morning,' she said eagerly.

'Then you shall continue the good work tonight, tomorrow morning, and thereafter morning and night until the whole thing is completed.'

'Slave-driver!'

But carried away by her own enthusiasm and stimulated by George's, Marian worked long, hard hours and completed *Amos Barton*, a much longer story than she had expected, within six weeks. George read it chapter by chapter and declared in the end that it was clear that Marian could indeed write good dialogue. He found much fun in the story but further declared that her pathos was even better than her fun.

'George, you're going to make me cry!'

'That is easily remedied, or do I mean furthered? *Amos* is merely the work of an apprentice, though a skilful one.'

'How good you are for me, George!'

'Good for you?'

'You will always prevent me from feeling conceited.'

'My dear Polly, If I had written this story I should feel in-ordinately conceited myself. But to business! Amos is too short to be published in book form, but not too short for serialisation. I think Blackwood ought to see it. I feel sure, with-out being over-confident, that he will want to publish it in his magazine.'

Pleased and excited, but overcome by her old uncertainty, Marian said: 'I beg you not to reveal the author's true identity.'

George Lewes laughed mischievously. 'I shall tell Blackwood when I send him the manuscript that Amos is the work of a friend of mine and give him the impression that the said friend is a clergyman.'

Marian rocked with laughter. 'I wonder what Marian Evans would look like in clerical garb?'

'Formidable.'

'I was afraid you might say sanctimonious.'

John Blackwood was the owner and editor of Blackwood's Magazine, to which George Lewes was a regular contributor. On George's recommendation he wasted no time in reading Marian's story. He liked it very much, he wrote, but he would rather see the other stories yet to be written before accepting it. George Lewes was disappointed; trying to force Blackwood's hand he re-plied that his 'clerical friend' was more than a little discouraged and hinted that there were other magazines. He added, however, that the literary clergyman would send the second story when he had completed it to his personal satisfaction. Blackwood wrote again, saying that he was glad to know that Lewes's friend was, as he had supposed, a clergyman: 'Such a subject is best in clerical hands.' And with that Blackwood offered the anonymous clergy-man fifty guineas for The Sad Fortunes of the Reverend Amos Barton.

'Do you wish to remain anonymous?' George asked Marian.

'Yes, and no. Make up my mind for me, George.'

'I'm all for you taking full and open credit, but my joke has carried me further than I expected. Blackwood could pos-sibly change his mind if told now that the author is a woman, not a clergyman.'

'That would be dreadful!'

'All in all I think we should wait and see how your Scenes From Clerical Life is received before revealing your true identity.

Meanwhile we must think up a pseudonym for the supposed clergyman.'

'His first name is George,' Marian said promptly. 'It simply *must* be George because of all the help and encouragement you've given me. But for you, dear George, *Amos* would never have been written.'

Lewes smiled on her fondly. 'And his second name? Evans, perhaps?'

Marian shook her head emphatically. 'In any case that might give the game away. Mr Blackwood is probably well aware that George Lewes is living with Marian Evans, and he must know that Marian Evans is an established journalist. We must think of some other name.'

Lewes grinned broadly. 'Why not "Isaacs" in memory of your estranged brother?'

'Certainly not!'

Lewes gave her an owlish look. 'May I suggest "Arbuthnot"? A really splendid name for a clergyman.'

'I should hate to be known as Arbuthnot,' Marian giggled.

'A name beginning with an "E" then.'

' "Edwards"?'

'Too commonplace. "Elford"? "Elgar"? Or what about "Eliot"?'

Marian seized upon 'Eliot' at once. 'I like it, George. It has a full-sounding ring and is easily pronounced. I shall enjoy thinking of myself as George Eliot.'

'And so,' Lewes smiled, 'George Eliot is born and christened.'

The first part of *Amos Barton* appeared in the January issue of *Blackwood's*. The year was 1875 and Marian was in her thirty-eighth year. She had already begun a second story and presently completed the series with a third. Meanwhile *Amos Barton* was well received and Blackwood wrote Marian some enthusiastic letters. In one he named a famous London club, saying that some of the men had wept when reading Milly's death scene in *Amos Barton*. It would be strange, he added, if George Eliot was a member himself and had listened to his own praises. It was clear from this that Blackwood doubted that her real name was George Eliot, but it was clear also, or so it seemed, that he still believed her to be a man.

Marian met John Blackwood when, visiting London briefly from Edinburgh, he came out to Richmond. She was presented to him as Mrs Lewes and, though he knew her to be Marian Evans, he accepted her as Mrs Lewes without reservation. She took an instant liking to him and found his Scottish accent fascinating. He asked her what she thought of *Scenes from Clerical Life* and she murmured, modestly she hoped, that the stories were improving instalment by instalment.

'My own opinion,' Blackwood said. 'I take it that you have met the author?'

Marian inclined her head. 'Yes,' she said, trying not to laugh.

'What manner of a man is he?'

'Rather shy and reserved.'

'But charming, absolutely charming,' Lewes added enthusiastically.

Blackwood turned to him with a wry smile. 'I think it most unfair of you to hide him from me. When, my dear Lewes, may his publisher meet him?'

'It really is unfair,' Marian said, when Lewes hesitated. 'George, if you would be so kind . . . ?'

'Sir,' Lewes said, his voice formal but his eyes twinkling, 'permit me to introduce my wife again. She is none other than George Eliot.'

Blackwood laughed softly and bowed. 'I must admit to having harboured a strong suspicion.'

Marian gave him a sharp look. 'Do you consider my writing feminine rather than masculine?'

'Your *hand*writing, at all events, Mr Eliot.'

'Ah,' Lewes sighed, 'we made a sad mistake there. I should have copied the stories for my wife.'

'So you should, man, so you should.'

'I beg you to keep my secret, Mr Blackwood,' Marian said urgently.

Blackwood shrugged. 'If you insist, keep it I shall.' He flung himself into a chair and sprawled out his long legs. 'And now, George Eliot, to serious business. Your stories are so successful that I want more than three for the series.'

Marian shook her head decisively. 'No, Mr Blackwood, I am rather tired of clerical life.'

'Please don't tell me,' Blackwood said, evincing deep concern, 'that your fiction writing is a mere flash in the pan.'

'No, not that,' Marian assured him. 'I have a subject in mind which could never come under the limitations of the title *Scenes from Clerical Life*. I aim at a larger canvas and intend to write a long novel.'

Blackwood's eyes shone with enthusiasm. 'Splendid, George Eliot, splendid! And while on the subject of novels, or rather in this instance books, *I* intend to bring out your *Scenes from Clerical Life* in two volumes. Subject, of course, to your agreement.'

Marian was too overcome to do more than stammer her thanks but Lewes, his mind on business, spoke up for her.

'How much?' he asked bluntly.

'Two hundred pounds.'

Well satisfied, Lewes opened a bottle of wine, a nicely matured madeira, in celebration of the coming event. Thereupon the three of them grew merry and loquacious, but Marian rather flushed and sleepy in the end. Tipsy, she thought, the Reverend George Eliot tipsy.

John Blackwood came to London again when the two volumes were published soon after Marian's thirty-eighth birthday. *Scenes from Clerical Life* was an immediate success in book form and would pave the way, Blackwood said, for George Eliot's first full-length novel. He asked if she was making good progress on it.

'I have the temerity to think so, Mr Blackwood,' Marian replied.

'And the title, have you a title yet?'

'Yes, *Adam Bede.*'

'Dickens,' Blackwood continued, 'is sure that George Eliot is a woman. Thackeray, always ready to argue with Dickens, is positive that no woman could possibly have written *Scenes from Clerical Life.* I think the time has come for you to reveal your true identity.'

Strangely Marian still shrank from this. 'Please, no, Mr Blackwood.'

'Ah, but wait! Somebody else is taking the credit and that we cannot have.'

'Somebody else?' Lewes asked indignantly.

Blackwood smiled whimsically. 'George Eliot has many admirers in Nuneaton. They are sure that the author is a man of that town, but nobody by the name of Eliot exists there. They even went so far as to consult a table-rapper.'

'How delightful!' Marian laughed.

'He rapped out the name Liggers. No Liggers either, but it was close enough to Liggins. Thereupon a Joseph Liggins modestly admitted to being the author of *Scenes from Clerical Life.*'

'The effrontery of the man!' Lewes said angrily. 'He must be contradicted.'

But still Marian hesitated. 'It scarcely matters, George. It was I who received two hundred pounds from Mr Blackwood, not Mr Liggins.'

Blackwood looked at her solemnly. 'Mr Liggins is a dissenting clergyman.'

Marian looked momentarily startled, then she burst into peals of laughter. 'George Eliot,' she gasped, 'can't possibly be accused of being a dissenting clergyman. Very well, Mr Blackwood, you have my permission to make George Eliot's true identity known.'

Blackwood rubbed his hands together. 'I thought that would do the trick.'

Marian finished *Adam Bede* just before her thirty-ninth birth-day and gladly accepted Blackwood's offer of eight hundred pounds for a copyright extending to four years. She felt rich if not successful and in gratitude dedicated the book to Lewes: 'To my dear husband, George Henry Lewes, I give the MS of a work which would never have been written but for the happiness which his love has conferred on my life.' Lewes protested, but emotionally, that she was being far too sentimental.

'If truth is sentimental,' Marian said warmly, 'then sentimental I am, but not too much so. You, dear George, are the prime blessing that has made everything possible for me. *Everything.* Only when I met you did I really start to live and write.'

'I could say the same of you, Polly.' But he wanted to make her laugh and added: 'Let us form a mutual-admiration society.'

Adam Bede was published soon after Marian's thirty-ninth birthday. It established her almost immediately as the leading woman novelist of the day and quickly went into a second edition, then a third. Its success was compared with that of *Jane Eyre*; it was even quoted in the House of Commons, and so pleased was Blackwood that he went so far as to make Marian the additional payment of four hundred pounds.

'Twelve hundred in all!' Lewes exclaimed. 'You're rich, Polly, rich!'

'No, George,' Marian corrected, '*we* are rich. Rich in many things other than mere money. Rich especially in our mutual love and trust. We can afford to live a better life, materially speaking, but our life was rich and full before this happened to us. Let us never forget that, George.'

'Never, Polly.'

'I am confident,' she said quietly, 'of greater success in the future.'

'Another novel, and another and another!'

But Marian grew sober and said, even more quietly: 'Let us not try to look too far ahead. More novels, yes, but let us give our hearts and minds to making the present better than the past and leave the future to look after itself. Please promise me that, George.'

Lewes took her in his arms. 'With a full heart, darling Polly.'

Epilogue
1871-1880

1

'I t was a beautiful spring afternoon in Rome. John Cross, his mother and his sister Elizabeth were strolling past the entrance of the Minerva Hotel. Suddenly Elizabeth Cross emitted a barely suppressed scream of excitement.

'George Eliot! Mother! John! Yes, it *is* George Eliot!'

Marian and George Lewes had just emerged from the Minerva and were looking this way and that, as if trying to decide in which direction to take a walk. Marian's glance fell on the family group and recognising Elizabeth she smiled in friendly greeting. George Lewes smiled in friendly greeting too, his smile embracing Mrs Cross and her daughter; John Cross he had not yet met. Nor had Marian met either him or his mother.

'Mrs Cross, how nice to see you again,' Lewes said warmly. 'You also, Miss Cross.' He introduced Marian. 'Mrs Cross, my wife Mrs Lewes.'

'An honour, indeed an honour, to meet the famous novelist,' Mrs Cross gushed. She gave Marian a direct look. 'I was madly jeolous when Elizabeth had the privilege of calling on you in London. She had never ceased to talk about your kindness.'

John Cross cleared his throat and smiled. 'I am, it seems, left to introduce myself.'

'Dear Johnnie, impatient as ever,' Mrs Cross laughed. 'Pray permit me, Mr and Mrs Lewes, to present my son John. He returned recently from America, upon which we decided to make a tour of Italy.'

'America, how interesting,' Marian said.

'Johnnie will be glad to tell you all about his experiences there,' Mrs Cross ventured.

'If given the opportunity,' young Cross said, his manner mock-solemn. 'It is practically impossible to get a word in edgeways when Mother is present.'

Mrs Cross smiled affectionately. 'And how,' she asked Lewes, 'was dear Herbert Spencer when last you saw him?'

'Guarding his health as carefully as ever,' Lewes chuckled.

It was through Spencer that he had met Mrs Cross and her daughter. The Crosses, old friends of Spencer's, lived at Weybridge, and there, during a walking tour of Surrey, he and Lewes had called on them. Lewes, on learning that Elizabeth Cross had just published a volume of poetry, had suggested that the young woman should call on Marian the next time she was in London. This she had done somewhat shyly but Marian, writing verse herself at that time, had quickly put her at her ease.

'I think,' said Lewes, glancing up at the sky, 'that we shall be caught in a rainstorm if we venture too far afield.'

Marian laughed heartily, the sky was completely cloudless. 'Dear George, he didn't really want to take a walk.'

'I'd much prefer a cup of tea,' Lewes said promptly. 'We shall all have tea. Come up to our suite. Tea, a chat about Herbert Spencer and some information, perhaps, about America.'

Marian and George's suite included a comfortable if ornate sitting-room. Marian sat on the sofa with Mrs Cross and found herself completely monopolised while John and Elizabeth Cross talked in whispers with Lewes at the other side of the room. They looked, Marian thought, like three naughty children whispering in church during the sermon. Always a good listener, Marian had never listened so relentlessly before, yet she found herself warming to Mrs Cross who, though she talked and talked, did so intelligently and with little touches of humour. They were much the same age, Marian being fifty-one, Mrs Cross two or three years older. From time to time Marian caught John Cross's eyes, seeing and enjoying his smile of tolerant amusement. He obviously adored his mother.

'Is your son married?' Marian asked, when Mrs Cross paused for breath.

'Married? Gracious goodness no! Johnnie is a confirmed bachelor.'

Catching her words John Cross smiled tolerantly again. He was unmarried simply because, at twenty-nine, he had yet to meet a young woman of whom his widowed mother approved, or he himself for that matter. But in any case he preferred the company of older women—women, as his mother put it, more or less of her own vintage, and intelligence too, of course. While trying not to stare rudely he studied Marian with the greatest of care and interest. He admired the fine brows framed in an abundance of auburn-brown hair and the grey-blue eyes which seemed constantly to change in expression as she listened to his mother and occasionally got in a few words of her own in earnest and deep musical tones. But what impressed him most, what seemed to indicate to him the depth of her artistic soul, was her fine if rather thin transparent hands. She was everything, he thought, that one could expect to find in the author of *Romola*.

'We Crosses are among your most ardent admirers, Mrs Lewes,' Mrs Cross was saying now. 'We find it difficult to decide just which of your books we like best. *The Mill on the Floss? Silas Marner? Romola?*' She knew that her son was growing impatient and drew him into the conversation at last. 'What do you say, Johnnie?'

'I change my mind constantly,' he replied, 'but on the whole I think *Romola*.' He crossed the room with quick, eager strides and stood tall and slender before Marian. '*Romola*, yes, until you write another book and throw me into confusion once again.'

Well used as she was to adulation, Marian blushed richly, causing John Cross to look pleased in a contrite sort of way.

'Johnnie,' Mrs Cross added, as if revealing a deep family secret, 'is better acquainted with the works of George Eliot than any other literature.'

'Your sister writes poetry,' Marian said to him. 'Do you also write poetry?'

'Gracious goodness no,' Mrs Cross interposed, 'Johnnie is a man of business with banking interests in London and New York.'

Marian smiled up at him. 'You must give me the benefit of your advice sometime. I am quite hopeless, or so my husband tells me, when it comes to managing my financial affairs.'

'I shall be only too happy, Mrs Lewes.'

Marian held his eyes for a moment. There was an earnestness about him which appealed to her. She judged him to be of solid character, a young man of delicate and generous feeling. If only she could have had children, a son in much the same mould as John Cross. Then she frowned involuntarily. She felt not in the least motherly towards him, as she did towards George's boys. Rather did she feel that they were much the same age and that a deep and abiding friendship had sprung into being between them in the twinkling of an eye. She smiled up at him again and came to one of her warm, impulsive decisions.

'You must visit us at The Priory, once we are all back in England,' she said. 'My husband and I are at home every Sunday afternoon. If you feel at all diffident about coming alone, Mr Spencer will be happy to bring you.'

'Providing his health will sustain the effort,' John Cross said, his manner mock-solemn again.

'Poor Herbert Spencer,' Marian laughed, 'he is sure to outlive all of us.'

'I quite agree, Mrs Lewes. A man so cautious is likely to live forever.'

2

JOHN CROSS had arrived early at The Priory with Herbert Spencer but the drawing-room was already moderately crowded. Marian and George, after moving several times, had finally found in the Priory, Regent's Park, a house very much to their liking. A two-storeyed house, it stood behind a brick wall in a spacious, rose-filled garden. The lease had forty-nine years to run; they had bought it for two thousand pounds and had quickly spent additional money making alterations and redecorating most of the rooms.

'As you will observe,' Spencer said, as if affecting the guise of a guide in the Palace of Versailles, 'it is a quite splendid, beautifully decorated drawing-room.'

'Spendid indeed,' John Cross responded.

It was a double drawing-room from which the usual folding doors had been removed. Owen Jones had decorated it, carefully placing on the walls the Leighton drawings for the illustration of *Romola*. A bow window, casemented down to the floor, looked out on the garden; the grand piano stood at the back of the room; two sofas and many easy chairs were scattered here and there, and there were several well-filled bookshelves round the walls. Marian, wearing a loose black velvet dress, sat in an armchair near the fireplace receiving her guests and now and again inviting a favoured one to sit at her side and converse with her. If she was deliberately holding court, John Cross decided, there was nothing ostentatious in her manner. As he had noticed in Rome, her eyes constantly changed in expression as she talked, and he thought that her head, when she bent it slowly in acquiescence, was the most majestic head he had ever seen. George Lewes approached unobtrusively and shook hands with Spencer, then with Cross.

'Welcome to The Priory, Mr Cross,' he said. 'I trust that you won't find the experience too overawing.'

Cross saw that his host's eyes were twinkling. 'Overawing, Mr Lewes?'

'Religious services at The Priory, that is how I sometimes describe our Sunday afternoons.'

Lewes glanced appraisingly round the room, quietly satisfied with the fact that more and more people prominent in society were making their way these days to The Priory and issuing invitations in return. There were many, of course, who still stood aloof but steady progress, due entirely to Marian's increasing fame as a novelist, was being made. If he and Marian were accepted in certain quarters as man and wife it was only because Marian insisted on receiving and visiting people who did indeed accept them as such. They were becoming something of a legend sheerly because of their devotion to each other—a devotion carefully and cunningly publicised by George Lewes himself. Theirs was no loose relationship, as their real friends, old and new, were happy to acknowledge; it was a true and holy marriage in the sight of God. Paradoxically they had gained and were still gaining respectability. Lewes was somewhat cynical about it, but he was happy and grateful for Marian's sake. But most of all he was grateful for the fact that his children, particularly Charles, now married and with children of his own, had accepted Marian from the first and spontaneously called her 'Mother', even on occasion and with greater affection 'Mutter'.

'Oh dear, oh dear!' Herbert Spencer wailed.

Lewes followed the direction of Spencer's gaze and shrugged tolerantly. 'Poor Edith Simcox again.'

John Cross had met Edith Simcox two or three times at bohemian parties to which Herbert Spencer had taken him as a means of enlarging his education and withdrawing him in part from the philistine world of commerce. Cross watched with interest as Miss Simcox, a well-known journalist and would-be social worker, pushed her way through the now over-crowded drawing-room to Marian's side. She wore flowing garments which seemed to belong to no particular period but which gave the impression of extreme flamboyance. Having achieved her objective, she curtsied deeply, then flung herself to her knees, bent low and kissed Marian's feet.

'Madonna!' she exclaimed, in a deep, throaty voice.

'She adores Marian, of course,' Spencer sighed.

Lewes shrugged tolerantly again. 'The adoration of a lesbian, I fear.'

'Dear me, dear me,' Spencer exclaimed, 'what have I done with my cotton wool?'

Glancing up in embarrassment Marian caught John Cross's eyes and beckoned. He hurried to her side, bowed and presumed to kiss her hand, thinking a trifle foolishly that it was more dignified than to kiss her feet. Then, at a nod from Marian, he helped the almost swooning Edith Simcox to her feet and placed her in a chair at the other side of the fireplace. She looked more like a bundle of rags now than anything else.

'Intruder!' she accused.

Marian beckoned again and invited Cross to sit at her side, which he did promptly. She asked after his mother and reminded him that he had not yet had the opportunity of telling her about America. He talked a little too quickly at first about his travels but Marian, sympathy and understanding shining in her eyes, soon put him at his ease. Later he gave her certain advice about banking and investing, and then, after they had conversed for the best part of an hour, he rose abruptly.

'Your other guests are growing impatient with me, Mrs Lewes. I seem to have monopolised you as thoroughly as my mother did in Rome.'

Marian smiled gently. 'The impression I gained was that *I* was monopolising *you*. But please come again to The Priory, come often.'

'I shall be going to New York again soon,' Cross said regretfully.

'Ah, in that case . . .'

While Marian hesitated he said boldly: 'Hospitality is meant to be returned, and I have accepted yours twice. I beg you to do us the honour, my mother and me, of visiting us at Weybridge before I leave for America.'

'Mr Lewes and I will do so gladly,' Marian delighted him by saying.

Marian and Lewes visited Weybridge a week or so later and spent a happy, tranquil day with the Crosses. Marian played the piano and another of Mrs Cross's daughters sang so appealingly that Marian's eyes filled with tears. They discussed plays and operas and literature, and Marian, who rarely discussed her work with anybody but Lewes and Blackwood, confided in her new friends that she was writing another novel, the title of which would be *Middlemarch*. When the time came for Marian and her husband to depart John Cross made a little impromptu speech, his voice, usually well controlled, charged on this occasion with emotion.

'Mr and Mrs Lewes, we have enjoyed your company thoroughly and sincerely. We feel that we have known and loved you all our lives. You came here to Weybridge as acquaintances; you are leaving, I feel and know, as lifelong friends.'

Touched and happy, Marian said: 'I have that impression too—Johnnie.'

Mrs. Cross smiled tearfully but she had a gay remark to make. 'For once my son has got more than *one* word in edgeways.'

3

IT was May in the year 1877. Lord Goschen, the celebrated Liberal politician, was giving a reception for one of the Queen's daughters, the Princess Louise, and Marian and Lewes had been invited because the princess had expressed a wish to meet George Eliot. John Cross, invited also, was an attentive if somewhat anxious spectator of the glittering scene about him. How, he wondered, would her Royal Highness receive his dear friend? Condescendingly, having been moved by curiosity? Graciously? Or in the easy and friendly manner for which she was well known? George Lewes stood on his wife's right, Cross on her left and a step or two behind her, all three waiting among the other guests for the Princess Louise's arrival. For the occasion Marian, persuaded to abandon her habitual black, wore a dress of grey moiré antique, an altogether splendid garment, Lewes had assured her, but she felt a little uncomfortable in it, not quite herself.

Glancing at Marian's back and the thinness of her neck, Cross thought in alarm that at fifty-seven she was growing frail. He had first noticed the frailty last Christmas (the Leweses and the Crosses always spent Christmas together at Weybridge) after the completion and publication of her last novel, *Daniel Deronda*. He was absolutely convinced that she worked too hard, but when it came to work she would listen to nobody. He admired *Daniel Deronda* but much preferred *Middlemarch*, the most successful of her books so far and the one which had brought her wider recognition than ever before. He hoped fervently that she would relax and find happiness at The Heights, the country house which he had found for her at Witley within easy reach of Weybridge. It was splendid for her to have a country house: The Heights, with its entrancing view of the Surrey Hills, for the summer months; The Priory, handy to the London scene, for the winter months.

A little wave of excitement ran through the drawing-room; the Princess Louise had arrived. Lord Goschen came to Marian's side immediately after welcoming his royal guest and offered her his arm.

'Her Royal Highness is waiting.'

Lewes and Cross followed at a respectful distance, the latter's anxiety growing apace. If the Princess Louise were merely condescending . . . !

Lord Goschen bowed before the princess. 'Your Royal Highness, permit me to present George Eliot.'

'No, no, I protest,' the princess said warmly, 'it is I, I insist, who must be presented to George Eliot.'

Marian, blushing quickly, could scarcely believe her ears. It was a signal honour and did much to bolster up her earlier determination to take a special stand with the princess, here in front of the highest of the high in society.

'If Your Royal Highness would be so kind,' she said firmly, 'I prefer always to be known by my married name, which is Mrs Lewes.'

The princess's eyes sparkled. 'Mrs Lewes it is, then. Come, my lord, present me!'

'Mrs Lewes,' said his lordship, gulping, 'permit me to present Her Royal Highness, the Princess Louise.'

Marian made to curtsy but the princess restrained her with a commanding look and held out her hand. Marian took it; they shook hands warmly.

'It is very pleasing, very heart-warming,' the princess said, 'to find so famous a woman sheltering modestly behind her husband's name. Her Majesty my mother will thoroughly approve when I tell her. Come, now, Mrs Lewes, let us sit down and have a nice long chat.'

Only by dint of great restraint did George Lewes prevent himself from cheering. He felt that he was growing taller, that his chest was expanding enormously. He was proud enough to burst. A glance at John Cross told him that his young friend felt much the same; they faced each other and shook hands, their faces wreathed in smiles. Later that evening, after a famous general and a saintly-looking bishop had been presented to Mrs Lewes, that lady came back to her husband's side.

'George,' she said breathlessly, 'we have been invited to dine with Lord and Lady Ripon. Among those present will be the Crown Prince and Princess of Germany, the Dean of Westminster and the Bishop of Peterborough. What do you think of that, darling?'

'I think,' Lewes chuckled, 'that my clever Polly has tamed the whole world.'

Marian sighed wonderingly. 'We have, as the Americans say, arrived.'

4

JOHN CROSS was too agitated at first by his own troubles to notice anything untoward in Herbert Spencer's manner. When at last he did notice that Spencer was more than ordinarily distraught he clasped the older man's hand and thanked him for coming out to Weybridge on this bleak and cold November day to lend his support and sympathy. Spencer looked momentarily puzzled, then he remembered.

'Ah yes, your poor dear mother . . . Her failing health . . . So sad, so very sad . . .'

'Everything possible has been done,' Cross said, his voice breaking, 'but the doctors hold out no hope whatever.'

'Terrible, truly terrible.'

'A matter of days only, Mr Spencer.'

Herbert Spencer looked even more distraught. 'Our dear Marian Lewes will be most distressed, but I doubt if it would be wise to tell her just now. While there is life there is hope. No indeed, not wise at all, under the present circumstances.'

'What do you mean by that, Mr Spencer?'

Then Spencer blurted it out, the reason for his hurried visit to Weybridge. 'My dear old friend George Lewes died yesterday.'

'Impossible!' John Cross exclaimed.

'You are, of course, as stunned as I am. It was all very sudden, very unexpected. The poor dear chap caught a chill, the chill turned to fever. His health had not been good recently. There was no resistance in him; he was too weak to put up a fight. Strange that he should have said only last week that the most desirable

217

end to a well spent life was a quick and painless death. Yesterday, my dear Cross. November 28th, 1878. A day his friends will never forget.'

'I must go to The Priory at once,' Cross said.

Spencer shook his head. 'Marian would refuse to receive you. She refused to receive even me. Apart from the doctors, George Lewes's son Charles is the only person she is willing at present to see. But write to her, write to her by all means.'

Cross wrote immediately, expressing as best he could his sympathy and personal grief. There was no reply. He wrote again a week later to tell Marian that his mother had died, that a mutual grief bound them together. Again there was no reply; Marian, said Spencer, had refused to open any of the letters which were reaching The Priory daily. However, through Charles Lewes she had sent Spencer a brief message to be conveyed to John Cross: 'Here we sit, sorrow and I.' She was in her 60th year, Spencer said, and felt that her life had ended.

Cross continued to write, feeling that now that his mother was dead only Marian remained: 'I turn to you in my grief, please turn to me in yours.' Two months after George Lewes's death Marian began to answer the accumulation of letters but still refused to receive visitors. To John Cross she wrote: 'Some time, if I live, I shall be able to see you, perhaps sooner than anyone else.' And a few days later, heartening and exciting him: 'I do need your affection and support; perhaps in a week or two I shall be ready to see you.'

Cross waited for the expiration of two weeks and then presented himself at The Priory without permission. The maid who opened the door to him refused him entry, but while he was arguing with her Marian appeared in the hall and quietly dismissed the girl. They looked at each other in silence, Marian Lewes and John Cross; it was several moments before either of them could speak. Finally Marian held out her hands.

'My dear Johnnie . . .'

He took her hands briefly in his. 'My dear Marian . . .'

'Yes,' she said slowly, 'I think the time has come for you to call me Marian. George would have wanted it. The "Mrs Lewes" was the only formality that stood between us.' She held out her hands again. 'I want you to go now, but you shall come again very soon.'

'Please let me stay a little longer.'

'No, Johnnie,' she said as firmly as she could. 'I can't bear too much sympathy yet. I'm a bruised creature and shrink from the

tenderest touch. I can but think that I shall die soon myself.'
'That is *unthinkable*, Marian!'
She looked at him affectionately. 'How angry you sound.'
'*And* feel, George Eliot. Your work, your high position in the world of letters, your *undying* reputation . . . The world expects you to live and continue to enrich its literature.'
'I care nothing for the world.'
'*I* expect it of you,' Cross said, quietly and simply.
'You are good for me,' Marian said, after a moment's pause, 'really good for me.'
A week later Marian allowed Cross to visit her again and at greater length. She told him that partly through his being alive to comfort and encourage her, she had decided to throw herself into the task of gathering together for publication all her late husband's unfinished manuscripts, and she discussed with him a plan for setting up a studentship in George Lewes's name.
'But how self-interested I must sound,' she said wryly. 'You too have suffered a great and untimely loss. How are you attempting to console yourself? Or should I say find distraction?'
Knowing that it would please and interest her, Cross said that he had embarked on an engrossing study of the Italian language as a means of keeping his mind occupied. Business no longer interested him and he had in any case a private income more than sufficient for his needs.
'I have made a start on Dante's *Inferno*,' he said, 'with Carlyle's translation to guide me.'
Marian had never been able to resist an intellectual appeal. 'I must read it with you, Johnnie. The *Purgatorio* too.'
'Seriously and critically,' Cross responded, 'examining every sentence carefully and minutely.'
They began their joint study of Dante that same day and continued it as, almost imperceptibly, Cross's visits became more frequent. Marian went eventually to The Heights at Witley to find solitude, she told her friends, and accused herself, none too severely, of making the move so that Johnnie would be able to visit her with greater ease from nearby Weybridge. It was a courtship, if only on an intellectual plane, but neither of them was ready or perceptive enough to recognise it as such or to wonder just who was courting whom. Marian, however, eventually came close to it herself and wrote to Spencer that there was a devoted friend who came continually to see that she lacked nothing. She added that her sorrow would never grow less but

that life, which her husband had enjoyed so intensely, was becoming intensely interesting to her again. She owed it to George's memory, she concluded, to go on living and striving for a steadiness in life, if not a complete happiness.

Marian returned to The Priory a year after George Lewes's death and began at last to receive all her old friends. Herbert Spencer was foremost amongst them. On one occasion he dined quietly with Marian and Cross at The Priory and Marian told him that with Cross escorting her she had been during the last week to a concert, to the National Gallery, to the Museums at South Kensington and to the British Museum.

'The weather was hideous,' Spencer protested, 'too hideous for Christians to be abroad.'

'Christians, dear Herbert?' Marian chuckled.

'Even agnostics,' he amended.

'We didn't notice the weather,' Marian said. 'Did we, Johnnie?'

'Indeed we did not,' Cross avowed.

'Interesting, most interesting,' Spencer said, glancing owlishly from Marian to Cross. Well aware that some of Marian's friends were gossiping avidly, he took a quantity of cotton wool from his pocket, the quite enlarged pocket in which he always stored his cotton wool. 'Could it be said,' he asked, stuffing cotton wool into each ear, 'that I am too old to play Cupid? Or, again, could it be said that I am playing Cupid too late in the day?'

Neither Marian nor Cross replied. Turning from Spencer they looked at each other in astonishment, each aware of the mutual revelation which Spencer's words had brought to the surface.

'Cupid or not,' Spencer continued perkily, 'I am not too old, indeed I am more than old enough, to play the chaperon.'

Marian rose and smilingly removed the cotton wool from Spencer's ears. 'We are in no need of a chaperon, Herbert.'

Cross rose too. 'Marian and I, Mr Cross, are to be married in the very near future.'

'Quietly, privately,' Marian added.

'Ah! Your swain has proposed already!'

'Not in so many words,' Marian admitted. 'In a sense he has merely issued an order.' She smiled fondly on Cross, then turned again to Spencer. 'It could be said that Herbert Spencer, a cunning and observant friend, has done the actual proposing for him. Heaven bless you, dear Herbert.'

When Spencer had gone Marian looked anxiously at her future husband. She knew instinctively that their decision to marry would arouse much criticism and possibly some unkind laughter at their expense. She quailed a little at facing what must be gone through, but she was tired of being set on a pedestal and expected not only to act wisely herself but to dispense wisdom on all occasions. After all, she told herself somewhat querulously, she was only a poor woman in need of love and constant companionship.

'Johnnie,' she faltered, 'are we doing the right thing?'

'The rightest right thing we have ever done.'

'You set my mind at rest. Whatever the world might say, we owe it to ourselves to live for ourselves.'

Cross took her hands in his and kissed her, reverently, she thought, on the brow.

'Darling Marian,' he said emotionally, 'I seek my happiness in dedicating my life to you.'

5

SEVEN months after returning from a Continental honeymoon Mr and Mrs John Cross moved from The Heights to a house in Cheyne Walk, Chelsea. Herbert Spencer was their first visitor. He found them in the library. Cross was in shirtsleeves, Marian was wearing an apron. They were in the midst of the task of arranging Marian's books of which there were several thousand. Spencer, the professional neurotic, looked at Marian in rather gleeful anxiety. He detected a shortness of breath in his old friend; he was sure that she looked drawn and tired and was on the point of collapse.

'Mrs Cross,' he said severely, 'have you consulted your medical adviser lately?'

'No, Herbert. I see no reason why I should have.'

'Pray let me take your pulse.' He did so, ignoring Marian's tolerant smile, and said despairingly, 'Much too rapid.'

'Merely the exertion of lifting and stacking so many books.'

'That should have brought a flush, if an unhealthy one, to your cheeks, but dear me. Marian, you're pale as death.'

'The sooner you start digging my grave the better,' she said cheerily.

Spencer shuddered violently. 'Pray don't joke, Marian. What distresses me most is that you should have grown so thin.'

She admitted that she had lost a fair amount of weight and

laughingly quoted the doggerel lines which she had sent recently to Charles Lewes and his family :

> 'Love to all
> Great and small
> From the feeble Mutter
> Seven stone
> (Her weight is known)
> When in heaviest clothes you put her.'

Spencer refused to laugh. 'I am most concerned, indeed most concerned, about your health,' he said weightily. 'You must take the greatest care of yourself, especially now that winter is upon us. It is going to be one of the most severe winters on record, I feel it in my ancient bones. I beg you not to venture forth during the cold nights that lie perilously ahead of us.'

Ignoring Spencer's warning, which she considered absurd, Marian continued her winter habit of going to concerts. She and Cross were at St James's Hall on Saturday, December 18th, to hear Adelina Patti sing. It was an extremely cold night but the interior of the hall was hot and stuffy. Feeling breathless and flushed, Marian slipped off her fur coat and lovingly told Cross not to coddle her when he asked her to replace it. At breakfast the next morning she complained of a sore throat.

'Dear Herbert should be here to remonstrate with me for the risk I took last night,' she laughed.

Her throat grew worse during the day and pained her severely on Monday. Cross called in the local doctor. He diagnosed laryngitis and ordered her to bed. She seemed better on Tuesday but on Wednesday suffered a relapse. Cross was alarmed by her apparent weakness and very rapid pulse. He called in the local doctor again, then Sir Andrew Clark, a specialist. Marian was struggling to sip beef-tea when Sir Andrew arrived at six o'clock in the evening. He examined her, concealed his alarm from her and took John Cross aside.

'I must be frank with you, Mr Cross. The severe chill has spread from Mrs Cross's throat to her heart. There is, I fear, no strength left in her to resist it. I regret to say this, Mr Cross, but I can hold out no hope at all.'

Marian fell quickly into a coma and without recovering consciousness died at ten o'clock that night. She and John Cross had been married less than eight months.

6

GEORGE ELIOT'S funeral was an occasion of almost national mourning. It was a bitter day with sleet turning to snow. All her friends, her brother Isaac, some of her detractors and many strangers were present at the service. It had been suggested that she should be buried in Westminster Abbey but Marian had left instructions to be interred in the next grave to George Henry Lewes's at Highgate Cemetery. Many people, including Isaac Evans, were in tears when the Unitarian minister concluded his address with a few lines from one of her poems:

'Oh may I join the choir invisible
Of those immortal dead who live again
In minds made better by their presence: live
In pulses stirred to generosity,
In deeds of daring rectitude, in scorn
For miserable aims that end in self,
In thoughts sublime that pierce the night like stars,
And with their mild persistence urge man's search
To vaster issues.'

Herbert Spencer, wearing a heavy overcoat and two thick scarfs, but forgetting for once to take his pulse, found himself standing next to Eliza Lynn Linton at the graveside. She, never having forgiven Marian for getting the better of her in the Chapman negotiations, was not in tears herself. Spencer, who had never liked her, detected a sneering smile and waited angrily for the words which were forming on her lips.

'Such a short marriage, poor thing. Obviously respectability was too much for her.'

'Madam,' Spencer said in a choking voice, 'you appear to me to be in the best of health, but I wish heartily, indeed I do, that you would fall dead at my feet.'